DAVID R. NORMAN 9/81

David A. Howard 9/9(?)

ACTION LEARNING

Action Learning is a management technique based on 'doing the thing' and not on abstract theories. From the beginning it met with resistance from self-styled management schools, its value and importance to industry only gaining gradual recognition. In recent years, thanks to Professor Revans's pioneer work, four foreign governments and a number of distinguished industrialists have implemented action learning programmes. But perhaps its greatest success to date is the recognition afforded its principles in the EEC Report entitled Management Education in the European Community, *where it is recommended that schools and organizations alike should embrace the ideas that inform this present work.*

ACTION LEARNING

NEW TECHNIQUES FOR MANAGEMENT

R.W. Revans

Blond & Briggs

First published 1980 by Blond & Briggs Ltd
London NW2 6LE

Copyright © R. W. Revans 1980

British Library Cataloguing in Publication Data
Revans, Reginald William
Action learning.
1. Management
I. Title
658.4   HD31

ISBN 0-85634-101-0

All rights reserved. No part of this publication may
be reproduced, stored in a retrieval system, or transmitted, in any form or by any means, electronic,
mechanical, photocopying, recording or otherwise,
without the prior permission of Blond & Briggs Ltd.

Printed in Great Britain by The Anchor Press Ltd
and bound by Wm Brendon & Son Ltd
both of Tiptree, Essex

Contents

To Norah and Andrew
for making endurable ten years
of exile in quest of educational
reforms

PART 1

The nine chapters of the first part of this book describe many
– but not all – of the action learning programmes that have
been run, or that are still running, since the ideas of learning
from experience in the responsible here-and-now were first
given operational form by the colliery managers in 1952. They
tell a little of what has happened in several countries, notably
Belgium, Egypt, Nigeria, India and Australia, to list them in
order of remoteness from the land of our theme's physical and
intellectual origins. These brief accounts show the innumerable
forms that action learning can take: in banks, factories, hospitals, mines, schools, trading and warehousing corporations,
government offices and every form of industrial and commercial undertaking, large, medium and small. Since our thesis is
that one learns best from whatever it is that one may be trying
to do, this infinite variety is not surprising: the Eskimo and
the Hottentot must do something in order to keep alive, and,
if they do have to do something useful, they can learn to do it
better by the very act of thinking of how they do it. That is
action learning. So simple an explanation must, of course, put
us on our guard; we must not fall into the trap of confusing
action learning with *words about* action learning. These chapters must be taken only as examples of what others have done
across the world, in order that we can try our hands ourselves
at the arts of learning by responsible doing; the fields of action
are open to all and one need pay no fee to explore them.

1.
Innovation at the Coal Board

The clever man will tell you what he knows; he may even try to explain it to you. The wise man encourages you to discover it for yourself, even although he knows it inside out. But since he seems to give you nothing, we have no need to reward him. Thus the wise have disappeared and we are left in a desolation of the clever.

When Demosthenes was asked what was the first part of oratory he replied, 'Action'; and which was the second he replied, 'Action'; and which was the third he still answered, 'Action'. (Plutarch, *Lives of the Orators, c.* AD 100)

There is nothing more difficult to take in hand, more perilous to conduct, or more uncertain in its success, than to take the lead in the introduction of a new order of things. (Machiavelli, *The Prince*, 1520)

Some impose upon the world that they believe what they do not believe; others, more in number, make themselves believe what they do not believe, not being able to understand the meaning of belief. (Montaigne, *Apology for Raymond Sebond, c.* 1580)

On the night of 31 December 1946 there occurred one of the most extraordinary events in the history of the British nation. At about 10 p.m. many thousand miners went underground employed by over 800 different colliery companies; they came up before dawn on New Year's Day, 1947, employed by one party, the National Coal Board. In a sense, an immense change had taken place; in other senses, nothing had changed at all. A long battle, fought by the Mineworkers' Federation of Great Britain, seemed to have been won; the previous owners of the capital assets of the coal industry had been bought out by the government for about £170,000,000, a first instalment towards paying for a reconstructed coal industry on which many times that orginal purchase price was to be spent. Each colliery was issued with a new flag and a notice board, telling the passers-by that it was now managed by the NCB on behalf of the nation; imaginative schemes were drafted – and a few put into effect – to bring about all manner of changes in an industry that seemed to lie at the very heart of our economy: schemes to rationalize the miners' wages, to introduce consistent pricing policies, to tidy up the relations of the new giant to the other state enterprises coming into existence, like the Transport Commission and the Electricity Authority, to modernize the mines themselves and to find and train a new generation of mining and other engineers to run them. All this was known and talked about (generally in a spirit of the meanest detraction) by a public influenced by journalists to whom the cultural history of British coalmining was as unknown as were the social customs of Tibet. What was not so well understood were the overwhelming difficulties of effectively changing anything with so vivid a recollection of its own past. When, as with the Irish, a community may look back a thousand years upon its grievances, the ministers of reconciliation are in for a rough time, and this was certainly what the Coal Board had to face.

For the nationalization of the industry revived in the most acute form a conflict that has divided humanity since the earliest times, that between the artisan and the scribe. The very act of trying to redress the long injustices of history demanded some form of administration to be settled on the industry; whatever form this might have taken in detail – supposing even that the miners' unions had been given seats upon it from the outset – would have called for some manner of bureaucracy. But those who, like miners, labour hard for their livings do not trust administrators, by whomsoever they are employed. I do not mean that the 800,000 men whose names were on our colliery books in 1947 all knew personally and detested heartily those particular office-workers set over them by the needs of the hour, even if there were such rumours throughout the industry as I heard in Cannock: that the members of the divisional coal board, meeting in Himley Hall (known locally as

Himmler Hall) several times a week, would drink to nationalization in warm human blood, and out of port-wine glasses
they had been obliged to take over at an outrageous price from
the coal-owning family that had once occupied the mansion,
namely, the Earl and Countess of Dudley. Every coal-field had
its legends; in one the top brass were personally ranked against
a scale of tonnage, Lord So-and-so a ten thousand man,
Admiral Such-and-such merely five thousand, while General
Bullyboy hovered uneasily between seven and eight thousand.
These were the quantities of coal production *lost* every time
they got close to one of the pits. In fact, not one of these
maligned persons, who were all gallant and courageous gentlemen, could have been personally known to the miners, and the
particular tonnages attributed to them could not in any way
have been assessed against their individual records. The
administrations that they diligently served were not being
judged by any evidence the miners had at their disposal; it was
the sins of their fathers that rose in slanderous voice against
them.

Among the oldest documents known to us is the Instruction
of Duauf; it is a copy of a writing exercise made by countless
Egyptian schoolboys three thousand years and more ago
(although the original text is much older), and in it Duauf gives
Pepi, his son, advice on entering the School of Books:

I have seen him that is beaten, him that is beaten: thou art
to set thine heart on books. I have beheld him that is set free
from forced labour: behold, nothing surpasseth books.
Every artisan that wieldeth the chisel, he is wearier than him
that delveth. The stonemason seeketh for work in all manner
of hard stone; when he hath finished it his arms are destroyed
and he is weary. The field-worker, his reckoning endureth
for ever; he, too, is wearier than can be told. The weaver in
his workshop, he fareth more ill than any woman; his thighs
are on his belly and he breatheth no air. Let me tell thee
further, how it fareth with the fisherman. Is not his work
upon the river, where it is mixed with the crocodiles? Behold,
there is no calling without a director, except that of the
scribe, and he is the director. (*A Study of History*, A. J.
Toynbee: abridgement by D. C. Somervell, OUP, 1946,
Vol. 1, p. 325)

Many parents today are, no doubt, still addressing the same exhortation to their sons and daughters as they leave school to enter the university departments of administration and management. We shall return in this book many times to the perceived advantages of escaping from the pit of toil, first, by becoming a master of the book and, second, by becoming a master of others; the miners in particular have long been aware of the gap that education seemed to offer the chance of crossing, just as many of its staff were aware of the dangers of the Coal Board embracing educational policies that might enable the miners to cross it. The board member who misread his script at the press conference was speaking for all scribes of all ages: 'I am here to *simulate* interest in this great and liberal measure . . .' as he announced a new scholarship scheme for young men from the pits.[1]

As director of education to the Coal Board I was well aware of the ambiguities that confused the relations between the miners and the new administration, but at no time was I able to convince the coalitions of power trying to run the industry that the ancient and formidable aversions of scribe from artisan might be the cause of some of them; some of the bureaucrats might well have been the overpaid and work-allergic nonentities the miners saw them as, but not all were quite as overpaid as the miners thought. Thus it was that, as soon as I had entered upon my mission of giving the industry some educational ideas, I started to ask how far we could forget the Instruction of Duauf and use the daily round of the pits (as well as the traditional books) to develop the new generation of leaders for which we had so great a need. If, in 1947, education still seemed to the administrators of the coal industry, as well as to the universities, what it had been three thousand years and longer ago to the schoolmasters of the New Empire, I felt obliged to seek for something more relevant and less aggressive. I detected enough antagonism in the industry already, without the class instincts of education still further depressing its morale. Thus it was that, from the outset, I was interested in any new approach to learning that could be seen to involve the doing of any job. None needs be disguised as a scholar.

In my search I was much helped by a celebrated colleague at

the Coal Board, Fritz Schumacher, who had made several visits to Burma, where he had become a friend of the Prime Minister and a student of the Lord Buddha. One passage attributed to the sage seemed to me to summarize the educational needs of our times:

> To do a little good is better than to write difficult books. The perfect man is nothing if he does not diffuse benefits on other creatures, if he does not console the lonely. The way of salvation is open to all, but know that a man deceives himself if he thinks he can escape his conscience by taking refuge in a monastery. The only remedy for evil is healthy reality.

There was healthy reality enough in the coal industry; the task was to make of it an educational remedy for its abundance of evil. Before the first year of public ownership had been completed we had started on the road to action learning.

Our first move was with the Institution of Mining Engineers, to set up with them and the education staff of the Coal Board a scheme of 'directed practical training'. Under this, several hundreds of promising young men with formal qualifications, such as degrees or national certificates, were given the extended chance of working, often for three years, under the personal tutelage of the industry's senior specialists. Most of these were mining engineers, but not all; eventually the scheme was extended to the training of accountants and other bureaucrats who would rarely have occasion to go near a pit, but at the outset it was strongly concentrated upon the control of the physical operations in and around the mines. The young men who profited from it were often from the coalface and had been given scholarships by the Coal Board to read some appropriate engineering or technology; many were the sons of mining engineers or of the managers of coke ovens, so that they took into the culture of higher education a powerful strain of healthy reality.

Their practical training, backed by constant seminars and residential week-ends, embraced two themes: first, so many months on the routines of the manager's daily chores – coalface organization, ventilation, roadway repair, haulage control, supplies and maintenance, wage negotiation, manpower deployment, accident prevention, reception and discussion of reports of under-officials, and so forth; second, field projects specific to particular troubles at particular pits, such as working through badly faulted ground, dealing with excessive water, isolating an underground fire, supporting a separated or fractured roof and any more of a hundred torments sent to test the most long-suffering of all human professions. Occasionally the field projects were positive, such as to reconstruct a shaft bottom without interfering with the daily output of the coal already being drawn through it, or installing machinery costing £50,000 on a coalface that had been laid out for handworking. I noticed that it was the field projects that drew the best from the apprentice engineers; they were obliged, alike by the complexity of the troubles and the absence of their bosses, to use their own powers of observation which, although among the most precious of human abilities, are not allowed much scope in the authoritarian trade of running coalmines. But the brass were generally so distracted by all the things they were trying personally to deal with – as they always had done in the expansive times of private ownership – that the young men were obliged to argue about what *they* had seen, what *they* had heard the miners say, and what answers *they* had had to *their* questions. When, on the contrary, the apprentice managers were merely being conducted around the industry to listen to their tutelary experts airing their opinions about how it ought to be run, the students merely had to listen and to copy, and occasionally to answer a few questions in the way that the answers were expected.

I was soon persuaded that a few important ideas were emerging from the projects – ideas that remained undetected during the didactic reverberations of the apprentice masters, but that are at the very core of action learning. Firstly, the apprentices had a sense of ownership of the field projects on which each served as general clerk, factfinder and record-keeper; this came out in unexpected ways, such as envying each other the possession of the other project. When, on the contrary, they were diligently trying to do what they had been told by their tutors or were taking to pieces something they had been told to take to pieces by some functional expert, they had no such incentive. Indeed, some of them were made to feel that, far from owning their task, they had become the property of their instructors, and they resented the patronage that had enveloped them. Secondly, their relations to the senior men under whose fitful charge they slogged on with the field projects – those to whom we later gave the title of *client* – were quite different from the relations with those confident but brittle specialists endlessly telling them the most astonishing facts about coal washeries, gate-end boxes or skip-winding. They held their clients in a sympathetic and compassionate respect, vaguely sensing that the senior men had been picked up by events they could not understand and that were forcing them to act their parts in a great drama for which there had been not only no rehearsals, but no agreed script. Their specialist instructors, on the other hand, they met with a languid hostility; the students did not warm to their self-assured inevitability, which seemed to drag not only their subject but also the students themselves through a professional mangle. As they put it: 'To be instructed, we must first be insulted – even if they intend to do neither.'

These divergent attitudes were, at first, hard to understand; the clients were in deep trouble, overworked and underpowered, unclear about the scope and limitations of their projects, not sure about how to use the apprentices they had been allocated, and yet they were respected. The experts, on the other hand, seemed past-masters of the technologies they practised and were never caught out expounding them; for all their infallible reliability, however, they were disliked. But what soon became clear among the apprentices, as in argument they relived their weekly experiences again, was that they began to know their clients *as persons*; they rarely achieved this level of familiarity with the specialists. They discovered that, in collecting evidence that their clients had no time to collect for themselves, they were often brought by their clients into a respectful consultation. Their personal views might be invited; they would be given side investigations to get on with on their own, or with one or two other trainees of their own choice; they would discover in these free assignments that some of the officials of the pits in trouble might hold opinions, and with great tenacity, totally opposed to those of their colleagues, and not seldom quite contrary to the laws of nature. The students even caught their clients letting slip an ignorance of things that the students knew at first hand, or making suggestions about next moves that were quite impracticable. Yet it was in discovering the senior men off their guard, or even in their dawning recognitions that the senior men might in fact be completely out of their depth without knowing enough about their trade to recognize it for themselves, that the younger men felt they were making the fastest progress. They were, moreover, prevented by their fellow students from becoming spoiled in the constant discovery of their clients' limitations, and it was in observing how charitable was the discussion of human frailty among a set of equal learners that I first began to envision its comradeship as the clearest expression of action learning.

The central idea of this approach to human development, at all levels, in all cultures and for all purposes, is today that of the set, or small group of comrades in adversity, striving to learn with and from each other as they confess their failures and expand upon their victories. Perhaps the mining industry alone, with its contemptuous indifference to the conceits of ordinary people, could have taught these resilient and mettlesome young men the humility essential to forgiving the infirmities of their bosses; had the students not received, in the daily pursuit of their own precious but challenging projects, those manifold lessons in humility that at once enable one miner to recognize another, these early sets might have become, like the case study of the business school, a flatulent self-deception. It was in being able to report, from one seminar to the next, what they had been able to do both to influence the client and to advance the project, that the more perceptive of the students made clear to me what they were truly learning; compared with the excitements of this, their assignments to the coal preparation experts or area workshops or divisional planning office were approached with a sullen contempt. Where all was so certain, so programmed and so much the same for every student, no matter what his past or his future; where one's opinion was not asked; where one could try nothing out; where the question to which the answer was unknown was simply never asked – namely, where those in charge never had anything to learn – then the visitors, too, lost any desire they might have had to do so.

These early experiences with the mining students stood me

in good stead when, at the end of three years as director of education, I became convinced that the coal industry – and probably all others – needed to question what it thought it was trying to do for the development of its existing managers. We had shown by bringing the apprentices together (in the course of tackling real difficulties to which their bosses did not know the solutions) that they were capable of learning with and from each other, if monitored by firm evaluation of their progress in the eyes of their fellows; this respect for 'healthy reality' shielded them alike from the insufficiencies of their own clients and from the impostures of the administrative theorists, who were, by 1950, starting to take up their loop-holes in the academic ramparts. But the more senior managers, who remained for many years the backbone of the industry, had no such apparatus of mutual protection. On the one hand, the technical knowledge of the mandarins who were trying to reconstruct the industry was so highly personalized as to form little more than a mythology, or, at most, folklore; in the early years of public ownership the industry was obliged to rely upon the professional advice of the Germans and the Dutch, both of whom had thriving and efficient industries. It was therefore most ambiguous to erect an educational policy upon the supposition that a central corps of competent practitioners could be identified to develop the middle ranks, although there was, of course, no shortage of able specialists and experts to run seminars on particular technologies, like roof control or hard-rock tunneling. On the other hand, the industry seemed unable to defend itself from the insinuations of the management professors; as a nation we had not yet enjoyed the refreshing disillusion of the early 1970s, and the socio-prattle of the behavioural scientists could still cram the lecture hall with gaping businessmen. I found it hard to believe that the mining industry would be taken in by such jack-o'-lanterns and their catch-penny methods. Nor, even if it were, could they do much to tackle the problems central to the pits, which were not those of mining technology but of the relations of management and worker. My own belief – which I still hold after thirty years, and which I argue later – is that these relations will be improved by action learning in which all in the pit work together on the identification, analysis and treatment of their

17

common problems. In 1950 it was impossible to secure a hearing for what is today becoming more generally accepted, especially after the frigid reception of the Bullock Report, namely, that only the parties themselves can do anything effective about the conflicts that they have themselves created.

In 1950, therefore, I decided that my views upon the needs of the industry for management education were an embarrassment to the Coal Board; since I thought they had embarrassments enough already, I left them to live among the miners of Cannock Chase. I had already convinced myself, on the evidence of the accident statistics supplied to me by Sir Andrew Bryan, Chief Inspector of Coal Mines, that we knew much less than we thought we did about the sociology of working underground, although some highly effective studies of coalface groups had been made by the Tavistock Institute of Human Relations; my own suspicion was, however, that the pathological condition of the underground community was most significantly determined by the way the mine was professionally managed and that the very managers themselves, whatever their level of education (or of acquaintance with the literature of behavioural science), were the persons most fitted to study the responses of their men to life in the pit. This is not the place to discuss the evidence for my belief at length; it is enough to refer to the figures later in this essay, particularly those of Chapter 10.

I therefore decided that I should invest a couple of years in an effort to persuade the colliery managers themselves to take in hand the study of their own operational troubles; in a manner that I could not clearly express, I wanted to see some sets of substantive managers, not of mining students, coming regularly together in the course of doing their ordinary jobs of running their own pits so that, like the apprentices, they could learn with and from each other by the exchange of advice, criticism and support. Since I had no idea how the managers themselves would take to such a proposal, I set about finding out for myself; it was for this reason, among others, that I decided to live in Hednesford and to deepen the acquaintance that I had made with several of the local managers while I had been on the headquarters staff of the Coal Board.

It was in visiting their pits and getting to know their under-officials that I began to form the impression that the managers, like the mining students, resented being told by superior persons what they ought to be doing, or what they ought to know; at the same time, they were puzzled by my suggestions that they might learn with and from each other – as the mining students seemed to be doing – on condition that what they thought they were learning was both *derived from* their own efforts to solve a real problem, and *checked against* their own progress in solving it. But in the course of time I found one colliery manager on Cannock Chase who said he would be willing, if permission were granted him, to help me organize a programme under which a small number of managers might, somehow, get together to help each other understand what might be going on in each other's mines. This was encouraging, and in trying to work out how I could exploit his willingness I was led into all manner of discussions with the managers about their troubles, and particularly about how slippery these seemed to be; no sooner had the manager started to work on whatever his torment appeared to be than it changed into something else altogether. Since, in fact, the problem itself did not change, it could only be the impression of the manager that changed – and that changed so quickly; thus it was that we needed more reliable diagnoses of our pit troubles before we set in hand the cures for them, and I was, at the time and even now, thirty years later, unable to see from where these diagnoses were to come but from those responsible for following them up.

On Cannock Chase I often contrived to get a small number of managers together at one particular colliery to discuss a local problem about which all could collect whatever evidence was needed; I could see that the manner of cross-questioning and the reliability of the support that these responsible men directed at each other was richer and warmer than the advice, however technically sound, the same managers would get individually from the staff of the area office or from the real experts at the divisional headquarters. At these local friendlies, all were learners; each talked about the troubles of the others, not only for the sake of them, but on his own account, too. By trying to understand his neighbour's obliquity of vision and infirmity of purpose, he might hope to learn something of his own. At the end of a year, I had already formed the design of the first action learning consortium of colliery managers; it was to create a small number of groups (later to take the canonical title of 'action learning sets', or simply 'sets') across the industry, sufficiently different in the size and geological structure of the mines from which they came to offer each other varied interpretations of similar problems, and able to learn at three levels: first, from the direct confrontation with the colliery conditions themselves; second, from the local (or 'set') discussions of what they imagined they saw either in their own pits or in those of their neighbours; third, from less frequent national gatherings of all the sets to exchange experiences from different coalfields.

These plans suddenly became a reality. There was a change of Coal Board and Sir Andrew Bryan became a member of the new administration; he immediately arranged for me to address the annual meeting of the National Association of Colliery Managers about the simple idea that the managers were as well qualified as anybody else to find out what was going on in their own mines, and better qualified than most to do something with their discoveries. In the event, twenty-two colliery managers formed the total consortium; their pits were of the greatest variety, from very large, with over 3,000 men on the books, to very small, with less than 50.

They worked in five sets and all started with the same four agreed operational troubles: the maintenance of machinery, much of which was very new, very expensive and very frightening; the control of materials, which were thought to be wasted and were known to be costly; the true efficiency of underground haulages, which were believed to be the main bottleneck to increased output; and the deployment of underground workers in face of an average absenteeism rate of 16 per cent. The project lasted for nearly three years, and produced, in addition to all manner of change at the participating pits, a series of nationally circulated recommendations by the managers upon forms of colliery organization. It was this association with the managers – and their under-officials with mining graduates attached to them for detailed studies of the local pit problems – that confirmed an impression I had first got on Cannock Chase: beyond such-and-such a size, pits become unmanageable. Little that we understand very clearly can be done to make an efficient or happy unit out of one that is already too large.

Looking back more than twenty-five years to this first action learning programme, we are obliged to ask why – apart from the score or so of managers whose mines became the objects of self study – no other persons, either within the industry or outside, were at all influenced by it directly. The changes and improvements in colliery organization that were introduced did not reach the other mines through exercises in action learning, but by administrative edict; no university school of management or mining expressed interest in what had been done; the staff colleges soon to be set up by the National Coal Board itself took as their models the American business school modified by the concept of the syndicate – a permanently constituted group that worked on what at first sight appeared to be practical problems until one found out that nothing they decided upon was ever to be tried out in reality. What was given in the way of affairs current to the production of coal was largely the rationalizations of misperceived experiences. The true condition of the industry was such that hopefulness was the most needed personal quality, and in some it was so buoyant that they found it not easy to distinguish between what they planned to do and what they achieved by trying to do it.

The traditional separation of theory and practice, of plan and execution, of book and tool, of administrator and artificer, suddenly exacerbated by the political necessity of nationalization, was hostile to action learning; in one coal-field alone was any sustained effort made to bring the directors and the labourers into fruitful contact, but this owed nothing to action learning – not, at least, in the form that it appeared to me. In the early 1950s we were still looking to the experts to save us; because the coal industry was only just emerging from utter dereliction it was no plausible hypothesis that the managers who were emerging out of the darkness as part of it might themselves have any suggestions worth making. Had they been thought to have any, what is more, of what value could they be compared with the propositions now on the tongues of the new élite, the professors of management science? Many years were to elapse – and many are yet to come – before the notion of autonomous learning, of managers helping each other as they

21

get on with their ordinary tasks was to be accorded attention, let alone to be accepted. It was still the expert who would step in at the correct moment and see that the ordinary men were not allowed to make fools of themselves. Elitism, whether by profession or by intellect, still dies hard, if it should die at all; in our latest economic mess it survives within the government, with its growing number of ministers who retain their special advisers. Whenever the camels of democratic policy jostle to get through the eye of the same budgetary needle there, surely, is work for the experts. But action learning would try a new combination of their skills; each would try to get, not the camel of his own minister through the hole, but the camel of another; we see in Chapter 8 that we owe this variation to the Public Service Boards of Australia.

When things are normal, by all means stick to the advice of your own expert, but, if ever they get troublesome, call for a general post; employ the man from the weather bureau to sort out the cabinet office and the man from the office to regulate the bureau. Beneath the expertise may struggle an intelligent mind; if there does, that expert mind may begin to learn and may even set off a collective learning process through the organization that it serves. But, if it remains rigidly cramped in the idolization of its own expertise, it will not learn much of the world beyond.

2.
Action Learning under the Trees

Fair weather friends soon fall to and make merry. But it is the comrades in adversity who provide us with the better example.

Every man takes the limits of his own vision for the limits of the world. (Schopenhauer, *Psychological Observations*)

To him who looks upon the world rationally, the world in its turn presents a rational aspect. The relation is mutual. (Hegel, *Introduction to the Philosophy of History*)

In 1964 I was invited, through the Ford Foundation, to Eastern Nigeria – later, during an unhappy interlude, to proclaim itself as an independent Biafra – to work with Professor Harold Martin, then of the Rensselaer Polytechnic Institute in Upper New York, and with his colleague, Simcha Bahiri, on a project run from the Institute of Productivity and Management in Enugu. It had been launched to improve the operating performance of about a hundred small mills set up in the surrounding scrublands to extract the oil from the nuts of the wild palm trees. It was before the development of Nigeria as a major source of petroleum, and Nigeria's trade was still largely in the sale of forest products and vegetable oil. The bulk of this was distilled from the nuts of the palm trees grown in carefully tended plantations, but there were still – or so it was believed – sufficient wild palms bearing fruit to make their organized exploitation worth while.

The mills set up to do so were primitive in the extreme and consisted of a few large vats of stainless steel-work, into which the nuts were loaded when properly ripe; they were then boiled and the precious oil was run off into drums, to be sold to a state trading corporation for further processing before export. Each little mill had two or three supervisors and about a score of general workers; the nuts were collected by girls who shinned up the trees, often with a baby on the back as well as a basket on the head. The girls sold the nuts to the mill managers at the best price they could get, although we had been told that there was a ceiling imposed by the central administration on the amount the managers were permitted to pay. The embarrassment of the development corporation was that, when the amortization of the capital equipment was charged against the expenditure of the total enterprise, the mills were losing money; since the price at which the product sold for export was fixed, the corporation could suggest nothing better to do than to close down the venture, although we were never able to discover what would have happened to the abandoned assets, nor whether any thought had been given to the social problems of putting a couple of thousand men out of work or depriving several hundred tree-climbing young goddesses of a lucrative and exciting pastime. It was to suggest action other than stopping what was going on that the three of us found ourselves in Enugu, the guests of an intelligent young Ibo lecturer, Dr John Iboko, from the Institute.

Although John Iboko had studied operational research at an American university he was, like Harold Martin, not anxious to play the role of expert consultant to the managers of the mills; he had agreed to my being invited to Enugu on the clear understanding that, if possible, the managers were to discover their own means of salvation, and this, we all insisted, they would do only out in the jungle. The managers whom we assembled in a vast and luxurious hotel in Enugu were considerably astonished to discover that none of the foreign visitors – Martin, a veteran adviser to productivity programmes across the world, retained by several agencies of standing besides the Ford Foundation and the United Nations; Bahiri, brought from Israel after spectacular achievements in setting up economically sound mechanical engineering factories in what, ten years before, had been a waterless desert; and myself, President of the European Association of Management Centres, a federation

24

of the forty or so European schools of university rank striving to raise the study of management to the dignity of graduate and postgraduate studies – had the slightest notion as to what seemed to be amiss with the enterprise. They were even more surprised to learn (and it took some time, since none of us spoke Ibo and none of the managers spoke English) that the three of us not only proposed to visit the mills themselves, but to do so in the hope of encouraging the managers to learn with and from each other what they ought to do about the mess they all seemed to be in. We found later that the officers from the central administration of the venture, who had advised the government to close it down and to sell its assets, had never been seen out in the field; it was difficult for me to believe this until I met the economic consultant to the corporation, when I discovered him to be an expatriate who graduated at a cele-brated management school in his own country, with many publications to his credit.

After a short talk upon the nature of observation, framed around studying the flow of materials, the rewards of labour and the recording of information, a first sample of a dozen mill managers, soon to be followed by a second dozen, were sent out to analyse their own operations and those of their fellows. Like the mining students many years before, they felt that much was expected of them, since they were clear that they would get little from the visitors. There, at each other's mills, sorting out each other's records more critically than if they were their own, watching and intervening in each other's operations, from the first bargains struck with the ebony god-desses balancing ten kilograms of fruit upon their heads to the final filtering of the precious oil from the reeking ooze, showing off ingenious gimmicks such as a corrugated iron sheet to sort overripe fruit to be processed at once from that which could be held for a few more days, explaining economies of method, such as getting the goddess to tip her load into a gravity-feed hopper at the head of a short flight of steps rather than to shoot it upon the bare earth, airing their favourite management principles and roaring together at their traditional jokes: there, out in the familiar field, they came alive. There, at each neigh-bour's mill, were the manifold variations of the problems they thought they knew so well in their own. In fact, the sweltering realities of their host mills became for an hour each more real than their own back home, for at each fresh visit what was novel was brought to them in a dozen different ways, reflected in a dozen distinctive images from the past experiences of a dozen different colleagues, like the kaleidoscopic snatches of a strip dancer seen in a dozen tilted mirrors. Each of these uncomplicated men, on his visit to another mill, fought a dozen times the battle of better managing it, and returned to think about his own task with new insight into his own professional experience. It was therefore little surprise for me to hear, some months later, that because of the improvements that followed, the corporation had changed its mind and was keeping the mills open. It took a civil war to close them, but only until the end of hostilities.

The convincing secret that each helped the others to unlock was, like so many other roads to virtue, obvious enough when they had first discovered it. It was not long before they found out that not all of the hundred units under the trees were losing money, howsoever their accounts were read. They were, all the same, considerably surprised to learn, in answer to their own questions, that the few who were actually making a profit were those who purchased their raw materials, the nuts, at the highest price, a discovery that seemed to stand the laws of economics on their head, and that was, moreover, disobedient to the instructions of the corporation's financial officers. But within a few hours they had also seen that the higher the price offered to the girls, the more nuts they were brought; indeed, the girls thought nothing of carrying their loads three or four miles through the scrub, from one mill to the next, should the first manager make too mean an offer for what they had brought him. A critical resource to the whole system – the time of the girls available to climb the trees for the essential fruit – was thus being wasted as they ferried their loads uselessly (for the system as a whole) along the network of paths on whose intersections stood the mills and the villages. A higher purchase price, moreover, brought more goddesses forward to gather the precious fruit, so that the managers who were paying above the prescribed price were working to their full capacity. Nor was that all. The effectiveness with which any given unit was conducted turned out to be highly sensitive to its total throughput; if this were too great, other troubles might arise that affected the quality of the crude product, and so the whole exercise among the twenty-four managers became one of mutual search for a common optimum. The experimental conditions for finding it were ideal, and the intervention of the Biafran war proved little more than a temporary setback; the Institute of Productivity and Management secured a thorough grasp of the notions of action learning and have done a service to its cause across the world.

The conditions making for the success of this first action learning project in a developing country are worth listing.

First, there was a powerful motivation to do something about the trouble they were in, namely, a threat of closure; as Samuel Johnson had observed 'Depend upon it, Sir, when a man knows he is to be hanged in a fortnight, it concentrates his mind wonderfully'. Most persons, not only managers, will try to learn soon enough when they need to do so, when the alternative to not knowing is sufficiently unpleasant.

Secondly, the learning of the managers was encouraged by their being obliged to think for themselves; there were no experts among them claiming to know the solution to their difficulties, confusing the current trouble with some other to which they had found, or believed they had found, the answer only last month. I had learned among the colliery managers of Britain that, when nobody present mistakenly clamoured to tell everybody else what to do, little time was wasted in doing useless things or in discussing empty assertions.

Thirdly, since there were no misleading suggestions from the outset, all suggestions needed to be thought about; some of these, howsoever ridiculous at first sight, such as that raising one's purchase price might also raise one's profit, were eventually given a trial, so that the managers saw the effects of their own suggestions or of their own objections to those of others. It is a cardinal postulate of action learning that only when the subject sees the effect of his own behaviour is there any chance of that behaviour being varied; the system that is to learn must receive inputs about its own outputs.

Fourthly, the constant arguments with colleagues striving to solve the same problems led each manager to review, often several times in a day, what he really saw as his past experience,

27

in the sense of how he used that past experience; this brought home to most of the men that their learning consisted more in reorganizing this experience than in acquiring fresh facts or principles from outsiders.

Fifthly, since so many different mills were involved in the study, any promising suggestions put forward were tried out many times with slight local variations, thus giving to the test a richer and more reliable evaluation.

Sixthly, and most important of all, in all the arguments about what they needed to do for salvation, the managers inevitably let each other have a few simple truths about themselves that they would not have learned in any other way; the community was fighting for its life, and any members of it who were being silly or obstinate or overbearing were soon made aware of their behaviour by their colleagues. In the less urgent setting of the management seminar, even the most perceptive of men may be slow in seeing himself as the fly in the ointment of the educational apothecary. The point is important, for it is the strength of the conspiracy, of which the English law takes a serious view. In a conspiracy one takes particular care to know the character of one's mates, for enterprises that may run a rope round one's neck are hazardous enough without being mixed up amid untrustworthy fellows. And, by the same token, one learns much of oneself and stands often to be reminded of it when things do not go smoothly. Comradeship in adversity may lack the risk of partnership in conspiracy, but it still may teach one much about oneself; when all must needs be serious, as closing an industry suggests, there is no virtue in behaving as other than the person one is. We may leave the point with a verse from Proverbs (ch. 27, v. 17): 'Iron sharpeneth iron; so a man sharpeneth the countenance of a friend.'

3.
The Hospital as a Learning System

Physician, heal thyself: whatsoever we have heard done in Capernaum, do also here in thy country. (Luke, ch. 4, 21)

Action learning is such a simple idea that it took those who set out to reorganize the National Health Service in 1969 almost ten years before they thoroughly misunderstood it; the mess they made in the upheaval of 1974 shows, nevertheless, that they had made some progress down the road to disaster.

In the Bible I read of a patient called Lazarus; he was brought to life again after being dead for four whole days. But he was discharged covered with bandages; our *Mr Armitage would never have allowed that!* (Lancashire ward sister on difficulties of working with surgeons, 1958)

You seem to think, Professor Revans, that the sisters in this hospital are fighting Death. It's not quite as simple as that: we're fighting the doctors! (Another Lancashire ward sister, 1958)

In September 1959, I presented a paper at the Sixth Annual International Meeting of the Institute of Management Sciences, held in Paris. The paper was entitled 'The hospital as an organism: a study in communications and morale'. In this I set out to show, from researches conducted in a number of hospitals in and around Manchester, that there were very wide differences between the stability of the nursing staffs at apparently comparable hospitals, on the one hand, and between the average number of patients discharged annually per available bed, on the other. In other words, each hospital had a recognizable character – similar to the metabolism of a living creature – that indicated its success in assimilating both its nurses and its patients. In general, this metabolism could be traced among nurses of all ranks, from matrons to assistant nurses, and among all diagnostic groups of patients, so that it was allowable to think of the hospital community as endowed throughout with a pervasive spirit.

The continuation of the researches over the next few years enabled me to publish in 1964 a tract, *Standards for Morale; Cause and Effect in Hospitals*, that suggested the organic characteristic to be the capacity of those within the community to learn with and from each other in the course of their everyday experience. Where the communications within the hospital were sufficiently open for each to help the other frame more precisely the questions they needed to have answered, the system was able to learn; not only did the nurses find their duties more interesting because they were more instructive, but the patients responded more rapidly to their treatment simply because this was based more accurately upon their clinical needs.

In 1964 the King Edward VII Hospital Fund, urged on by its Assistant Director, Janet Craig (later to become the first secretary of the Action Learning Trust) undertook to promote the Hospitals Internal Communications Project (HIC); this was supported by the Department of Health and Social Security and aided by the Department of Community Medicine at Guy's Hospital Medical School. Just as in the coalmines and in the jungle, our aim was improved performance by better understanding, with the better understanding achieved by action learning through a joint attack upon common problems. Hospitals, we thought, help patients to get better; nobody *cures* patients (any more than anybody else *teaches* managers), although somebody must provide the conditions in which the natural processes of revival and improvement built into each of us by Almighty God are given the best chance to exhibit their merits. If an illness is clearly diagnosed and an appropriate programme of care built upon it, these natural processes may be encouraged and so speeded up; if a faulty diagnosis is made or the patient treated with the care intended for another, the strivings of Nature may be brought to nothing and the

30

recovery of the patient impeded – perhaps for good. Thus members of hospital staffs who help each other to perceive more clearly what may be going on around them, from doctor to porter, from matron to washerwoman, from administrator to ward clerk, might bring the patients rapidly to the point of recovery and hence of discharge. We may therefore assert that one evidence of collective learning is a slow decline in the average length of patient stay; this may, of course, be translated into other measures, such as the use made of available beds, which, in practice, seems to be strongly correlated with the mean length of patient stay in the corresponding clinical division of the hospital.

Evaluation of the outcome of an experiment in action learning by the trends in this simple measure is, in practice, rather complex, for even in those hospitals that volunteered to join the HIC Project not all the consultants wanted to get involved. In reading the records of the hospitals across the period of the exercise we had therefore to discriminate between the records of the different patients according to whether or not their consultants were participating in the supposed learning processes. Moreover, across the decade, 1964 to 1973 inclusive, in which I trace the effect of the Project (which ran from 1965 to 1968) many other influences bore upon the National Health Service, helping to cause a long-term decline in the average lengths of patient stay in all hospitals throughout the country, and not only in hospitals that tried action learning. This complication must be allowed for, but it still leaves us with other things we need to think about. Action learning is a novel, and therefore a threatening, experience; I examine at length in another part of this book (Chapter 19) some typical responses of the coalitions of power that may be caught up in the more robust developments of self-awakening, and some of them do not like what they begin to learn; action learning is felt as an intolerable strain, and those who do not like it may not have the courage to say so in public. One might then expect to see their ambiguous involvement in the programme reflected in the records of their hospital's performance.

In the event, the management committees of ten large hospitals in and around London and their senior staffs volunteered to try the idea of learning with and from each other; seven of the ten were acute generals and strictly comparable, and they were joined, to add variety to the inter-hospital discussions, by a university teaching hospital, one for the mentally ill and another for sick and mentally handicapped children. Each hospital nominated two teams, each of three: doctor, nurse and administrator. The senior teams spent three days together discussing the problems, as they saw them, of running large hospitals, and the measures they took to deal with such problems; these discussions were preparatory to receiving in their hospital the junior team from some other hospital in the consortium. The junior teams spent about three weeks together discussing such matters as the conduct of free interviews, the search of data and the preparation of flow process charts; they tried their hands at visiting another hospital to find out from the resident staff what they imagined to be their problems and what they thought needed to be done about them.

Each hospital, working with its neighbours in the consortium, then selected a small number of problems internal to itself and formed a number of operational teams from those caught up in these problems; these worked in co-operation with the teams from other hospitals, and sometimes with students from local colleges to undertake the donkeywork of collecting the responses to questionnaires or of studying in some detail a hospital service. In this way, and over three years of sporadic effort, the ten hospitals tackled nearly 40 perceived sources of malfunction; some of these projects involved several hundred members of the staff of the hospital, either in the original collection of data or in the later efforts to change the system under review.

In the evaluation of the outcome of the project using the data of changes in hospital performance (for there are other evaluations of the experiment written by the staffs of the participating hospitals themselves),[2] we use only the statistics of the seven acute general hospitals, since the other three are not comparable among themselves. Since there were eighteen other large acute general hospitals in and around London that did not come into the experiment, we are able to compare the trends in the experimental seven with those in the other eighteen. In fact, I have chosen to compare the trends in the experimental seven with those in all other hospitals in the South-

East of England, as I feel this to give the more representative measure of the national shortening of the length of patient stay over the decade. And in comparing the trends in the experimental seven with those of all other hospitals in the same four regions, I have further treated the seven as two sets, of five and of two respectively. The two hospitals, in an evaluation of the programme made before the end of the experimental period, said that they had found it disappointing; they implied, entirely honestly, that they had been somewhat misled in joining the consortium in the first place. Since they reported this several years before the evaluation made in 1975, we are entitled to treat the records of the two separately from those of the five, whose staffs soldiered through to the end and who now, ten years later, still write appreciatively of their experience.

Hospital	Type	Divisions involved		Divisions not involved	
		GM	GS	gyn	obs
I	AG	−4.44	−1.18	+2.32	−2.28
II	AG	−1.43	−5.25	+1.74	+0.34
III	AG	−2.93	−0.68	−1.45	+0.84
IV	AG	−6.23	−2.26	−0.31	+0.88
V	AG	+0.31	−0.89	−1.45	na
VI	AG	−0.13	−0.10	+1.26	+1.32
VII	AG	+4.93	+3.07	+2.87	+1.73
VIII	Ch		−8.56		
IX	MI		−3.76		
X	UT	+3.73	+1.12	−1.53	+3.44

(Source: DHSS Form SH3)

Table 1: Results of HIC Project 1964–73. Changes in days per decade of mean length of patient stay relative to similar patients in all other Metropolitan region hospitals, or, for Hospital X, in all other London teaching hospitals. Key: AG acute general; Ch Children's; MI mentally ill; UT university teaching; GM general medicine; GS general surgery; gyn gynaecology; obs obstetrics.

The grand means for Hospitals I to V for divisions involved and not involved are respectively −2.498 and +0.070; the significance of their difference is about 1.25 per cent and is thus unlikely to have occurred by chance. For *all* entries of Hospitals I to V and for Hospitals VI and VII they are respectively −1.282 and +1.869; their difference is significant at below 1 per cent and is even less likely to be random. Our experiment does therefore not disprove the assumptions of action learning.

The relevant findings, from which the project is finally evaluated, are given in Table 1. It employs the data for four only of the clinical divisions in the seven acute general hospitals, but since there were no obstetric patients at Hospital V there is one empty cell in the matrix of seven hospitals by four clinical divisions. The four have been chosen because they are the largest in most hospitals, accounting for over half the total discharges in 1973 out of thirty specialties in all. The detailed percentages in 1973 were: general surgery, 18.8; general medicine, 13.5; obstetrics, 11.9; gynaecology, 9.2. Twenty-six other specialties account for the remaining 46.6 per cent of the total inpatient discharges at all hospitals. The choice of the major four to make our comparisons between trends at the experimental hospitals and trends at the others representative of the hospital service as a whole can thus be readily justified. Of these four specialties (clinical divisions), one pair, general surgery and general medicine, alone contributed consultants to the HIC Project; it attracted no gynaecologists and no obstetricians. This therefore entitles us to show, as we do in Table 1, the data for the four main specialties in separated parts of the table. Moreover, on the admission of the staffs themselves of Hospitals VI and VII, we are entitled to consider them as negative towards the project, whereas the staffs of the other five acute general hospitals we shall count as positive. For sceptical readers who suggest that, were action learning of any real merit, there would be no negative respondents to it, I suggest a study of the chapter in this book already mentioned (Chapter 19). Our tables shows the key results for the 60,000 inpatients who passed every year through the seven acute general hospitals; the entries are, in days, the relative changes in length of patient stay across the decade, 1964 to 1973 inclusive; the analysis finishes in 1973, simply because in 1974 the National Health Service underwent a momentous reorganization, the effects of which are hard to appreciate and are at the present time under examination by a Royal Commission. By 'relative' changes in length of patient stay, I mean 'relative to changes in the length of stay of patients in the same clinical divisions (specialties) but in hospitals that did not join the HIC Project'. The control hospitals were all others in the South-East of England, except the university teaching hospitals.

34

The display of data is impressive. In the five acute general hospitals in which the consultants participated, the clinical divisions in which they did so shortened (relative to other hospitals in the South-East) their length of patient stay by about sixty hours. In the same hospitals, the change in relative length of patient stay in those clinical divisions in which the consultants did not participate was slightly to increase it, by a non-significant amount of less than two hours. For the two acute general hospitals that joined the project but were disappointed by their experience of it, there was a statistically significant lengthening of the relative patient stay.

If we confine our remarks to those hospitals that seemed to profit from the experience, we may go a little further and roughly estimate the cost-benefit of the endeavour. Thirty-five thousand patients a year over the decade were generally speeded through the general medical and general surgical divisions of the five positive hospitals, achieving a final reduction of sixty hours (and so an average of thirty hours) in their mean length of stay. Three hundred and fifty thousand patients were thus discharged about ten million hours sooner than they would have been had they not benefited from the experiment. Since the cost of this was £62,500 – not, of course, counting the time of the staff engaged on what were common hospital duties – the hourly price to be paid for getting the patients home more quickly was about three-fifths of a penny, or fifteen pence a day. We should ask ourselves whether, if by local co-operation the teamwork within a hospital can be so improved as to get the patients home more quickly, this is a fair price to pay for doing so. If we ask the less extravagant question as to what might be the marginal cost of the food, bedlinen and soap (but not the overheads such as salaries) for ten million hours of bed-occupancy, we should be bound to conclude that, howsoever assessed, it would exceed £62,500 considerably. And from where does that saving come? It comes from the unused skills and motivations of those already within the hospitals themselves, effectively marshalled by action learning.

These financial exercises are as illiberal as they are useless. The main benefit of the HIC Project is to prove that, given the will to allow those responsible for our hospitals to discover for themselves how to run them more autonomously, they might soon learn how to do so. The National Health Service might become just as skilled in diagnosing the afflictions of a sick hospital as its doctors are in identifying those of a sick patient; such insights and their appropriate cures might well be developed area by area, hospital by hospital, and all could learn with and from each other. But vast cultural changes must first be secured; public administration in general, and that of the social services in particular, is still dominated by the authoritarianism of the Middle Ages; it is still for the professor-popes and the bureaucrat-emperors to tell others what to do and how to do it. If there is one thing we can no longer ignore, it is that the Health Service has had all the expert attention it can stand and that the hour of self-aided convalescence is long overdue.

Soon after the Hospitals Internal Communications Project had been completed, the question was raised about treating other branches of the social services beset with ill-defined and obstinate problems. There were, in particular, many expressions of disquiet about the miserable experiences of the mentally handicapped and their families; it was a confused and contradictory tale that was usually told, since the personal character and professional integrity of the officers censured for the unhappy incidents so titillating to the press were always beyond reproach; such staff invariably were overworked and not seldom underpaid. It seemed grossly unfair for society, which had made peace with its own conscience by unloading its responsibility for protecting the disadvantaged upon a handful of willing professionals, to call down retribution upon them when things went seriously wrong.

With the further support of the King Edward's Fund for London, therefore, a small group from the Hospitals Internal Communications Project worked for three further years on an action learning consortium to improve the services offered to the mentally handicapped. The main efforts were those of the staff of seven local authorities – Gateshead, Nottingham, Hull, Oxford, West Suffolk, East Sussex and the London Borough of Hounslow – and others locally concerned with the mentally handicapped, such as the Regional Health Authority and the general practitioners, as well as the voluntary organizations and the parents. About 150 professionals joined the work of the consortium – paediatricians, doctors, mental welfare officers, health visitors, teachers from special schools and training centres, record officers and administrators – along with the parents and voluntary workers, to study the needs of a 5-per-cent sample of the mentally handicapped still living at home. They came together nationally to discuss what questions they thought they should ask, working in professionally homo-geneous groups on some occasions and across professions on others. They prepared questionnaires incorporating the results of these self-searchings, and for every person whose needs and experiences were under review collected the facts as they were seen by six different parties – parents, general practitioner, health visitor, mental welfare officer, teacher and the official files kept with the medical officer of health or his successor.

The consortium met regularly to discuss the results of the study and finally produced a report to which all in some degree had contributed; they gave to it the ironic title: 'I thought *they* were supposed to be doing that!' because they dis-covered, parents and officers together, that the topic of co-ordination between the many parties there to help these unfortunate families, although continually complained about, was almost never taken in hand. It is an interesting coincidence that the study was completed over here at exactly the same time as the study by the Rand Corporation of the social and economic troubles of New York City (see Chapter 17); it is less interesting to discover that the two enquiries reach the same conclusion about the needs to involve both staff and clients in the formation and discharge of welfare policies. I believe that the only difference between the two studies lies in method-ologies: whereas the Americans were calling upon one of the most sophisticated research agencies in the world, we in Britain were getting those who must deal with the disadvantaged in the normal course of their employment to identify and to deal with their common troubles as part of the daily round. Action learning pretends to be nothing more: learning by action, or doing better tomorrow by asking how well the job is being done today. As in all high-order evolutionary processes, the attempt to improve the services to the sick and to the dis-advantaged must begin with the attitudes and skills of those who serve in them; even those sovereign lords of social research agencies, the writers of the Rand Corporation, recognize that they can do nothing without the personal backing of those who provide the services, and for whom the services are provided. The apostles of action learning would take the American thesis one stage further: it is for the expert researchers, if protocol demands that they are to be involved at all, merely to suggest the conditions in which those with the operational responsibility can do the whole job from start to finish.

4.
Belgium breaks through

Things they don't understand always create a sensation among the English. (Alfred de Musset, *The White Blackbird*)

If any man wishes to keep a school in Ghent, and has the knowledge and ability, he may do so, nor shall any man be able to say him nay. (Charter of Ghent, granted 1191 by Mathildis of Portugal)

Edward III . . . sent secret emissaries into Flanders . . . to tell the Flemings 'how happy they should be if they would but come over into England, bringing their Mystery with them, which would provide their welcome in all places. Here they should feed on fatt Beef and Mutton till nothing but their fulnesse should stint their stomacks: yea they should feed on the labours of their own hands'; and, as a result of the arrival of a large number of Flemings, 'English Wool improved to the highest profit'. (McKisack, *The Fourteenth Century*, OUP, 1959, p. 367)

Action learning? You don't know what is action learning? If there's money in it – and it has anything at all to do with training managers – then it's action learning! (Any management professor, 1978)

At about the time I was suggesting how the grosser problems of the hospital service might be tackled by action learning – by the staffs trying to learn with and from each other by throwing open to their comrades in adversity their own internal chaos and confusions – there was becoming apparent in Britain an awareness that all was not as well as it might be with management in general. It was not only the National Health Service that seemed to be breathing heavily; various business analysts were pointing out that those firms in Britain run by the British throughout did not seem to be doing so well as those of foreign ownership, with some foreign element in their management and direction. Various delegations, concerned with productivity, quality, design, costs and other aspects of an industrial economy, had visited America, Japan and other exporting countries in the hope of discovering the reasons for their growing superiority as manufacturers of the goods traditionally made and sold by Britain. Managers of all ages were sent to courses at American business schools to learn the convincing secrets of their educational superiority; experts in 'organizational theory' from Boston, Cleveland, New York, Pittsburgh and San Francisco came with instant plans for restructuring British corporations so that almost everybody, by now reporting to somebody else, would at once become more efficient than he or she had ever been in their previous tasks.

So overwhelming did the evidence eventually become that the mandarins of British industry decided to set up in this country the counterparts of these celebrated American institutions; we were to have our own management professors, dispensing the new wisdom from our own centres of national excellence. The possibility that America's natural resources, internal markets and ruthless competitiveness were so great that her productive economy was able to afford the extravagance of ruinously wasteful business schools, pretending like cocks that crow at the rising sun to be the real driving force behind it, never crossed the minds of all those, so clever and so financially interested, who wanted to see business schools set up in this country. And yet this seems to have been the only proposition that, fifteen years later, has been proved by the establishment of such mammoth academies in Britain. The availability of millions of pounds to the new élite set off what at the time I called the Academic Klondyke:

Management education is one of the fashionable activities of the age; hundreds of courses are offered throughout Europe, in universities and colleges of technology, by management foundations, educational trusts, industrial consultants, federations of employers, registered companies, nationalised industries and, most vigorous of all, the eternal ambush of commercial exploiters that awaits each passing fashion. It is prudent to enquire of all who purvey this latest art, whether teachers or not, how they made a living yesterday, for a new trade has sprung up overnight, and thousands now support themselves, either wholly or in part, by professing to show existing and potential managers how better to do their jobs. (*The Theory of Practice in Management*, Macdonald, London, 1966, referring to an address of 1963)

It was impossible, in these conditions, to encourage even those who were putting up the money to stop for a few moments and ask themselves what they imagined all this activity was going to do – except provide each of many quick-witted academics with a lot of money, a sports car and a cottage in the country. My own thesis that there is and can be no such subject as a 'science of administration' was dismissed as the envious maundering of one who had read neither economics nor psychology : my evidential proof that, beyond certain magnitudes, the organizations we were trying to run rapidly declined in effectiveness (and thus the doctrine of economy of scale was just an illusion) was contemptuously dismissed by the experts.[3] My proposals for establishing at the Manchester College of Science and Technology a consortium of managers to tackle their local troubles by the mutually supportive methods of the mines and hospitals were thrown out with the comment that they would 'divide the faculty'. All hopes were pinned upon the new business school. But as soon as I knew into whose hands the control of this was to fall, I resigned my chair and resolved to leave the country.

I therefore offered my services to the Belgians, and spent the next ten years in exile. I worked for a singular institution, founded and run by a remarkable man; the institution was the Fondation Industrie-Université and its managing director was Gaston Deurinck. Although the developments of action learning were, during those ten years, confined almost entirely to Belgium, it is also clear that a slow cultural preparation was maturing all over the world; business was awakening to the fact that management cannot be taught by professors of management. When the work of Gaston Deurinck and the Fondation was ready for the world, the world, in turn, was ready to

41

receive it. I am well aware that it was the Belgians who took the risks in giving action learning the extended trial it was granted, although Gaston Deurinck had, independently of me, already reached some of the same conclusions about the futility of academic teaching; he had, indeed, been somewhat rasher and had invaded each of the major universities of Belgium with schools of active management research, bringing real managers to examine real problems in real time in the company of the academics. Nor was this all. Belgium is a highly industrialized country with little natural resource; it lives by efficiently converting expensive imports into yet more valuable exports, a policy that must recognize good management as an extremely precious asset. Since the factory system grew to maturity in Belgium long before it did in Britain (the cloth mills of Flanders processed the wools of Suffolk sheep many centuries before the Industrial Revolution), the Belgian industrialist does not need to be persuaded about the importance of effective management. Moreover, the unhappy history of Belgium as the cockpit of Europe has led this redoubtable little nation to understand that only its own people are going to save it; the slogan of British productivity missions, turning their eyes to America, 'Salvation by Aliens', has no appeal to a virile country rich with its memories of uninvited aliens shelling its cities. The idea that its businessmen might learn with and from each other by working together on their various problems was thus at once accepted and forthwith developed.

Although several different programmes in action learning were started in Belgium – including one to inject more realism into the work of doctoral candidates likely to finish as management professors, and another in which senior managers studied their own jobs in ways that enabled them to exchange experiences with other managers studying theirs – it is sufficient in this introduction to describe briefly the Inter-University Programme, at least in the form in which it was first launched. It is a strength of action learning that the programmes it evolves are continuously changing; systems that do not, or cannot change, do not, or cannot learn. However this may be, the programme started around the five major universities of Belgium and twenty sizeable enterprises; the smallest of these was a wireless telegraphy concern that maintained the equipment on board most of the vessels belonging to the Belgian merchant marine, and the largest included international steel companies employing of the order of 100,000 workers.

The most enthusiastic supporters of the programme since it was set up over a decade ago have been the banks, of which Brussels, as the administrative capital of the European Economic Community, has several; engineering, chemicals and papermaking, oil refining, insurance, metal blending and smelting, electricity generating, locomotive building and a dozen other industries have participated in the programme, which has three broad purposes. First, to enable every enterprise to make better use of its existing resources, by trying to engender within it a social process of learning calculated to help it identify its internal strengths and weaknesses, to understand better its inertias and its dynamics, and in other ways to make more effective use of its stored experience. Second, to encourage a selected class of senior managers, men of 35 years of age, who have already demonstrated their abilities to run their own department or division of their concern, to prepare themselves for the open-ended responsibilities of policy-making; the programme attempts to change confident experts, who by role and training are equipped to implement the policies of the directors for whom they work, into members of the policy-making boards themselves. Those who have proved themselves capable to carry out the policies of others are to be equipped by the programme to form policies on their own account; those who are able to answer questions are to learn how to pose them for others to answer. Third, to encourage a change in the self-perception of professional management development experts; the teacher of management is to recognize the futility of his mission, and to see himself no longer as an instructor of novices, but as a mature person trying to contrive the conditions under which managers learn from their own experience. Management education is no longer to be a craft pursued in schools and seminars, although these may survive as supporting media; the development of the manager is to be seen as a natural outcome of his successful daily practice; by tackling today's problems more thoughtfully, he automatically learns how better to tackle tomorrow's.

We shall in a later chapter analyse the structure of action

learning programmes of this kind (see Chapter 21); it is enough for the present to outline its cardinal points.

First, the chief executives of a score of Belgian companies were invited to submit to the programme both a major inter-departmental problem (or opportunity) to be worked upon, together with the name of a senior departmental manager. The problem had not to be a mere puzzle, namely, something to which a solution could be said already to exist, provided some specialist acute enough could be let loose to find it; a problem is some embarrassment to the top management to which different reasonable, honest and experienced men would suggest different approaches, according to their personal value systems and individual past achievements. The senior managers, too, were expected to reveal, as the result of stringent interview before a jury of chief executives, that they were not investing up to nine months of their lives at this critical age in order to become merely expert in more management techniques, such as computer programming, financial analysis or sophisticated mathematical methods. The encouragement to be given to these senior men, to be known as fellows, was that they might be able, in conditions where nobody around them could see what to do because they had not before encountered such conditions, to suggest what might be the more useful questions to pose.

Secondly, having nominated both a problem and a fellow, the participating enterprise had to prepare itself to receive into itself a visiting fellow *from another enterprise* in the pro-gramme. The first step in preparing for this was the appoint-ment of a client, a member of the senior staff – perhaps even the president of the enterprise – who could be said, more than any other person, to 'own' the problem nominated for attack. It might also be necessary for the enterprise to identify a counterpart to the visiting fellow, and it would be essential for the client to make it thoroughly known throughout the enter-prise that its top management was serious about the project and expected the support of all concerned with it.

Thirdly, the fellows were brought together, with some of the chief executives of the participating enterprises, to decide upon the programme of exchanges; there are certain simple rules to govern these, if the learning of the visitors *and* of the visited is to be worth while.

44

Fourthly, the twenty fellows were then allocated to the five universities, and built into sets; the only rule we found important about the constitution of sets was that they respected the language, French or Dutch, which the participants regarded as their mother tongue, howsoever well they spoke the other.

Fifthly, the fellows were given a short induction course, to prepare them to enter their receiving enterprises with an opening balance of self-confidence; this course has been progressively shortened as the programme has matured, and is now no more than three weeks, one-third of its original length. For the next three months the fellows were four days a week in their receiving enterprises and came together on the fifth in their sets, to discuss their problems and their progress with the other three or four members. This first spell of three months is called the 'diagnostic' phase of the programme; during it the fellows are expected to identify the nature of the problem they have been posed and to outline an action plan that might be implemented with the support of their clients – and of any other resources whatever available within the programme as a whole. At the end of the diagnostic phase, alike as an incentive to their exhausted spirits and as a critical monitor to their achievements and to their proposals, the fellows are taken to America, where they are able to present their accounts and proposals to the business school experts and to receive what are often usefully different interpretations of their experiences and of their prospects. At the end of the American visit, they return to the 'therapeutic' phase of the programme, to spend a further three or four months on persuading their receiving enterprises to put their plans into effect; if the fellow has gained the confidence of the client, and of a powerful client group (*structure d'acceuil*), during the diagnostic phase, so that the proposals he takes to America are as much those of his receiving enterprise as they are the products of his own ingenuity, the therapeutic phase can be rewarding.

Finally, the visiting fellow is to review with his client and client group what outstanding is left to be done, and to suggest with them what organization they should themselves set up to see that it is done.

The conditions in which the Inter-University Programme

45

was started could not have been more favourable to the educational experiment it was; Belgium is a small country, and its captains of industry are well known to each other. The programme therefore opened with strong social support; every participating chief executive knew that his colleagues would be judging the quality of his enterprise and the soundness of his personal judgement by the calibre of the fellow whom he sent to exhibit his talents in attacking the conundrums of another firm. There was no fear of the programme becoming (as other programmes are not seldom seen to become) a kind of academic Sargasso Sea for assembling the managerial driftwood away from the commercial trade routes. Belgian industry is so varied and yet so concentrated that there was no trouble in exchanging oilmen to work in banks, or insurance directors to take up the strategic hopes of innovating steel concerns; the opportunities for those who had become more than expert in one industry – or even in one specialism within one particular industry – to redress for nine months the unseen problems of a totally different sector of the economy were available on the doorstep, unlike in India, where some years later the fellows worked upon the problems of receiving enterprises many hundreds of miles from home. But it was the close association with the universities of Belgium that gave the programme an intellectual rigour of its own; since there were five participating schools, the five sets of fellows developed along their own lines and, at the monthly gatherings of the whole consortium, displayed in each other's progress both a friendly competitiveness and an anxiety to learn from a different dialectic. The research traditions of the universities also directed much attention to the underlying logic of action learning, so that we are able to present a repertoire of theoretical credentials (see Chapter 20) such as does not encumber the bill of all-star turns that is so frequently offered as a management programme. Finally, the setting of the programme, in one of the busiest cities of Europe – if not of the world – meant that it became fairly well known, if not always fully understood, and it is from Brussels that the notions of action learning have now diffused around the globe. The first occasion to take the essentially English idea of learning from observable experience through a cultural barrier arrived in 1969, when a small party from the first round of the Inter-

University Programme raised the flag of action learning in the principal city of the Arab world.

Before closing this brief account of my ten years in Belgium, however, I must mention the doctoral programme that evolved out of my association with the universities of that country. A number of generous bursaries were awarded every year, between five and ten, for students wishing to become teachers of subjects with a strong managerial concern, such as engineering or accountancy. They entered whatever might be the department of the university appropriate for their doctoral researches and, supported for four years by the bursaries (one of the years being spent abroad), prepared what is regarded as a normal thesis. It had been, nevertheless, a condition of award of the bursary that each candidate, in the submission of the thesis, would pay particular attention to the four following points:

(a) In what ways can the contents of this thesis – insofar as they have any bearing upon the problems or opportunities of contemporary Belgium – be made intelligible to men of practice? It must not be forgotten that some doctoral researches may enter realms of argument so remote from the everyday business of ordinary persons that even a university committee monitoring the award of degrees may be frustrated in its search for suitable examiners; it is not unknown for a dissertation to be sent to another continent for final evaluation because there is no professor in Europe able to understand what it is about. It was for the Belgian candidate to satisfy the committee for doctoral awards about the continued intelligibility of his work.

(b) Through what manner of practical action – setting out budgets of cost, inventories of resource, programmes of time and so forth – could the conclusions of the thesis, either in whole or significant part, be tested? It is generally acceptable for a doctoral thesis to conform to the conclusions of other doctoral publications; the demands of the Belgian committee of award go substantially beyond this, and ask that the doctoral candidate will prepare, in collaboration with industry, commerce, public administration or any other recognized authority, a detailed plan for implementing his conclusions.

47

(*c*) Apart from the substantive issues around which the thesis is drawn, what contingencies would need to be provided for in this submission to practical application? For example, if the argument to be tested has anything to do with a factory, the preparations to be made for testing it will, in some way or another, involve alike the trade unions and the present work flow, to name two adventitious influences only. The specification of (*b*) above would be incomplete if these were not listed; the present demand is that their interactions with the thesis issues should be examined with foresight and diligence.

(*d*) What, specifically, has been the effect upon the doctoral candidate of investigating and treating the three questions set out above? In what manner, for example, have they caused the argument of the thesis itself to be modified; or taken the candidate into operating sites that he might never have visited; or confronted him with persons not normally to be found in or near the traditional academic setting?

When these conditions were first suggested – and their observance was to be the consideration for the very substantial value of the doctoral award – they encountered the most formidable opposition from some of the faculty, especially those in the management departments. To keep the peace, it was finally decided the substantive thesis need make no reference to them whatever, even by implication; they formed a distinct submission.

5.
The Nile Project

The educational mission of the West is not to instruct the African in the achievements of its own past; still less is it to lay upon him the veneer of an alien culture. (Journal of Management Studies, May 1967, p. 169)

Professor H., who supplemented his income by lecturing to Ethiopians about the Ricardo–Marx–Solow models of Capital Accumulation, used to mug up his notes on the aircraft; it is also related that dogs drink from the Nile while running beside it, for fear of being snatched by the crocodiles.

One action is worth a thousand words. (Arab proverb)

In the early 1960s I was invited to the University of Khartoum to act as an examiner in the school of business studies; these seemed to consist largely in lectures (of great interest to cultural anthropologists), by expatriate professors on remote subjects; one of these was by a New York accountant about the regulations of the Stock Exchange, and I watched its content being diligently copied down by a hundred attentive students, not one of whom could be discovered to own more than a part share in an aged camel. The law, it is said, exists for the benefit of the lawyers, but there were American professors drawing more for giving one such lecture than the average Sudanese earned in a twelvemonth. Such is the overwhelming force of management education.

Following my series of visits to Khartoum, I prepared an application for financial help for the Sudanese to conduct an experiment more relevant to their needs for future managers and administrators; my draft was inspired by the National Plan that had been accepted by the government (*Journal of Management Studies*, May 1967, p. 169):

> But, particularly as those engaged with the plan are aware, there is a gap between goal and starting point, between the roads and the factories foreseen on the pages of the plan, on the one hand, and the barefooted African still carrying his simple produce to the local market, on the other. The problems of translating intention into reality reflect the contrast between Africa and Europe, for it is unrealistic to delay the development until, by formal education, the African is more adapted to the assumptions that underlie the industrial economies of Europe. The historical preparation necessary to the growth of our factory towns cannot be repeated in Africa, and so can never provide the African with the learning experiences that have moulded twenty generations of Englishmen. The African has to acquire whatever cultural change is necessary to the success of his economic policies in the very act of putting those policies into effect. It cannot be gained from academic education. On the contrary, it must be secured through the attack upon his present poverty. He must learn, not so much from the scholarship of the European, as from solving the problems that lie before him in Africa. And the educational task of the West is not to instruct him in the achievements of its own past, howsoever successful these may appear to be; still less is it to lay upon him the veneer of an alien culture. It is simply to help the African tackle his own problems as he perceives them, to reach the goals that he has set himself, and to give him advice both appropriate to the point he has already reached and indicative of the goal after which he presently strives.

The application was refused by all the authorities, official and voluntary, to whom it was submitted; where reasons for this were given they invariably included my omission of such as my New York accountant and similar experts.

The likelihood of persuading the Arabs, however, to work towards a more active role in the solution of their own socio-economic problems and in the training of their own managers arose in 1969, when the Development Centre of the Organization for Economic Co-operation and Development staged a seminar in Cairo to discuss productivity in the Middle East. I was invited to speak at it, and took the chance there of renewing my acquaintance with Professor Saad Ashmawy of Al Azhar University, Cairo, who had been my doctoral student in Manchester. I returned, in my address, to my earlier themes – that only Africans can understand and develop Africa, that Africans can effectively learn only from their own responsible study of African problems, and that, if the intervention of Western professors is not to be actually harmful, in addition to being unconscionably expensive, a lot of thought must be given to their role. These arguments appealed to the director of the Central Training Organ of the Egyptian government, Dr El Abd, and a close relationship developed between Brussels and Cairo; since the Inter-University Programme had been based on the study and treatment of the current problems of the Belgian economy, public and private, it seemed to Dr El Abd that both Belgium and Egypt might have something to gain by working together. Managers from Belgium thus went to Egypt to help launch a similar endeavour, called here the Nile Project; Egyptian managers have visited the participating enterprises of the Inter-University Programme in order to present to them their project work and their more obstinate problems.

One difficulty central to the staging of realistic programmes, based on the study and treatment of what is actually going on in the world, is that of access; one cannot begin to understand what one's troubles are, or how they may differ from any 'solved' in the textbook, unless two parties are concerned to do so. Those in charge of the organization in difficulty as well as the interested therapist must both be ready to face the risks of confronting reality; the first may suffer the annoyance of seeing his embarrassment get worse by being ineptly tinkered with, and the second may suffer the humiliation of being proved a mere theorist, or even an ignorant theorist. It is, to some extent, the hesitation of both parties to face these risks that has preserved management education from becoming contaminated by the unforeseeable; if businessmen are reluctant to admit professors to the theatres of action while continuing to send their managers to the lecture hall, the professors may not only come to believe that it is unnecessary to know what is going on in the enterprise: they may finally conclude that too close a contact with reality is harmful. In a culture even more dependent upon books than is our own – for Duauf himself was an Egyptian – the task of diffusing action learning may be formidable.

Thus the first step in Egypt was to interest the presidents of some major industrial corporations; it was essential for them personally to support the field examination of their here-and-now troubles by their own managers. Although Dr El Abd and the Central Training Organ provided introductions and administrative support, the main task of inspiring the key figures of the Egyptian economy fell to Professor Ashmawy, who spent literally hundreds of hours during the early part of 1970 importuning top managers and their henchmen of every kind. It was not unknown for him to spend a whole hour in a telephone conversation to persuade some president to turn up at a meeting to discuss the programme. It was also necessary to seek the support of the other bodies in Egypt financially interested in the spread of management education, of which there were many. Professor Ashmawy also set out to attract his own university colleagues, not only to get their support in running the programme (although their efforts proved an anachronistic disappointment), but in the hope of interesting the universities in general to take some interest in the current torments of Egyptian society. For this, the climate was more favourable; the schools of medicine and of engineering had both for some years been insisting upon the need for their professional studies to have some regard for the relation of theory to practice. And to lend colour to Professor Ashmawy's arguments with the Egyptian presidents, I arranged to bring to Cairo a couple of senior Belgian managers who had been through the Inter-University Programme; I was sure that if Professor Ashmawy could assemble enough businessmen to listen to his proposals, it would not be academics who would convince them. For men of practice are to be converted – if they can be converted at all – only by other men of practice, and these, moreover, must speak from their own hearts a straightforward message, free of surprises. Ferdinand van Assche was a senior officer of the Kredietbank and Pierre de Smet the chief technical designer of Traction-Electricité, one of whose recent contracts was the construction of a nuclear power station at that time among the largest in the world. Both fellows, representing finance and technology, were practical men of the highest reputation, and they were listened to with attention and respect at public meetings in Cairo and Alexandria.

Although I had some experience of African involvement in action learning from the jungle programme of Nigeria, it had not been necessary in this to explain to any senior executives or public officials just what the programme was intended to achieve; indeed, action learning had emerged from Nigeria rather than been taken to it. In Egypt – a culture almost six thousand years old but only recently escaped from Western domination and more than somewhat allergic to the further insinuations of Western schools of government – it was essential to disclose our testimonials. We were, after all, in the city of a thousand mosques at a time of Islamic revival, and we were due to visit Alexandria, traditionally so single-minded in its attachment to the Koran that the burning of its famous library was saluted by the comment: 'If what is in those books is true, we have it in the Koran. If what is in them is false, we do not have it in the Koran. All of them may continue to burn.'

There is nothing more likely to test one's own belief in an idea than to try carrying it across a cultural barrier, and to succeed in this the idea must be stripped of all that is not central to it. The message we brought to these conferences is that men learn to manage only by needing to manage: necessity is not only the mother of invention, but also the mother of development. Thus we planned to confront selected managers each with a real problem to identify, to observe, to diagnose and to treat. Even if the given problem could not be solved in the sense of being finally disposed of, at least it might be understood well enough, by those remaining with it, for collective action economically to be taken about it. The programme was to be essentially action-oriented, helping those in the presence of the problems to take and to implement specific decisions at specific times and in specific conditions; it was not to encourage some gathering of students to discuss possible actions that might be taken by others in general on some future occasion

that might never arrive. We stressed how the Belgian programme had obliged each participating enterprise to come with
its own complex and unsolved affliction, about which the
president was worried but did not know what to do for the best;
we showed how the score of enterprises had put into a common
pool a set of projects differing among themselves as much as
twenty animals drawn at random from the Cairo Zoo. But it
was our insistence upon the need to exchange the twenty
fellows between the Belgian enterprises that produced the
greatest effect upon the Egyptians, and that most sorely tested
our veracity in the court of their collective opinion. The effect
of this particular text in our gospel was quite dramatic; the
controversy it started was prolonged and acrimonious, but in
the end proved conclusive. The local management development
experts, who saw the proposed Nile Project as a threat to their
livelihoods and who had come to the public meetings to oppose
us, fell out among themselves in trying to sway the opinions
of the businessmen against us. It was history repeating itself;
the soothsayers of the Pharaohs had gone down before the
prophecies of a foreigner almost four thousand years ago.

Thus it was agreed that the Egyptian managers, drawn from
enterprises ranging from soap to banking, should be allocated
to concerns of which they had had no past experience and on
problems with which they were in no way familiar. Since the
programme was so novel, it was agreed to simplify the range of
projects, and these were confined to the study and improvement
of motivation and to the relevance of industrial training. An
effort was made to secure high-level fellows by demanding of
each a university degree, ten years of senior management
experience and at least two years of service in his present
concern. Each was seen to be a key man in a key role, by
temperament creative, persistent and ambitious, and likely, by
the opportunity of the programme, to be able to carry further
responsibilities. The selection processes were extremely severe;
each man had to make his own case for being chosen, and had,
in particular, to convince the selection jury that he would
collaborate cheerfully and constructively in a pioneering programme certain to produce unseen and discouraging setbacks
for all who joined it. For a number of reasons, mainly because
the fellows felt for the security of their own jobs were they to

leave them full time for several months (a piece of caution that turned out a blessing in disguise), it was decided to pair the enterprises and the fellows; they then served, like Box and Cox, alternate weeks together in each other's enterprises. In Week 1, any two fellows would be working in Enterprise X; they would return there together in Weeks 3, 5, 7, etc. In Weeks 2, 4, 6 and so forth, they would be together in Enterprise Y. When in Enterprise X the fellow from Enterprise X would largely be getting on with his own job, although he would be interested to help the visiting fellow during that same week from Enterprise Y; in the next week both fellows would be in Enterprise Y, when the fellow from that enterprise would be getting on with his own job, although also doing what might be needed by the fellow from Enterprise X. The model, which was encountered for the first time in the Nile Project, has been extended to making the same man both the client in his own firm and the visiting fellow to another, thus adding further richness to the action learning experience.

The Nile Project programme proper opened with a part-time induction course mainly concerned with the skills of interviewing, and with such ideas as self-awareness, the nature of learning and the origins and reinforcements of resistance to change. It touched upon general system notions such as input and output, cost-benefit and flow-process charting. The design of a simple introductory course aimed primarily at helping a vigorous manager to read in communicable terms what may be going on around him proves an instructive exercise for even the most self-assured of professors, to whom the robust artlessness of action learning is so elementary that it may take several years completely to misunderstand. On the other hand, the sophistication of the academic models was generally such that the managers could not comprehend them, so that a compromise was eventually reached; the professors were persuaded to discuss examples of industrial practice in which they themselves had personally been involved, and to abandon their textbooks, particularly those which they themselves had written and were, it seemed, marketing on their own. The sessions at which the academics talked only about their own pieces of research or consultancy proved immensely popular; they were greatly appreciated and the fellows drew from them many ideas in representation and modelling that they were able to apply in their own projects.

The quest for structure also encourages two other vital qualities of top management: 'How can men be helped to listen to what is being said to them?' (see also Chapter 11) and 'How do we help men to pose simple questions about what is going on under their noses before encouraging them to seek sophisticated answers to other questions that nobody is ever likely to ask?' (see also Chapter 18). The success of the induction course in this is illustrated in the opening paragraph of the final report of the taxation specialist of the Eastern Tobacco Company, who worked upon the problems of training in the Tanta Oil and Soap Corporation, where he sets forth the following questions to be posed to the senior staff: 'What *is* training? What do you think it is? What does your boss think it is? What does your training officer think it is?' It takes a secure person to ask such questions and to press for consistent answers to them. For the second phase of the programme, that lasted three months, they spent half the time in their receiving enterprises securing the answers to such primary questions, in forms that enabled them to make recommendations about what ought to be done about the problems that had been offered them at the outset. During this time they met regularly in three sets, two studying problems of motivation and the other the needs of training; one set met in Alexandria, the others in Cairo. Their business was to discuss their progress and their obstructions, in the light of the information they had collected in the previous week and of their intentions to use it in the following.

By the end of the year, each had drawn up a report upon the conditions he had found in his receiving enterprise, and upon what he thought should be done to improve upon them. These reports were then, very courageously in the view of one of the Belgian managers who had been invited back for the presentation, offered at a series of semi-public meetings, chaired by Dr El Abd, to which all presidents and other parties interested in the programme were invited. At these meetings, each of a set of fellows, backed by a few counterparts, gave an account of his findings and his recommendations, outlining his methods, his programme, his evidence and so forth. The frankness with which some of the visitors described what they had seen, supported by the conviction with which they urged their recommendations for action, had never been anticipated and aroused more than a little defensiveness and recrimination. While the witness of a perceptive but disinterested manager from elsewhere may provide useful suggestions about how to deal with one's troubles, the enthusiasm for applying them may be dampened if they are dwelt upon too much in public. At the same time, most of the presidents had agreed that they should not hide from any in the programme those shortcomings that, although revealed only in one enterprise, were probably common to all.

The thoughts of most of them were probably best expressed by the president of the Eastern Tobacco Company, who cooled down the heated meeting with the following memorable lines (translated from the original Arabic by Professor Ashmawy):

At first I refused to accept the fellow's report about my company. Then I tried to find reasons for persuading myself not to accept it. I thought – and how sour were my thoughts! – that the criticisms were against us, against my staff, and against me. But as I hear it in this room tonight, the same criticism is being made by all the fellows, against their own companies as much as against the others, since they all worked in pairs; it is a common feature of the whole programme. We are all of us in the same boat. This makes the findings of all the fellows very important and very relevant. I want to say, here and in public, that I have a lot to learn, that we all have a lot to learn. So much that is critical goes wrong under our very noses and we do not notice it. Why? Because, at whatever level we work, we become absorbed by the trivialities of our day-to-day troubles. We all need this programme. Otherwise we shall soon be saying that we cannot see the River Nile because it is covered in water.

Apart from the stimulus of such common sense as this, there were more tangible results; the reports on training, for example, none of which had been prepared by a professional training officer, made clear that training was seen as Napoleon had seen liberty – something to be confined to the speeches of ceremonial assemblies. The work of the hard-headed engineers, lawyers and accountants who had studied the discrepancies between the real needs of training (by spending days out in the cotton fields and on the floors of the repair shops with the labourers who did the physical work), the supposed policies of training (by visiting the training schools and by examining the staffs who worked in them) and the budgeted resources allocated to training, led Egyptian industry as a whole to see the grave imbalance between what was called for and what was supplied.

One enterprise took the unbelievable step of at once multiplying its training grants – *tenfold* – although that may have been a testimonial to the choice of problem in the first place rather than to any admission of remorse as the facts emerged; it also agreed to raise the status of the officer-in-charge of training by two whole promotion grades, even although he had resented the study of his department by a non-expert from another concern. This is one specific outcome of the programme; others are described in the literature,[4] but perhaps the outcome that gave to the assembled presidents the most satisfaction was the discovery (to be so frequently repeated in other countries) that their enterprises had an impressive supply of unused abilities, that the managers of Egypt were perfectly capable of producing well-argued policy briefs, backed with precise recommendations about putting them into practice.

Despite these undoubted achievements of the Nile Project, however, it was in the second, or implementation, phase of the programme that we were first forced to give attention to the pathological elements at work to prevent true fulfilment in the micro-political labyrinths of industrial administration; our grasp of action learning at the time was not such as to enable us to see what we might have learned from the senior managers at Factory B (see Chapter 12). We did not, during the development of the Nile Project, appreciate the importance of the client group for the implementation, or therapeutic, phase of the projects; the Egyptian fellows were not advised to make a team out of those who could be called to answer the questions 'Who knows? Who cares? Who can?'. Nor had we at that time made the analysis that has since enabled one to write the chapter on managerial climatology (see Chapter 19); we had not then learned how to use action learning itself to develop action learning. For it is not only that one manager may learn with and from the other by their participation in the same set; sets, too, may learn from other sets, just as we now see that one programme can learn from – and only from – another. Our ignorance of the implementation process was brought home very clearly when, at the end of their first Nile Project, most of the Egyptian managers came to Belgium to compare progress with the fellows of the Inter-University Programme. At the meetings they had together, despite their language difficulties, the two companies could see how deeply they shared the exasperations of having rejected their careful and efficient strategies, by receiving managements that were afraid to face up to the political consequences of changes within their own organizations that were already long overdue. Perhaps the most important outcome of the Nile Project, set out in the original draft report of November 1971, was the stimulus it gave to finding a general theory of project implementation (see Chapters 18 to 22).

After organizing a second programme in action learning from his own university in Cairo, Professor Ashwamy was invited by the Libyans to experiment along similar lines at the University of Benghazi; here, under great difficulties, he has run two more with the help of some of the fellows in the first Nile Project. The most acute and unrelieved handicap to success in Libya – and it has been encountered again in Saudi Arabia – is a shortage of managers so grave that it is virtually impossible to keep those who join the programme from leaving it as, almost immediately thereafter, they find some other and more lucrative appointment. Cities like Benghazi and Jeddah, growing as a consequence of the petroleum boom as no cities have grown in the past, give the impression of a fairground set up on an opencast mining site, and it is a testimonial alike to Professor Ashmawy and to action learning that he has managed to complete three programmes there with increasing success; the 1977–78 consortium in Saudi Arabia began with seventeen fellows and finished with them all. Participating enterprises included, as well as a few private merchants, the national airline, Saudia; the Saline Water Conversion Authority; the Municipality of Jeddah, and the University Hospital; Petromin, the national bailiff of the vast mineral and petroleum reserves of the kingdom as they still lie in the ground; the National Cement Corporation and several others. At the end of their first programme, about fourteen of the participants visited Western Europe to fraternize with the fellows from programmes run in Ireland by the Irish Management Institute with Trinity College, Dublin; from the Inter-University Programmes of Belgium; and from the General Electric Company's programmes in Britain.

At the time of writing, Professor Ashmawy is working with the Saudis on setting up in Cairo a Pan-Arab Programme for Managerial Self-Development, and proposals have also been put forward for a World Institute for Action Learning primarily to help the underdeveloped countries both marshal their own strengths more effectively, and reduce their dependence upon the not-seldom-bogus expertise of the foreign consultant. It is gratifying to acknowledge the support that this simple thesis now draws from the later efforts of the intermediate technologists. What, in the opening paragraphs of this chapter I refer to as 'the veneer of an alien culture', has many ingredients; it may be true that the most obvious of these are to do with engineering and machinery, such as the motor cars that fill the ditches and the broken-down air conditioners that obstruct the natural ventilation of the supermarkets. But behind these inevitable eyesores lurk the more insidious contagions, such as university education and professional sport, environmental irresponsibility and cultural disintegration; these, and a score of others, slither in behind the expert and the tinker, the consultant and the peddler, the professor and the quack. Action learning, autonomous and local, alone will offer defence against the charlatan, the turner of the quick buck and the other wolves in sheep's clothing. Expressed as intermediate technology it could make yet another promising departure.

6.

Sir Arnold offers Encouragement and GEC shows the Way

I think we know pretty well how to train experts, or those who ought to be able to find the best answers to questions that are already more or less intelligently posed. I am not so sure that we know how to train leaders, or those who know how to pose such questions in the first place: to lay bare the risks involved in trying to do something and to recognize what you do not know can be a masochistic business. Perhaps the Belgians even got to like doing it . . . Anyhow, we might see if we can develop the idea in GEC; then, in five years, it could be taken up by other British companies. (Sir Arnold Weinstock, at an interview in November 1973)

Late in 1973 one of the television services of the British Broadcasting Corporation presented a discussion on the state of British management education; I had been invited to take part in it, largely, I believe, upon the recommendation of Mr Alistair Mant, author of a famous report upon the condition of the same subject, *The Experienced Manager*, published by the British Institute of Management in 1969 (see also Chapter 14).

I was careful enough to turn up at the television studio with a real manager, Gilbert van Marke, from one of my Belgian programmes. I recalled the trouble that Christopher Columbus had run into when he came back from having discovered America, namely, that none would believe that he had ever been there until he was able to show them three Red Indians the like of which had not been seen by European men before. I felt of all the evidence of action learning I might produce, nothing could be more convincing than a live Belgian able to recount his experience of it.

Sir Arnold Weinstock, Managing Director of the General Electric Company of England, happened to be watching television during a short spell of indisposition and at once invited me across to London to talk about the management development policies of his own company. Since these already incorporated the essential ideas of action learning – that evaluated experience alone helps senior managers to accept the risks essential to their trade – it did not take more than fifteen minutes to agree that *using the existing staff of GEC* I would in the shortest possible time build on the company's accepted assumptions of how their risk-bearing men are shaped; I emphasized my conviction that only the staff of GEC could improve GEC, and asked that any agreement into which I entered with the company specifically stated that in no conditions would I be asked to run a second programme for it. If my ideas upon how an organization learns from the study of its own treatment of its own problems could not be grasped by the officers of the company within twelve months, I saw no virtue in staying with it. This proposition considerably surprised the staff of the company, but it had the effect of making them sufficiently interested to understand what action learning was intended to do. For what possible reason, they asked, did I not seek a long-term and lucrative contract with so rich a firm?

At the time of Sir Arnold's invitation I had been eight years away from Britain; in that period Belgium had staged not only the Inter-University Programme but had also started to experiment (through an inter-university college for doctoral studies in management sciences) with the award of doctoral degrees through researches that paid attention to the practical application of whatever the researches claimed to be illuminating (see Chapter 4); action learning had entered the Middle East through Egypt and Libya; it was being discussed by the Swedes and the Norwegians, and I had spent a month in Dallas, Texas, helping to initiate a programme agreeable to the American academics. But nothing had been tried in Britain and, if I had asked for the most spectacular introduction of action learning to the land of its contemptuous rejection, I could not have thought of one more fitting than that Sir Arnold would have been its backer. For his opinions of the business schools and of the professorial brotherhood were, if anything, somewhat more unequivocal than my own; it was his declared policy on taking over any enterprise to stop whatever was going on as management education; he had stood aloof from the campaign of precipitate alogy that culminated in the Franks Report and the setting up of the business schools; above all, he believed that if his staff had the courage and the integrity to face the stresses of running their own shows, then it was not for him to tell them what to do. This had led GEC into an extreme policy of decentralization: the London office of a company with a ten-figure annual turnover could all get onto a London bus.

Having given to his field commanders so great a liberty of independent action, Sir Arnold believed that they might well be ready to learn with and from each other in the very effort of dealing with the problems of their daily encounter. When, in the course of the next few weeks, I met some of these field commanders and assured them that nobody was trying to teach them how to do their jobs but that they themselves might be interested to contrive the conditions in which they could make the most of their adversities, they threw fifty-five problems into a pool and nominated thirty-six middle managers to work on them. This promising response of the field commanders was seconded by three fortunate auguries: Michael Bett, later the first chairman of the Action Learning Trust, had just taken over as personnel director of GEC and had an entirely open mind as to the kinds, if any, of management development he was ready to back; David Pearce, the management development manager responsible to him, had not even joined the company when Sir Arnold had noticed the television show; and Dunchurch Industrial Staff College, that GEC had recently acquired in its merger with the English Electric Company, was under new management and ready to try something fresh.

Those who know how effectively any camarilla of petulant time-servers can bring to nothing even the wishes of Napoleonic figures like Sir Arnold Weinstock by misrepresenting the operational plans of his advisers will understand my wonderful fortune; my university experience had convinced me that only the death (which was too unlikely to hope for) or the retirement (which was to be too long delayed) of my opponents would open the way for innovation in the academies, and I was then to discover that at GEC no rearguard action was to destroy my effort, waste my time nor misrepresent my ideas. No rearguard action needed to be fought; alone of all the hundreds of organizations with a concern for management education, GEC had no rearguard. No fortifications of behavioural science repelled my simple ardour, no networks of administrative theory ensnared our lowly mission; we just went round the factories and persuaded people to help their colleagues work upon their troubles. There was no more in it than that. The story is told by the participants themselves in a most readable book, *More Than Management Development*, edited by David Casey and David Pearce (see p. 317), who saw that the programme ran, and who held the coats of the managers as they got on with the task of learning with and from each other while helping to diagnose and treat the real-time problems that had been put forward for examination.

It took about eight months altogether to launch the first GEC programme; numerically and structurally it was not much unlike the first Inter-University Programme of Belgium, with twenty-one participants and four sets, as against twenty-one fellows and five sets. But the range of options was much wider, for in Belgium we had insisted upon all fellows undertaking an unfamiliar task in an unfamiliar setting, whereas in GEC the other three options (familiar task in a familiar setting; unfamiliar task in a familiar setting; and familiar task in an unfamiliar setting) are all encouraged. If action learning is to help, quantitatively as well as qualitatively, find the world a few more managers, the contribution from top level exchange programmes will be meagre enough. There are something like four thousand managers in GEC today, and it would be quite inadequate to set out to train these through exchange programmes alone. If the fundamental assumptions of action learning are valid, and managers learn best with and from each other while working so closely together on related problems that each can become for the others a source of acceptable advice and criticism, then they should be able to offer that support without necessarily having to move far away from

64

home – or even away from home at all. Hence it was that the GEC programme first enabled us to explore new options, such as the fellow studying his own job while continuing to do it; or the fellow studying an entirely different job and its problems, but in his own firm or factory; or the fellow studying the troubles of an exactly similar job to his own but in a different firm or works. Provided that each fellow still receives the constant advice, criticism and support of other fellows – or comrades in adversity, as they came to be called – meeting week by week in the same set, and provided that each followed a properly sequenced programme of diagnosis, prescription and therapy, reporting with relentless and uncomfortable accuracy his success and his failure, his advances and his delays, then it seemed to make little difference to his insight into his own learning and the micro-politics around him. In the same way, the very size of GEC, with its several hundreds of factories, suggested that once its own staff had picked up the idea of action learning – which that staff rapidly did – there was no virtue in running one nation-wide programme; the company now has a number of regional consortia spread across Britain, and is ready to admit to its community of learners all who are ready to subscribe to the central belief.

The GEC programme, which on account of the immense fame of its principal backer has attracted a lot of attention, was also cardinal to the setting up of what were first called 'management clinics', but are now propagated as the management action groups (MAGs) of the Institution of Works Managers. This purposeful professional organization, with about 17,000 members, is pioneering a totally new service to its branches. Like the majority of the engineering and scientific institutions, it was originally set up to attract the professional works manager by offering – or by trying to offer – three useful services to him: first, the force of political unity essential to advance his career interests; second, the assurance that his trade would not be diluted by the entry into it of unqualified persons, simply by setting educational standards and ensuring that they were observed; and third, by offering to members a regular programme of lectures, seminars and other socially agreeable activities designed to spread a professional understanding of the nature of works management. But in these iron times it has become necessary for the Institution to ask whether this programme, even supported by the other two services, was sufficient to maintain its membership. In reply, its education committee set out to encourage a few of its branches to organize action learning among their members (or with others locally interested), and the most popular option of project adopted within the MAGs so constituted is that first tried by GEC as the study by the fellow of his own job.

The promise of the departure made by the Institution of Works Managers is almost unbounded; already some groups are confined entirely to chief executives, who have discovered within their arduous responsibilities not only a new support, but also a new incentive and a new knowledge. At the present moment Alan Lawlor, who has been the field officer backed by the Institution to explore the conditions under which its members are able to learn with and from each other, is sowing the seeds of action learning among the farmers; if ever there were an occupation that might profit from the structured opportunities of those who follow it to learn with and from each other while continuing to do it, that occupation is agriculture. If it could be contrived that across the whole of the country those who carry the real responsibilities – and I at least am clear as to who those people are – for our manufactures and our husbandries were supporting each other in their common production of wealth by their common membership of management action groups, we would have taken the first major step towards democracy at work. Managers who have learned to share their interests and their talents with other managers and from other walks of life will have moved well down the road to sharing them with their own employees. The 'Own Job' option of the GEC programme was a landmark – even for action learning.

To return to the words of Sir Arnold quoted at the head of this chapter: there have been developments elsewhere in Britain of the ideas that originally attracted his attention, and a handful of other enterprises are now engaged in exchanges after the Belgian model. But the developments most likely to influence Britain as a whole are not to be explored on these sophisticated levels; as with the action groups of the Institution of Works Managers (and the variety of options set out in

66

Chapter 21), GEC itself has taken a lead in decentralizing its programmes. By 1978, after the five years of incubation foreseen by Sir Arnold, the pioneering enterprise was running a series of local programmes across the country; that in Scotland involved co-operation with the trade in alcoholic liquor, that in Lincoln, a cathedral city, with the police force and the education authorities. Such must be the expression of local character and of local need if action learning is to become a true instrument of local growth. The Lincoln experiment is, in part, the inspiration for the regional consortia proposed in Chapter 9; it makes its point with a ruthless clarity: If the education system of Britain seems to be turning out children allergic to industrial effort and likely to embarrass the police (an assumption rather than a demonstration), then only those who run the schools, the factories and the precincts can do anything about it. What they do, moreover, they had best discover for themselves, for then – and only then – will they do it with understanding, conviction and resource. The burgesses of Lincoln are suggesting by their collective efforts the conditions of such discovery; they are committed to learn, with and from each other, the four cardinal declarations of Buddha which introduce the next chapter. But they are adding something of their own: each is concerned not with his local suffering alone, but also with the sufferings of his comrades in adversity.

It may be yet too early to describe what Lincoln is after but, when the last rhetoric of social science echoes around an empty exchequer, it will be the citizens of Lincoln who save their kids and who encourage others to do the same. Perhaps there is, looking down upon the latter-day sons of our cathedral city, the approving eye of the magnificent Robert Grosseteste, Bishop of Lincoln from 1235 to 1253, vigorous advocate of the observation of particular facts, of the use of measure and classification in the formation of argument and of the practice of experiment in testing the reliability of belief, the indefatigable opponent of all who sought guidance from abstract deduction. This great patron of action learning, with his unswerving respect for what is possible in the here-and-now, has been rated as having 'had a greater influence upon English thought and English literature for the two centuries that followed his age' than any other person; Wyclif put him above

Aristotle, and Roger Bacon, father of experimental method, applauds his understanding of science. But he was, first and foremost, interested in action as distinct from *talking about* action, and is referred to by Matthew Paris as 'the rebuker of pope and king, the corrector of bishops, the reformer of monks, the director of priests, the instructor of clerks, the patron of scholars, the preacher of the people' (*Cambridge History of English Literature*, vol. I, pp. 204–5). The GEC initiatives of 1978 could do worse than take so redoubtable a pioneer as their example. We shall see in Chapter 13 that the teachers, employers and constables of Lincoln may well be able, in the 1980s, to pay due homage to their great precursor.

7.
India seeks Educational Independence

*Once the Buddha was living at Kosambi, near Allahabad, in a
simsapa grove. He addressed the monks:*

> *'And what is this, monks, that I have
>   declared?*
> *This is the suffering – this I have
>   declared.*
> *This is the arising of the suffering –
>   this I have declared.*
> *This is the cessation of the suffering –
>   this I have declared.*
> *This is the path leading to the cessation
>   of the suffering; this I have declared.'*

*To understand this unequivocal utterance is to understand the
entire teaching of the Buddha. (Buddhism: A Living Message;
Piyadassi Thera, Colombo, Sri Lanka, 1967, p. 27)*

It is also to understand the gospel of action learning.

In 1973 Dr John Marsh, formerly Director-General of the
British Institute of Management, gave to Mr Praxy Fernandes,
Director-General of the Bureau of Public Enterprises of the
Government of India, a copy of the Nile Project. Mr Fernandes
at once saw the significance of action learning and, with the
official help of TETOC (the Council for Technical Education
and Training in Overseas Countries) I was asked to discuss
with the Indians the possibilities of action learning as a medium
for them to make more effective use of their immense talents.
Mr Fernandes was not only a shrewd administrator – and he
has since become the director of an international centre for the

development of public enterprises, run by the United Nations in Yugoslavia – but also a considerable philosopher. I found his views upon the nature of knowledge as welcome as an oasis in my academic Sahara, for I had been raised in the austere school of experimental physics which taught that one could never know what the atom *actually was*; all we could hope for was to observe how it *apparently behaved*. Action learning descends from this ethic: something exists not for what it *is*, but by what it can *do*. It is idle, indeed, fraudulent, to take students through the contents of books except as the overture to application that can test the rigour of the argument.

Mr Fernandes was in a tricky spot; on the one hand, he inherited the ancient culture of Indian philosophy, for ever seeking the essential nature of things – their quiddity, including the quiddity of quiddity, and the quiddity of the quiddity of quiddity, and so forth; on the other hand, he was supposed to be doing something about India's endeavours to turn herself into a modern industrial nation so as to raise the quality of life among her 600,000,000 population, the majority of whom were existing at the levels of poverty that misfortune can soon transform into destitution. He illustrated his concern in our first conversation, by comparing India with Japan. 'Recall,' he said, 'such conversation with an educated Indian as you can. Was ever there talk more subtle and refined? What question did it leave unanswered, what issue unexplored, what school of philosophy unplaced, what ambiguity unexplained? . . . But then remember when you were with several educated Indians together, warned well in advance of your common purpose, and all prepared to treat of the agenda. Was there ever such confusion, such obstruction, such perversity, such concentration not upon the wrong issues but upon no issues whatsoever? How can it be that those so individually insightful and informed can, by the mere circumstance of coming together, set off so great an avalanche of calamitous destruction? And then remember your most lucid argument with the most illustrious of the Japanese, in which you strove with all your might to relish the full magnificence of the Chrysanthemum. What can you repeat of it? Nothing. What did you understand of it at the time? Nothing. What do you expect of your next encounter under the flag of the Rising Sun? Nothing

But then tell me what happened after you had met that party of Japanese – not just one scholar to whom you could give the whole of your attention and in return receive the whole of his – but the delegation of twenty who saw you all together? Then what was the outcome? Within a week you had a message to say that they had introduced action learning with success in every university and business house throughout their nation.' He paused and sought my confirmation. 'I want action learning in India for this very reason. It will give us the chance to talk with our accustomed brilliance and to bring the artillery of argument against our comrades. But your programmes will force us to argue with each other about what we are doing and what we are achieving. Nobody will ever cure us of our fatal loquacity; action learning will make use of it, and all will be able to join in on equal terms and with equal promise of reward.' The Director-General of the Bureau of Public Enterprises was a keen epistemologist; he saw that what his firms needed to know was not the nature of existence, but the essences of action.

In the summer of 1978, the Bureau was ready to launch its third programme. A score or so of projects, now organized regionally, but launched with aid from New Delhi in previous years, have shown that managers in India are every bit as capable of learning with and from each other as are Europeans; there is a strong motivation among the Indians to develop their own programmes along their own lines, and it is likely that issues regarded as somewhat more than delicate in this country, such as the relations of management and labour, will be studied by action learning approaches over there as they could not be in Britain unless some powerful example is set. I also believe that action learning will develop in India for the study of such serious social problems as urban poverty and the quality of village life; projects to tackle both of these by the kinds of involvement referred to later, in discussing the troubles of New York City (see Chapter 17), are now in draft. Indeed, there is a powerful case to be made (and not only in India) for using action learning to supply the national planning agencies with ideas as well as with realistic descriptions of the problems that burden the heart of India's productive economy. If, as I believe, within a few years the main supply industries of the subcontinent – coal, oil, food, cement, fertilizer, machinery and engineering, electricity, aircraft, pharmaceuticals and so forth – have worked among themselves, learning with and from each other what their problems really are and what resources they can muster to deal with them, it will have become impossible for central planning bodies any longer to ignore the help of those who not only know what the field problems are, but alone might be able to deal with them.

These are questions for the future, and, no doubt, India will have something to tell the world about them in due course. To me, the interest of working with the Indians has come from the speed and clarity with which the ideas of action learning have been picked up; only the Australians have moved faster. But when one considers the differences of size and of culture between the two nations, the Indian achievement is still astonishing. By an investment of my time over there, negligible compared with what I have exhausted in Britain, I have been rewarded to see action learning take root not only in the organization of India's factories, but in the dialectic of her scholars.[5] For the present book it will be enough, however, to give a short account of the programme of activities, organized with the help of TETOC and of the Bureau, that has enabled such rapid advance to be made. The written proposals that I originally made to get started, dated March 1974, are given as an appendix to this chapter.

My first mission was to make the contacts with the Indian managers at all levels as suggested by the meetings specified; at each of these gatherings it was left for the participants to decide what follow-up arrangements they wished to make, such as which chief executives were ready to bring their organizations into the proposed consortium and which academics were ready to help in the staffing of it. Out of about eighty executives who accepted invitations to hear what action learning was trying to do, about fifteen eventually sent fellows into the programme; despite the enormous difficulties of organizing a single programme on the scale of India, with projects as far apart as Bombay, Delhi, Bangalore and Calcutta, the idea of action learning has been taken on, and attention is now being concentrated upon setting up programmes of a regional order.

After the implantation of the first seeds of interest, and a suitable lapse of time for them to strike root, about four months in all, I returned to India to meet those who had actually committed themselves in order to plan the field operations; the design of these efforts is most readily expressed in the memorandum I sent to the Bureau of Public Enterprises in preparation.

Proposed Workshop for Organizing and Supervisory Staffs

Objective
(1) This workshop is to ensure that the field preparations for the projects essential to the first action-learning programme are completed. Experience shows that schools drawing mainly upon the traditions of book-learning do not always see how much detailed care must be taken to launch successful practical exercises that involve real people in real problems and in real time. In this programme there will be over twenty projects, since some enterprises are sending more than one fellow; we may co-ordinate them through four centres of university rank. The workshop is to satisfy personally those responsible for the programme, therefore, that the total investment of time, effort and money in the venture has been prudently made.

Workshop Participants
(2) (a) from enterprises: the public enterprises committed to the programme will contribute and receive between them about twenty fellows; each enterprise should thus be represented by one or more senior officers, both to plan the detailed design of his local project and to speak on behalf of his enterprise for the fellow or fellows delegated to work elsewhere. There should thus be about twenty enterprise representatives at the workshop.

(b) from universities: four academic centres (Ahmedabad, Delhi, Hyderabad and Bangalore) should each send two nominees, making eight in all.

(c) from Britain: it is expected that four visitors from Britain – from the University of Leeds, from TETOC, from GEC, and myself, will help with the organization of the discussions, and reply to questions.

(d) administrative staff: we can expect a dozen visitors, from the Bureau and from the Standing Conference of Public Enterprises, as well as from ministries and such bodies as the Indian Productivity Council.

73

Residential accommodation should be available for about forty persons.

Time Table
(3) The workshop, lasting about two weeks, should be run in three phases:

(*a*) preparatory: all participants would spend three whole days together, but most of the time split into the four groups concentrated on the four academic centres; the enterprise representatives would each have the fullest chance to present to the others in their group a detailed account of the project they had to offer. These presentations should make it clear to those in each group that adequate preparations have been made not only to receive the visitors but to involve the senior staffs of the enterprises likely to be interested in the projects on which they are to work; the academic staffs will gain from these presentations some advance impression of their weekly obligations in helping the participants.

(*b*) verificatory: after three days the participants will disperse; the enterprise representatives will return to the project sites where each will organize on one of the five succeeding days a conference involving all those who will play a role in the local project; they include:

the local or resident general manager;

the client who owns the problem around which the project has been designed;

the co-ordinator, or official on the staff of the client, who can attend to any questions of organization or procedure that might arise outside the scope of the project as such;

members of the receiving organization likely to be caught up in the project as well as the client himself (it is usual for at least a dozen persons to be involved in the implementation of what the visiting fellow eventually has to recommend, although it is not suggested that more than two or three possible collaborators will be identified so early in the programme);

the personnel or training officer of the receiving unit;

the visiting fellow (from another enterprise coming to work on the project);

the delegated fellow (should one be nominated from the particular site to undertake a project elsewhere);

a representative of the university centre to which the visiting fellow will be attached; and

74

a visitor from **Britain** with previous experience of action learning.

The purpose of these site conferences is to bring home to the key staffs of the receiving enterprises what may be expected of them. In particular, *it is to introduce the notion of the project being a learning experience for the local enterprise* as much as for the visiting fellow. All previous experience suggests that, although most receiving enterprises grasp this point for themselves, they usually do so too late to get all the benefit they might otherwise have done. Since the primary objective of TETOC is to encourage the Indian enterprises to become independent of British support as soon as possible, every site meeting should also be run as an opportunity for the local management, helped by its own training staff, to envision how it might organize its own independent and internal action learning programmes in the future.

It is thus of great importance that proper records of these site meetings be kept to encourage the diffusion of action learning, not as an educational abstraction, but as a series of exercises to be undertaken by engineers, chemists, miners, bulk food handlers and so forth.

(c) confirmatory: the last two days will be reserved for confirmatory presentations, within sets, by the enterprise representatives concentrating upon modifications of design that have been made at the site conferences and outlining the possibilities for enterprise development that have emerged from the site discussions.

This timetable leaves no opportunity for academic inputs, but there will be plenty of chances for individuals to raise personally their needs, as they feel them to be, for reading or coaching assignments with their academic advisers. The omission of any predetermined syllabus of instruction is deliberate; the programme proper, intended for the fellows alone, will attend to this, and will start with a short induction programme on project design and evolution, with references to appropriate research methodology.

These two series of conferences were separated in time by several months and served quite different purposes: the first was strategic, the second tactical; the third, or operational phase, was the programme itself, that began about a month after the site meetings and their aftermath had been disposed of. To those readers who find my memoranda about them somewhat commonplace, I can only say that action learning starts at the beginning: those who are to be caught up in the programme must themselves have helped design it at the level of tactical detail.

The prognostications of Mr Fernandes with which I open this chapter turned out to be not inaccurate. Many of the themes proposed for investigation and treatment by the fellows were somewhat less specific than they might have been; one of the three largest concerns in the country, for example, saw the opportunity offered by the presence among its higher management of a senior man from a totally different industry as a self-analysis. Could not the score or so of summit executives ostensibly working together for the good of the enterprise clarify among themselves – with the help of this non-competing observer – their suspicions that, as a directorate, they were much less efficient than they knew they could be? Another enterprise of the same order of magnitude, recently formed through the amalgamation of four high technology companies respectively of Russian, American, German and British origins, asked its visitor to help them set up a more satisfactory administration for making the best total use of so diverse a quartet. A third organization, concerned with overseas trade, invited its visiting fellow to suggest why those within it appeared so fearful of using their delegated powers; agents at the major ports, given authority to settle deals of a lakh of rupees, insisted on referring the papers to their bosses in New Delhi. A fourth wanted advice as to why it was so far behind in its capital development plan. And so the rest . . .

Now, although it might appear that action learning is a highly unsatisfactory way of dealing with issues so vast and so diffuse, and that a couple of hours with a first-class Western consultant would have shed all the light necessary to understanding and to action upon these labyrinthine confusions, the outcomes of such assignments were all that had been hoped. The fellows and their clients learned from this first programme to recognize those questions that were worth debating – in that useful action might follow the debate – and those vaster generalities about which little could be done, such as, for example, the need to employ quite ordinary persons, and even to accept the fact that they might sometimes try to evade responsibility and at others try to exercise too much. But there were several projects that, having been put up by engineering enterprises, were more specific than the other examples set out above. A firm building aircraft found it more than difficult to equalize its production month by month; instead of making two units a month throughout the year, the annual output was bunched into the first three months of the calendar year. What were the identifiable reasons for this and what ought to be done about it? Another enterprise in the biochemical industry was concerned with the low capacity at which some of its critical assets were being used. What were the reasons for the excessive down-time and by what managerial action could the plant occupancy be raised? The makers of very heavy steam-raising plant, employed to drive turbo-generators, were taking forty months to build jobs which they knew from first principles ought to be finished within twenty-four. Why was this and what ought to be done about it? These are all complex, interdepartmental problems, well charged with opportunities for accusation, acrimony and all else that is negative in the inventories of human nature. Yet they were ideal for the Indian top managements, being both specific enough to anchor the argument to the concrete and the real-time here-and-now of such and such a group of persons locally responsible for getting something done, *and* general enough to bring together the key figures from a range of professions and a range of industries, so that they could engage in the very discussions essential to the integration of Indian industrial policy as a whole.

In its third phase the programme of the Bureau of Public Enterprises has dropped the exercises in generality that, as Mr Fernandes expected, were choices inevitable to the introduction of action learning into India. The insistence upon specificity of outcome while preserving an organic or corporate range within the projects themselves has been emphasized by the concentration of sets within regions; they were formerly made up nationally in order to give the programme an All-India reputation. Moreover, now the industrialists are able to appreciate that action learning involves not simply the fellows alone, but perhaps a dozen or more well-placed men in each receiving enterprise able to support their visitor and, by their personal efforts, strongly to influence the outcome of the whole project, they have started to use the programme as a means of spotting talent – perhaps the nation's most critical resource. Nothing is likely to arouse interest more quickly in the programme among the senior managers than the suggestion that one's contribution to its success might be a considerable testimonial. Since private industry, as among the Australians, is now taking heed of the Bureau's experiment, we may expect its reputation as an index of talent not to decline. Nationalized industry in Britain, too, may have much to ask.

APPENDIX TO CHAPTER 7
Written proposals, March 1974

I should appreciate an opportunity for the following meetings:

 (a) with the minister or permanent secretary of any govern-
      ment department, or with the president or chief
      executive of any industrial or commercial undertaking,
      that proposes to make use of, or that might consider
      making use of action learning; the interview, which
      should not take more than fifteen minutes, would make
      clear that I see the development of their managers as
      the responsibility of the managers themselves, encour-
      aged and supported by their own superiors, and that,
      although the existing training staff retain a responsi-
      bility, it is not that traditional to them (I believe it
      important that those in charge of industrial and com-
      mercial development should change their perception of
      the personnel function, as much in the training of
      managers as in the treatment of labour; neither are
      purely 'expert' or 'professional' side-lines to be com-
      mitted to specialists, like, say, book-keeping or materials
      handling);
 (b) with a number of chief executives of operating firms,
      units or divisions, preferably in a group of ten or so
      and with their chief personnel or training officers, to
      elaborate the idea that management development
      depends upon the mutual support of men faced with
      complex and stressful decisions; it must be among such
      key executives that any arrangements for such mutual
      support would need to be agreed in principle; each
      meeting would need about two hours;

(*c*)   with virtually any number (up to, say, a hundred) of management teachers, heads of staff colleges, consultants or advisers in training and staff development, research workers in the social and economic sciences, industrial course organizers, personnel managers and any others concerned professionally with the development of executives, managers and supervisors in the public and private sectors of the economy; this meeting, intended to spread conviction as well as information about action learning, should take the form of a workshop and should last at least six hours, with suitable breaks, and should present testimony from real managers who have participated in real action learning programmes; the workshop should not be so heavily loaded with the training staff of one particular undertaking, nor with the academic staff of one particular academy, that they might collude to defeat its purpose should action learning emerge as a threat to their present interests or activities; (experience shows that professional teaching and training staffs are willing – and not seldom anxious – to consider fresh approaches to their tasks so long as there is no chance of spontaneous co-operation, usually at a subconscious level, to reject them; even if not seated together and also without previous collusion, a network of colleagues from the same organization, faced with what they believe to be an attack upon their present practices, can soon destroy a meeting out of which the rest of the participants are hoping to gain something);

(*d*)   with from six to ten unit managers and their immediate subordinates, representing the small number of undertakings likely to co-operate in the same action learning set, so as to discuss the organization of projects, the choice of fellows and clients, the progress of diagnosis and implementation, and so forth, with particular reference to the support expected from the line managements; allowance must be made for more than one such meeting to be held among the representatives of the same set of enterprises, since discussion may vary the choice of projects, of fellows and of clients;

(*e*)   with as many managers of all ranks who might conceivably be nominated as the fellows for the first programme, in order to explain as clearly as verbal communication only will allow that action learning differs unrecognizably from traditional teaching, and that it calls for the reorganization of the participant's existing knowledge with the help of other participants rather than for additions to that knowledge by professional teachers; such meetings should, if possible, be run in two parts and offer the widest opportunity for the potential fellows to discuss this new approach among themselves.

8.

Australia snatches the Lead

*You ask, 'What has gone wrong with the universities of today?'
Those of Europe are in trouble, you complain? Why is it, do
you imagine, that in the hour when your country has no alternative to using better her own wits, the nurseries of her
intelligence are falling into disrepute? Because their traditional
product is no longer among the marketable truck that the
world is looking for. And what does that traditional product
remain? A kit of ready-made opinions to help the owner pass
himself off as somebody he is not and never could be . . . The
world has no need of such nurseries any more; in any case, we
could provide our own.* (An Australian public servant discussing an action-learning programme at Deakin University,
Geelong, 1977)

*Trustworthy advice, my dear Professor, fit for the quarterdeck
of any sinking ship.* (The same person, a few minutes later)

I have tried for twenty-five years to get action learning into the
British public services, for, having been an education officer of
a county authority and also director of education to the
National Coal Board, I feel I know some of the troubles that
beset those called upon to run our public business. I am well
aware of how many institutions there are of renown to help
them with training courses, such as the Royal Institute of
Public Administration and the Institute of Local Government
Studies at the University of Birmingham. But at a time when
central and local administrations alike are under the stress of
unprecedented change, and when there are now persons neither
malicious nor deranged to organize themselves in demanding
that the payrolls of government be reduced – so that one might
expect to see in the public service new modes of training and

81

procedure – it is still the ancient doctrines that endure. Like little Pepi almost five thousand years ago, the aspiring bureaucrat still voyages to the School of Books, and like those who ran the cities mentioned in Ecclesiasticus one must still be conversant in dark parables to appear before princes (see Chapter 14). We must not be surprised if those with so long a start in the traditions of book-learning continue to manifest a steadfast opposition to all new ideas; we may regret that the government training colleges regard action learning with contemptuous dismissal, but at least there is a rational explanation for why they do so.

Nevertheless, there is an awakening interest in action learning abroad. In May 1978 I had the privilege of talking with about a hundred senior officers of the Department of Personnel and Administrative Reform of the Government of India; it seems well known enough that the Indians have inherited their present civil service from the British Raj, but not quite so well known that thirty years of independence have not left India entirely as she was in 1947. She herself is seeking to change; my advice is that only an attack, by Indians themselves, in India and on the here-and-now problems of India, will help her public services to escape the slumbering encumbrance of Oxbridge immutability. The Public Service Board of the Australian State of Victoria is also baring my credentials to the world, even if its try at better government just by embracing action learning as an instrument of managerial development can be of no conceivable interest or value to those concerned with Whitehall and local government. It might therefore be out of place to report at any length here upon the advances of the Australians: the short reference that follows, however, is not included in the expectation that it will – or even might – have any interest for, say, the Civil Service Department or the Local Government Training Board, but because the private sector in Britain might like to know that the action learning programmes of the Public Service Boards of Australia are of such appeal that industrial enterprises are seeking to join them. A statement about these experiments by Dr Roy Gilbert is included as an appendix at the end of this chapter.

The speed with which these programmes have been introduced – and with which the senior civil servants have taken up an interest in them – might well arouse the suspicions of experts in the teaching of administrative science, were it not for the well-known fact that Melbourne (although no longer the capital of Australia) is the city of metropolitan rank farthest away from Whitehall, and therefore least likely to fit the analysis made by Arnold Toynbee of civil servants with whom he had long worked:

> To tend the machinery of a highly organised state, administering many millions of subjects, was as soul-destroying a task as the performance of any typical set of scientifically managed physical movements in a factory. Red tape, in fact, could prove more restrictive than iron; and red tape had now entered into the civil servant's soul, while the part played by formalities and routine in an overworked civil service was being played by an increasingly rigid and disciplinary party-system in overworked elected legislatures. (*A Study of History*; abridgement by D. C. Somervell, OUP, 1957, Vol. 2, p. 337)

When we remind ourselves that it is nearly thirty years since Arnold Toynbee made this evaluation, in an age that, compared with today, may safely be described as leisured, so that the conditions which then he judged already to have paralysed the administrative spirit have since worsened by an order of magnitude, we must conclude that the innovative actions of Australia are not likely soon to be taken up in Britain. As the economic autumn closes in upon the academic rabbits, so will they be less inclined to scour the neighbouring meadows for the unfamiliar; they will sooner seek the comfort of their hutches and fawn upon the hands that feed them. For despite Dr Gilbert's modesty in declaring that action learning sells itself once its initiatory programme succeeds, he has had to display immense physical vitality and emotional courage to recruit organizations so potentially inert by virtue of their size, and so naturally self-satisfied by virtue of their invulnerability to criticism – and, what is more, to recruit them to a cause that demands as a prime condition the civil servant abandoning the security of his own desk. Those with even the most fleeting acquaintance with our British administrative tradition are aware of its tenacity of routine and worship of recondite formality, whether in Whitehall itself, or in the offices of the most remote of rural district councils.

The magisterial inanition that has yet to be overcome if action learning is to receive any kind of a trial in the British public service is particularly discouraging to those who have sensed the eager and sparkling vitality of the Australians. Granted that the Premier's Department of the State of Victoria does not handle half the business even of the office of the Chairman of the Greater London Council, it is, judged by British standards, little short of spectacular how, within six months of its first acquaintance with the idea of action learning, the Department was arranging for an officer from the Commonwealth capital to pass several months within it on so unlikely a task as sorting out its grosser infelicities. Melbourne is far away and the journey there, even by jumbo jet, an exhausting trial, calculated to unhinge a mind of iron. I found myself reciting, all the way from Singapore to New Delhi, Walt Whitman's *Leaves of Grass*, as my febrile imagination flitted from the British public service at one pole to the Australian at the other. But from what dark and opaque recesses of my memory stole forth the interfering error?

> I think I could turn and live with Australians, they are so
>   placid and self-contain'd;
> I stand and look at them long and long.
> They do not sweat and whine about their condition;
> They do not lie awake in the dark and weep for their sins;
> They do not make me sick discussing their duty to God;
> Not one is dissatisfied – not one is demented with the mania
>   of owning things;
> Not one kneels to another, nor to his kind that lived thou-
>   sands of years ago;
> Not one is respectable or industrious over the whole earth.

Was it, perhaps, because Whitman had lost his job in the Department of the Interior for having written *Leaves of Grass*, saturated, as he describes it, 'with the vehemence of pride and audacity of freedom necessary to loosen the mind of still-to-be-form'd America from the folds, the superstitions, and all the long, tenacious, and stifling anti-democratic authorities of

Asiatic and European past'? I do not know, for I cannot trace the springs of revelation.

My return to Australia was not long delayed. I spent three weeks in September 1978 visiting the Public Service Boards of three States – of Western Australia in Perth, of Victoria in Melbourne and of New South Wales in Sydney – and of the Commonwealth in Canberra. Like most other government bureaucracies in times of economic stress, all were under attack, relentless and ill-informed, from every mouthpiece of public opinion. But it was not such criticism alone that was inducing them to turn to action learning, alike within and between different branches of administration, leading one State board to declare that it would have five hundred of its staff engaged in action learning projects before the end of twelve months. Such had been the outcome of its first experiments, seeking not only the more effective use of the existing resources of the community but also the development of the political judgement of its officers, that the permanent heads of the government departments, for reasons best known to themselves, had already met to enquire in what ways they themselves ought to be engaged for their own benefit in action learning. This is a remarkable inversion of the cultural belief: 'How wonderful a thing is education – provided it is for the other man!'

In a lifetime spent on trying to propagate ideas, my recent Australian experience was the first ever of the boss class asking for its own enlightenment; the condition that action learning encourages it to shine autonomously, for each to illuminate the darkness of his brothers, does not make the request any the less impressive. I feel that the efforts now to be made inside the civil services of Australia, in which the current administrative and managerial perplexities of economic failure are accepted as the syllabus of a new understanding, will teach all who are ready to learn. How better might we be instructed to respond to the challenges of national mischance?

APPENDIX TO CHAPTER 8

The following statement about these Australian experiments was prepared on 5 May 1978 by Dr Roy Gilbert of the Public

Service Board of Victoria, and is included here with his permission:

External Action Learning Programme

1. Genesis of programme

I heard Professor Revans talk at Deakin University in February 1977; I supported his philosophy and so decided to experiment. A small group of Public and Private sector managers met after the Deakin University seminar with a view to running an action learning programme. Five organisations, the Victorian Public Service Board and four private sector organisations, agreed to participate in a programme commencing in July 1977. Unfortunately, the other four withdrew at the last moment. The very next day I was approached by the Commonwealth Public Service Board to arrange a four months' secondment for one of their officers to our Premier's department. I saw the opportunity. I explained to them the principles of action learning and then asked them to give me two officers in return for two of our people. They agreed to the experiment. The programme commenced on 25 July and finished on 25 November 1977. An evaluation of the programme is attached. The information gained from the 1977 programme is currently being used to entice private sector organisations to participate in further programmes this year.

2. Scope of the Projects

The two projects in the Victorian Public Service were submitted by the Public Works Department and the Premier's Department. They were stated as follows:

(a) Public Works Department

Problems exist in the timely delivery of contract and non-contract furniture and equipment which conforms to agreed standards and client requirements. The Public Works Department has responsibility for the purchase and delivery of furniture and equipment for its clients, and although the principal responsibility for delivery of contract furniture and equipment on time at the lowest cost lies with the chief supply officer and his branch, a number of other branches in this Department and other organisations are involved. The visiting fellow is requested critically to examine the processes and procedures in this Department, in the client Department, and in any other organisations involved in the delivery of furniture and equipment to primary, high and technical schools, and to recommend any change considered necessary to ensure the most effective performance of this function.

(b) *Premier's Department*

The Victorian Government is aware of the need to coordinate its various agencies and to ensure that the agencies are aware of and give due cognisance to the functions and responsibilities of each other. A visiting fellow could assist in the consideration of the procedures that enable each of the agencies to exercise its functions, having full regard to the responsibilities of all the other agencies. For example, in the Western Port Catchment, the Western Port regional planning group, the State Coordination Council and the land conservation council have a responsibility in the planning and coordinating field.

The two projects in the Commonwealth Public Service were stated as follows:

(c) *Meteorological Service*

To maintain the quality of service in Regional Forecasting Centres, and in the Observation and Traffic Sections, in the light of financial and staff cut-backs.

(d) *Australian Public Service*

To examine problems in the promotion and transfer of staff in the Australian Public Service.

3. *Strategies for Implementation of Results*

My comments are restricted to the two projects within the Victorian Public Service. Although all four were satisfactorily completed, I am more familiar with those in Victoria.

(a) *Public Works Department*

The detailed modes for implementation are outlined in the attachment. In addition, an officer of the Department has been given the responsibility of carrying on the work of the visiting fellow. Arrangements are also being made for the fellow to revisit the Public Works Department and discuss progress.

(b) *Premier's Department*

The visiting fellow developed a new system for the State Coordination Council. Once again the Department has given an officer responsibility for continuing the fellow's work. Furthermore, a special committee comprising four permanent heads of government departments has been asked to review the fellow's work; he has also been invited back to discuss progress.

4. *Problems encountered*

(i) Selling the concept of action learning to management: it sells itself if the initial programme is successful. For the initial programme the trainers themselves must have the ability to find managers with the courage to try something new.

(ii) Resistance to solutions found by outsiders: the level of this depends upon the quality of the solutions and the mentality of the line managers. This has not been a major problem in our first programme, although the chief supply officer in the Public Works Department is not entirely in favour of the fellow's proposal. The chief supply officer wanted a bigger store in Port Melbourne, while the fellow's solution meant a much smaller store. I deal directly with the Permanent Head, and, with him on my side, any sensible recommendation is likely to be implemented. Resistance has not been a problem at all in the project in the Premier's Department; this, like the Public Works Department, is pleased with the results of action learning and intends to participate in future external programmes. Both are also participating in the Board's internal programmes. (Perhaps a significant factor in the success of our programme has been my own personal position. I am head of the Recruitment and Staff Development Division of the Public Service Board, and as such deal directly with all the Permanent Heads. I was also the set adviser for the four project fellows. If, therefore, there are any problems arising while implementing the recommendations I can immediately talk with the Permanent Heads and remind them of the need for action. My dual role ensures continuity.)

Internal Action Learning Programme

The Victorian Public Service Board conducts an internal action learning programme, namely, through action learning in one's own job. Two Public Service Board officers are seconded for one month to two Departments to take over the line responsibilities of two departmental line managers in administration. A set is formed of these four men, with a set adviser. The project is to improve the efficiency and effectiveness of the departmental work units, and during the month the set meets twice weekly for about two hours at each meeting. The two line managers work full time on the project while the two Board officers take over their jobs. These two officers spend one week with the line managers before the programme proper begins, in order to familiarise themselves with the jobs they are to take over, and with the operations of the work units.

The first such internal action learning programme was conducted during December 1977. It was so successful that we intend to run them frequently. A second programme commenced on 17 April and a third is to commence in June. Departments that have participated, or that are down to participate, include Conservation, Public Works, Premier's, Education, Law, Local Government, Crown Lands, State Rivers and Water Supply. No problems have been encountered in this programme. Any recommendations are automatically implemented because the head of the work unit in the project is a member of the set. There is no imposition of ideas from outside. People participate because they seek the opportunity to step out of their job for a month.

Management Development Programme
Action learning principles have also been introduced into this more traditional programme. It is now designed as follows: A group of 20 relatively senior managers are nominated by their Departments, and first meet for half a day. At this seminar they must spell out the aims, functions and criteria for performance evaluation of their own respective work units. They work initially in five groups of four, and then report to the total group. One week later they meet as a group of 20, for a period of three days, to discuss general strategies for improving efficiency and effectiveness. This three-day programme is opened by a Minister of the Government or by a shadow minister of the opposition. On the last day they break up into the five sets of four to develop specific strategies for their own work units. After a further six weeks the five sets gather again to discuss progress and difficulties, and after twelve more weeks the total group of 20 meet for a day to discuss progress with an invited Permanent Head. Unlike those within the internal action learning programme, the 20 managers must carry on with their own day-to-day work during the twelve weeks. All Departments are now participating in this programme, whereas before the action learning elements were introduced only a minority of Departments did so. It is learning by doing. It gets results.

9.
Prospects and Possibilities

Not to test in action what one might have learned is like a woman putting on her make-up without a looking glass; only in Britain does everybody get away with it.

Behold, thou . . . knowest his will, and approvest the things that are more excellent, being instructed out of the law; and art confident that thou thyself art a guide of the blind, a light of them which are in darkness, an instructor of the foolish, a teacher of babes, which hast the form of knowledge and of the truth in the law. Thou therefore which teachest another, teachest thou not thyself? (1 Rom. ch. 2, vv. 17–21)

Every tree that bringeth not forth good fruit is hewn down and cast into the fire. (Matt. ch. 7, v. 19)

The interest in action learning now being shown in so many parts of the world demands that we try to foresee how it will develop after its long and reluctant period of gestation. In struggling to form this vision of the future we must not be too optimistic; what appear at the time to be decisive and spectacular gains for our approach are frequently forgotten a couple of years later, for unless the seedlings are continuously nourished by those who have set them they are soon choked by the tares of scholastic ridicule and pinched by the frosts of managerial neglect. We may quote an example of such oblivion from the United States, where what seemed at the time to be a most promising nursery for the common sense of action learning has been wiped without trace from the slate of local memory.

In the early 1960s I found myself addressing the American Psychological Association in Washington, D.C. There was in the audience a young man who was retained by a businessman's club in Milwaukee to run a regular programme of discussions for them, introducing topics of immediate relevance to the management of their own small and medium-sized firms. My thesis, that all businesses had a great deal in common and so much to learn by working together on related troubles, struck this young psychologist with the force of divine revelation. He saw at once that the discussion programme of the club could write itself, without the injection of outside expertise or advice, if only the members would be willing to give their attention, not to artificial and purchased case-discussions, but to the here-and-now evidences of each other's perceived afflictions. I found myself within a few hours on an aircraft to Milwaukee, and next day in the company of half-a-dozen or so of the Wisconsin managers, some of whom came down from Green Bay, a hundred miles away, to meet me. After a short discussion the club agreed to try action learning. What then happened is best described in the words of a local professor – not, we observe, from a school of management, but from a university department of speech communication (see appendix to this chapter).

However this might have been, the Milwaukee experiment inspired no further innovation. Neither Executive Committee Group I nor the Speech Communication Center has, to the best of my knowledge, followed up what seemed to have been interesting at the time. When, some years later, at a celebrated business school in Chicago, to which I had taken a few of the fellows from the Belgian programme, I mentioned the failure of the Wisconsin kite to stay aloft the dean observed rather knowingly: 'Well, professor, over here the whole venture was a violation of the law of the United States. The Sherman Anti-Trust Act was passed as long ago as 1890 to stop companies from getting together in conspiracies against other companies.' His observation is interesting, because the precise purpose of the Sherman Act has always been difficult to define; according to two leading authorities[6] the law has been a broken reed. To me, perhaps, it is little more than another obstruction to the spread of action learning.

Progress in America has been very slow altogether; the regular visits of the Belgian fellows to the leading business schools of the East Coast have led nowhere, although there was, very recently, a proposal by one of the country's largest public utilities to initiate a programme with a score of other large enterprises on Manhattan. The American Management Associations are promoting *More Than Management Development*, giving an account of the GEC experiment (see Chapter 6), and by all accounts the book is selling better in America than in Europe. The American Productivity Centre staged the first international conference on action learning, convened in Houston, Texas, in April, 1979. A programme of action learning among undergraduates, held in 1972 at Southern Methodist University, Dallas, which took me there several times, seems also to have survived the departure of the dean of the school, Jackson Grayson, who left to become chairman of the Price Commission set up by Richard Nixon as part of his Economic Stabilization Programme. Some of these setbacks, nevertheless, are not totally discouraging. I am sure that they are no more than the ups-and-downs of what is a longer-term epoch of cultural preparation, and that the nation of the pragmatists, Peirce, James and Dewey, will eventually take up action learning on an impressive scale.

I am also optimistic about the future of action learning in the development of the social services in Britain, despite the opposition from the established bureaucracies and the belief of our civil servants in what is called 'administrative science'. Now that the carefully explained application of this to the 1974 reorganization of the National Health Service[7] seems to have led to little more than the need to set up a Royal Commission to enquire what has gone wrong with it – and I am not implying that all the tribulations of our health care systems can be traced to that single calamity – there may be a chance that action learning will be brought to the rehabilitation of the mutilated Hercules before long. The sketch outlined in an earlier part of this book (see Chapter 3) shows that action learning might have done a little to improve the use of the resources of certain London hospitals, whose staffs co-operated to examine and improve their internal communications and, with these, their services to the patients. As long ago as 1970 I suggested that, in exactly the same way, the National Health Service itself might try what had been achieved by the individual hospitals. My argument, although rejected by the administration at the time, is worth repeating here, since it demonstrates specifically how hard it may be to engender new modes of perception – let alone of analysis or decision – in the Punch and Judy shows of our Establishment. I quote from my original proposals, *The Green Papers, 1970*, written at the invitation of a celebrated charitable foundation attempting to influence the policy of the government towards the impending reorganization:

We remember that administration has no claim to be a science. Nevertheless, to the empirical observer with experience in fields other than medicine there are two striking peculiarities of this great public service. The first is that its effective technological power (and to a lesser extent its political) lies at its base, among the doctors who are its front line; the second is that it is conducted in a climate of anxiety, often concealed, sometimes forgotten, frequently ignored, but never absent and always keyed to discharge its tensions . . .

We should thus set out to enquire how the very doctors themselves, the practitioners out in the mission field, can be brought, inside the terms of the Green Papers and of the proposed Health Services Advisory Council, to take an effective part in the description, analysis and improvement of what is actually provided at the cutting edges of the health services. It is a wrong reading of the problem to imagine that 'objective studies', conducted solely by professional research workers, usually economists or sociologists, who do not share the clinical responsibilities of consultant or general practitioner, can have any *significant* effect upon the quality of the services they provide. It may, of course, have *some* effect, but it is unlikely much to improve what actually goes on unless it secures the voluntary commitment of the doctors.

I interrupt the quotation from the memorandum of 1970 to draw attention to these words, since the effects of the researches referred to are by now perfectly well known. *The Times* of 8 June 1978 carries a headline: 'Health service has top-heavy structure and should be simplified, commission is told'; the article it adorns mentions a report by a professor from Brunel University – the institution that supplied the 'principles' on which the 1974 reorganization was based – which recommended that each region and area (of the NHS) should review its struc-

ture with a view to simplification. I continue my quotation of
1970:

> But, in addition to this elevation of what is already going on
> [*Note of June 1978:* this means the HIC and related
> researches in action learning for which I was responsible in
> 1970] into a settled and continuing attack upon the prob-
> lems of management and administration, more positive
> measures are called for. At least three can be suggested.

> (1) every area health authority should be given powers,
> defined by earmarked grants (and should be obliged to use
> them by being designated as a scheme-making authority) to
> conduct research into its own administrative and managerial
> functions; such powers should permit them to work in co-
> operation with other authorities or institutions (such as
> universities, colleges of education, technology or commerce)
> interested in management, administration or allied subjects;
> they should include powers to second their own staffs for
> such work, and to engage substitutes to fill vacancies so
> created. To make these measures effective, the Minister
> should require each area health authority to submit annually
> its proposals for using such powers . . .

> (2) to give such a movement a professional as well as a
> bureaucratic or administrative significance, a number of
> prizes or prize-lectures should be founded, preferably under
> the aegis of the Royal Colleges, for the doctor or group of
> doctors from a given area judged to have conducted the most
> interesting piece of research; in such awards regard should
> also be had for the support of others, such as nurses, with
> whom the doctor, or group of doctors, had worked . . .

> (3) in the settlement of merit-awards the record of any par-
> ticular candidate in having contributed to the study or
> resolution of the para-clinical problems of the hospital shall
> be taken into account . . .

Seen in the context of the previous eight chapters of this book,
the argument advocated for the reconstruction of the National
Health Service is both logical and consistent. I do not base it
entirely upon my belief that there is no science of administration, namely, a body of coherent laws drawn from empirical
observation enabling competent persons to make predictions

from it. My argument follows from the intense localism which lies, and which *necessarily* lies, at the heart of all effective patient care, on the one hand, and it follows, on the other, from the all-pervading anxiety in which that care is sought and provided. The area organization best suited to patient care delivery in such-and-such an area is a matter for those within that area, not for a cockpit of academics or a kitchen of management consultants. If the service were partitioned into a hundred local areas and each of them were made responsible, by action learning projects both *within* and *between* themselves, for the constant monitoring and development of how it ran itself, we should learn more about practical government within a twelve-month than from a wilderness of behavioural scientists and their familiars.

We hear, from time to time, of oversights in the building of new hospitals or in the closure of old ones. If the planners of a new facility costing twenty million pounds in, let us say, Liverpool were having to co-operate with those also planning innovations (whether of the same or of a different nature) in, say, Newcastle, Stoke-on-Trent, Plymouth and Colchester, after the manner of an action learning set, there would be less divergence between what was really needed and what might be provided – or retained. What is more, the exercise would bring honesty alike to the support of devolution and to the clarification of economic policy. It would become the responsibility of the central administration to ensure that the localities learned with and from each other in a fashion so far unheard of. Local administration, at present a dialogue of abuse carried on between monkeys up adjacent trees, would become, like all who participate in the study of each other's real problems, a model of imaginative prudence and sceptical enthusiasm. What is more, I believe that I shall live to see it.

It is our need to get away from generality worn as a mask to disguise our ignorance that is met by action learning. After the Eastern Nigerian Development Corporation, looking at the total profit of its hundred little mills spread through the jungle, takes the *general* decision that they ought to close (there was no profit, only a residual loss), the climate is favourable to *specificity*. A problem incomprehensible at the level of the corporate book-keeping may have meaning to those who struggle with the nuts, as it proved in practice. This does not mean to say that the corporate book-keeper ought to be shot for suggesting that several thousand people might be deprived of their livings; it does not even imply that he ought to be sacked, since he would only be replaced by another, who might be still more of an expert. But it does mean that the relations between the headquarters of the Development Corporation, on the one hand, and the hundred managers out under the trees, on the other, need to be rethought on other than the 'principles of administrative science'. So with Britannia's Punch-and-Judy show; it may be kept as entertainment, but, like the corporate book-keepers of the Nigerian jungle, it needs help from those who do the real work. It is the mission of action learning to discover how the manifold parties are best brought together in fruitful achievement.

The need for the establishment to shake itself free of stale and misleading generalizations seems to be widely spread; it is not confined to the National Health Service nor to the Nigerians. As we shall see later (Chapter 17), an investigation of the afflictions of New York City by the Rand Corporation suggests that both the field staff of the municipality and the neighbourhood groups they serve must be brought into the formation and discharge of city social and economic policy. Now that action learning across the world is starting to prove how local and specific resources can be brought to the understanding and treatment of diffused and general questions, we ought to ask how it can help the Punch-and-Judy show. My present suggestions are for regional consortia that bring local government, including education and police, industry and commerce, the social services, including unemployment, health, welfare and benefits, voluntary organizations of all kinds, helped by the appropriate professional agencies, into the same fruitful co-operation as saved the oil mills of the jungle and promises to help the public enterprises of India and Australia. Already a few Regional Management Centres are in league with each other to ask themselves what such consortia might be able to do, and what help they might need to get it done: help from such as the Manpower Services Commission or the Department of Education and Science in the way of finance to get started, and from the manifold participants on their local doorsteps to mount the attacks upon the intractable problems that loom up in front of us. It is possible that the notion of self-help by the regional consortium is still premature; none can tell before it is tried whether or not the employers, the trade unionists, the shopkeepers, the residents, the police and the schoolteachers of any English city drawn at random are sufficiently concerned about, say, adolescent violence to wish to study it in all its local specificity, and to learn with and from their fellows in two or three other cities something of its cause and cure. The scope and promise of action learning, as the previous chapters suggest, are wide and unexplored. In due course, they will be given a trial, simply because, in the complex societies in which we live, the Punch-and-Judy show is losing its popular appeal. There will, of course, be efforts to revive it. Latter day Diocletians will draw the sword on its behalf and renew the persecution of those who embrace the participative cause; they may even at this moment be taking up their position alongside Dog Toby as the British Brookings Institution. Whether they will pop up before or after the appearance of this text – or whether they will pop up at all – remains to be seen.

Even if the evidence (see Chapter 13) shows the attitudes of those about to leave school towards those in authority to vary significantly more *between* schools than *within* them (so that the school is the main influence in determining such attitudes), the family still has to live with its own rebels. Despite the influence of the school, some parents may still wish their children to grow up less hostile to authority in general. A few parent-teacher associations may thus like to experiment with action learning consortia in which all work together, either upon the problems of their own delinquents or upon those of their neighbours', to learn with and from each other how to help more effectively the young tearaways. It is the promise of the Lincoln experiment described in Chapter 6 to make this possible.

APPENDIX TO CHAPTER 9

The Milwaukee Consortium was a cooperative project involving six Wisconsin companies. It was a joint venture of Executive Committee Group I and the University of Wisconsin-Milwaukee Speech Communication Center. I (Professor Carl Larson) served as Project Co-ordinator. The project proper began with the selection of analysts from each of the participating companies, all of whom were top executive officers. These analysts attended a two-day orientation program in which they acquired some basic interviewing skills and developed a research plan which would guide the collection of data in the participating companies. The general focus of the research plan concerned the discovery of communication problems between supervisors and subordinates.

After the development of an interview schedule, a pilot study in a non-participating Milwaukee company, and the selection of representative samples from each of the participating companies, the analysts returned to the participating companies and completed their interviews. Each analyst interviewed employees of every company other than his own. At the completion of the interviews, the analysts gathered for extensive analysis meetings in which they compiled their results, identified both unique and common problems, and translated their findings into standard forms. At the completion of these meetings, each company analyst (with the combined findings from all the standardised returns relating to his company from the other analysts) conferred with the appropriate chief executive officers to outline action programs directed toward the solution of the problems discovered in the interviews.

My observations on this project were:

(1) The company analysts felt, intensely and consistently, that they had benefited greatly from the interviewing orientation program, from the opportunity to compare their own operations with those of other companies, and from the information that other analysts provided fully about problems within their own companies.

(2) The problems identified were markedly similar from company to company and in most cases were sufficiently grave to be extremely valuable discoveries for the participants.

(3) Participating companies have undertaken serious action programs to correct the problems which were discovered.

(4) The program was unique in that the companies discovered for themselves their own problems and were in a good position to evaluate realistically both the extent of the troubles and their abilities to do anything about them. In other words, there was little resistance to accepting the results of the interviews and very little difficulty to understand their implications. The staff of the Speech Communication Center have engaged

99

in many research and consulting programs for business and professional organisations, but found that the usual resistance originating from an academic institution was missing in this project.

(5) We encountered no difficulty with any of the employees, nor were any problems created by the design or conduct of the project.

PART II

The four chapters of the second part of this book set out some of the researches, admittedly of an academic kind – in that their primary purpose was to secure for each research worker some postgraduate qualification – that have illuminated the growth of action learning into a code of practice both logical and consistent. The first studies upon the deficiencies of large organizations – made at a time when the economists were hell-bent on 'the economy of scale' – threw up the notion that, like the dinosaurs of old, the big organization could not adapt because it could not learn. Its liability to be continually on strike led into the study of morale at work, and this into the study of internal communication; if people are to adapt they must understand to what it is they are adapting, and this requires that they are able to question what they see going on. Big enterprises have difficulty in keeping in touch with themselves and therefore in learning; since bigness affects all, managers and supervisors as well as those on the shop floor, morale at the top, in the middle and among the workers, tends to be much the same throughout the whole organization.

The researches reported here stress the learning characteristics of the community, and so put action learning upon a sound base of empirically proven rules. The study of morale among school children with which this part of the book closes shows very clearly a relation between the teacher perceived as a friendly person and the teacher perceived as a medium in the learning task; there is an exact correspondence between the school and the enterprise as learning communities. Our studies show that, until those who work in the organizations are called upon to put them right, we shall continue to waste our time and to defeat our purpose by expecting their rehabilitation at the hands of uninvolved or expert consultants.

10.
Small is Dutiful

And it came to pass on the morrow, that Moses sat to judge the people: and the people stood by Moses from the morning unto the evening. And when Moses' father-in-law saw all that he did to the people, he said 'What is this thing that thou doest to the people? Why sittest thou thyself alone, and all the people stand by thee from morning unto even?' ... 'The thing thou doest is not good. Thou wilt surely wear away, both thou and this people that is with thee: for this thing is too heavy for thee; thou art not able to perform it thyself alone.' (Exod. ch. 18, v. 13ff)

A state cannot be made out of ten citizens, and one which is made out of ten times ten thousand is no longer a state ... Who can be the general of a mass so excessively large? And who can give it orders, unless he has Stentor's voice? (Aristotle, *Ethics*, Bk IX, ch. X, para 2; and *Politics*, Bk VII, ch. IV, para 11)

The first thing therefore necessary is, that a city should consist of such numbers as will be sufficient to enable the inhabitants to live happily in their political community: ... what is its proper limit experience will easily show, and this experience is to be collected from the actions both of the governors and the governed. (Aristotle, *Politics*, Bk VII, ch. IV, para 12)

My experiences as director of education to the Coal Board, with its involvement in the directed practical training scheme of the Institution of Mining Engineers to ensure our next generation of colliery managers, brought me to question whether the senior brethren of the industry could teach their successors much worth knowing, since so many seemed largely incapable of learning anything themselves. The more I saw of the planning that went into the reconstruction of the mines, much of which was done by those who had been nominated to supervise the younger men under training, the more I doubted whether anybody knew what, in the first place, we ought to be teaching. A powerful caucus of intelligent and far-sighted men at headquarters was dedicated to rebuilding the industry using the most advanced technology in comparatively few mines; they were supported in their hopes by the prevailing spirit of the times, believing the victories of science to have won us the war and anticipating them to win us the peace. The plans of this expert staff were to be fed down to the coal seams through a national administration, and, granted the assumptions on which they were framed, it was impossible to deny their elegant self-assurance. But things did not seem to work out as foreseen; one felt uneasy about so many people biting off more than they could chew; aspiration was always just beyond capacity, and the industry seemed littered with unfinished jobs. These may have been praiseworthy shortcomings: for thirty years the unhappy industry, cut up by hundreds of different owners, starved of capital, no longer attractive to young men of ability, had done nothing to modernize itself. With the advent of nationalization, therefore, and its promise of un-imaginable resources, those who had grasped the levers of power at once embarked upon expansive plans of rehabilitation. Since it takes about ten years to sink a pair of shafts and to open up the coal measures, there was no time to lose; plans had to be made and work had to start forthwith. And, despite all the muddle and all the acrimony, it eventually produced results; it may, for example, be overlooked – as we congratulate the Coal Boards of the 1960s for their statesmanship – how their successes were assured by rasher men fifteen years before.

There seemed, at the time, to be evidence enough to suggest both the need to reconstruct the industry in terms of big mines with highly concentrated internal production units – drawing a lot of coal from a few intensively mechanized faces rather than many districts more widely scattered across the same pit – *and* to push through the reconstruction plans at the earliest possible moment. To justify the claim for bigness were the examples of the Germans and the Dutch, both of whose mining industries were held up for us to emulate and whose individual mines were, on average, far larger than our own, whether by tonnage raised or by manpower employed. To justify the claim for speed of development were both the appetite of industry for power and the menace of alternative sources to supply it; so confident were the nuclear experts that we were about to enter an epoch of unlimited and inexpensive energy, and so optimistic were the estimates of the geologists about the coming gluts of oil and gas, that the mining engineers in charge of colliery development could hope for nothing better than getting there first. We refer more fully to what eventually happened to our coal supplies in Chapter 17; for the present it is enough to say that the Coal Board put its head down and pushed forward with its plans.

The political needs to show early results were so imperative that there could be no time for carefully examining the thesis that production must be concentrated into comparatively few units. But already by 1950 some of the trainees attached to the planning engineers were quarrelling about the progress of the developments on which they were working, and one could hardly dismiss some of the misgivings they expressed about their assignments. It was not so much that they saw the technical design as inelegant – for they were in no position to judge this; they were, moreover, very loyal to the bosses they saw themselves as helping. Their doubts were always about the feasibility of the construction programmes endlessly unrolling before them, whether the job could be done in time or at the estimated cost; they lived with the practical men on the sites, assessing delay, investigating breakdowns, chasing strayed deliveries, listening to the miners, and all in no very definite role, without definable contract. But they often came together to compare notes. From these unprogrammed adventures they gained an unshakable conviction that many of their superiors were incapable of learning from their own experience; those in charge were seen as drawing upon a fund of fixed ideas immune to all external influences, such as whether they might work in practice.

In particular, any contract calling for more than face-to-face communication between those responsible for it was bound to get into trouble; only when two or more conflicting interests were able to meet was there any likelihood of accommodation, since written requests or instructions were generally ill-framed, often misdirected, and usually interpreted in senses totally outside the imaginations of those who originated them. Personal arguments, often abusive and occasionally violent, seemed essential to open the vision to other points of view; so many minds had set so hard under the concrete of experience that only in physical collision might their defences be breached.

In a culture that thought with its muscles, whose followers measured their tasks with the length of their strides and the reach of their shovels, and who settled their accounts on the nail, the complexities of national reconstruction were impossible to measure; they were seen as the insinuations of the devil, imported overnight: the subtle abstractions of paper work, all programmes and deadlines, the contracts entered into with non-mining men far away and even abroad, the decisions taken in London where nobody could hear the dawn chorus of the miners' boots in the street outside, and the harassments of the new administrative controls. The old and trustworthy ties were broken for good; unsigned agreements about what to do when things went wrong were no longer enough; everybody dealt with so many details and charged them against so many accounts that they seemed to spend all their time filling in forms of which they had no later recollection. Indeed, at one point in our researches, trying to estimate the stress under which the managers were working, we chose as one index the number of official returns upon which their signatures appeared upside down. To put it simply, the elegant self-assurance of the plans prepared by the high-level experts was no match for the robust vulgarity of the colliery yard; in many instances it had also to face ridicule and opposition.

Despite this evidence that the coal industry, by virtue of its ancient and tactile heritage, needed time to accommodate to the demands of centralized technical planning, with its implications of complexity and change, the plans to construct the very large units were pushed relentlessly ahead. The authoritarianism traditional to the industry, and derived from the rights of the landowners to exploit their own coal reserves in their own fashion, was used to promote the new gospel of 'economy of scale'. It was not confined to technical affairs alone, but was also used to rationalize the innumerable wages agreements that the Coal Board had inherited from the 800 and more previous owners of the industry. The enforcement of new contracts in these fields might also run into trouble, but since the opponents were more likely to be miners' lodges than local mining engineers the conflicts would be more serious. Such was the case at Grimethorpe Colliery in August 1947; here the Five-Day-Week Agreement did not work out quite as planned, and the whole Yorkshire coal-field was stopped for the first time since 1926. It was easy – and to some extent excusable – to dismiss this particular conflict as the natural growing pains of the reinvigorated giant, and to remind the critics that, such had been the dereliction into which the industry had been allowed to fall, the very agreement under dispute had been signed by candlelight because there was no coal to run the power stations. And, even if the strength of the National Union of Mineworkers allowed them no alternative, it did demand courage of those at the Coal Board to sign such a treaty.

But something more than courage, particularly the courage bred of authoritarianism, was needed to transform the industry; faced with the need to change not only the methods of coal production, helped by technical planning, but also the relations between the management and the miners, helped by new wages agreements, we also needed the will to learn. If half a million men are to do something today that they could not do yesterday, or if they are to do tomorrow what they cannot do at present, then they have something to learn. Our misfortune was that, in 1947, there were plenty within the coalitions of power trying to run the industry who could see the needs for new technology and new agreements; there were few who could see the need for themselves, and for others, to learn. Neither the Grimethorpe dispute nor the constant stream of reconstruction difficulties out in the coal-fields could be seen as evidence of the industry's inability to learn from experience, whether past, present or (it seemed) future.

I shall produce later on the evidence to suggest that the doctrine about 'economy of scale' needs to be radically rethought – should there be any who may still believe in it. Thirty years ago, however, it was the accepted wisdom of economic and social theorists, so that it was impossible, within the administration of the coal industry – exactly as it is impossible today within the administration of the National Health Service – to open up any discussion of such size-effects as communication, morale and autonomous learning. The suggestion that any organization ought to be able to learn from its own everyday experience, simply by asking itself what it thinks it is trying to do, what is preventing it from doing it and what measures it might take to overcome its problems and to move nearer to its goals, is still regarded by students and practitioners of administrative science as unrealistic nonsense. To most servants of the Coal Board in 1950, as to those of the National Health Service today, the key to successful reorganization has nothing to do with the capacity of its employees to learn from their experiences of success and of failure; it is still a matter of the 'right' central plans fed into the 'right' administrative structure. When the organization at any level, headquarters, divisions, areas or working units is so large, so inflexible and so opaque that nobody can tell what the 'right' plans ought to be, nor even what the existing structure is (let alone what the 'right' one ought to be), then the doctrine of 'economy of scale' is dangerous claptrap.

My early studies, first published in the *Political Quarterly* in 1956, were based upon the manifest confusions of the rejuvenated coal industry; two years later I was able to demonstrate their validity in quite different fields, including health care and manufacturing industry, further justifying the practices of action learning which had by then been developed. For the moment it is enough to say that the researches that were the basis of these early papers on the disastrous influences of organizational scale led always to one conclusion: by not being able to understand what was going on around him in the large unit, the miner (or other worker, including the nurse) was no longer able to understand where his responsibility might lie; if the conditions of work are unintelligible, whether by virtue of ignorance, confusion, rumour, ambiguity or other failure of information or guidance, then those who face such conditions cannot contribute effectively to the ostensible aims of such work. Even if they are initially well disposed to the organization that employs them, the unintelligibility of their tasks will soon lead to their disaffection; they will not care for anything but their own interests, and will have no sense of duty towards their organization. Since the evidence in 1956 was that the big units tend to have poor communications and so high unintelligibility, we must associate our sense of duty with the smaller concern.

The title of my first paper on this topic was *Industrial Morale and Size of Working Unit*. For obvious reasons it should have been called *Small is Dutiful*. My next attack upon the subject, published by the North Holland Company in 1958, in a series, Human Relations and Modern Management, was entitled *Human Relations, Management and Size*. The general thesis was developed first at the Coal Board; apart from discussions with colleagues at headquarters, however, it made no impact whatever upon the industry and the operational measures that flow from it, now called action learning, remain foreign to its authoritarian culture. Logical proof holds nothing for practical men.

There was, however, one great man out in the coal-fields who had firmly grasped the need for the industry to learn from its experience, and who had done so without any prompting from me. Sir Hubert Houldsworth had begun his professional life as a research chemist and had moved upwards into the law. The laboratory and the court had both taught him the value of an operating plan based on specific facts, verifiable from alternative sources, rather than upon the general principles of the academic or the accepted wisdom of the professional administrator. At the Coal Board this gave him a reputation for poor sportsmanship, where the bureaucracy would no more think of stiffening its arguments with truth than a boxer would sink to pack his gloves with a pair of horse shoes. Even when his division was carrying the entire industry upon its financial back, a squalid campaign of detraction was conducted against him, and from its unamiable exercises even some members of the Board itself did not always stand aside. For Hubert Houldsworth, whatever his own self-esteem, knew that coal had to be drawn up the shafts of collieries, that only the miners could cause it to be so, and that in the process managements are more dependent upon their men than the men need be upon their managers. It was this clarity of vision that took him constantly into every colliery manager's office and into every miners' lodge in his division, always ready to be told what, if anything, he ought to be doing to help those in the pits to identify and to solve their problems as they themselves saw to be proper and efficient.

The consequences of his participative approach, that made every pit in his division into a collective learning system, are traced in the next few pages; he personally led a remorseless campaign to involve both his colliery managers and their trade union branches in the reconstruction and improvement of their own pits. He kept all central bureaucracy to the barest minimum and constantly experimented with forms of delegation and involvement unknown in other coal-fields. So we must read the lessons in morale that he taught the industry; so we must read, set out below, the sharp decline of the accident rates in his division; so we must read the immunity of his miners to the septic angers of Grimethorpe that stopped the whole of the neighbouring coal-field; so we must read the steady fall in his wages cost per ton of coal raised relative to the national trends. And when, in the course of time, he left his division for the headquarters in London and his mode of participative leadership, from which all were able to learn, had been replaced by the ancient realisms and the traditional bossmanships, his former command could no longer withstand the corruptions of morale that spread from the adjacent coal-fields. Without his support of their own learning, his pits lost the lustre of their early achievements; nevertheless, in the strike ballots of both 1972 and 1974, long after Sir Hubert was in his grave, the miners of his division cast relatively more votes for peace than did most of their fellow trade unionists, so that some long-term effects of his example may still endure.

To make clear the contribution of Sir Hubert to the cause of action learning, it is necessary to say a few words about the organization of the industry following its nationalization. The great Midland coal-field, a reserve of fuel energy far richer than that of North Sea oil, stretching from Leeds to Leicester, was formed into two administrative divisions, Yorkshire and the East Midlands; these were further partitioned into areas, eight in Yorkshire, seven in the East Midlands. Sir Hubert was the first chairman of the latter, with about a hundred thousand men under his leadership. Although it is impossible strictly to compare any two sets of mines, it is safe to assert that any differences between the two halves of the Midland coal-field due to geological or other physical factors are certainly less than those between either half and any other coal-field in the industry. And in some particulars the differences between natural conditions in Yorkshire and in the East Midlands are entirely negligible. For example, immediately to the north and to the south of the administrative boundary created to divide them lie six and eight pits that are as similar to each other as can be conceived; all fourteen were sunk just before the First World War and, at the time of Sir Hubert's chairmanship, all worked but one and the same seam of coal. Thus, more than twenty thousand men worked underground in these fourteen mines in conditions that were as nearly as possible homogeneous across them all. We are therefore entitled to ask whether those north of the line responded to the experiences of public ownership differently from those to the south of it, and, if so, in what way. For if Sir Hubert's efforts to interest his miners in facing their problems constructively were significantly therapeutic – as the theory of action learning would suggest – while the traditional authoritarianism of the expert bureaucracy north of the line remained as it always had been, contagious and envenomed, the records of such large samples of men would be certain to display the differences between them.

The story is told in Figs. 1–4. For simplicity their contents are much abbreviated, but readers with a deep interest in these remarkable findings will be able to elaborate them in detail, since the individual figures are still available from the Coal Board.

Figure 1 shows the annual average rates of compensable accidents at the fourteen comparable pits over ten critical years, three before and seven after nationalization. It is not merely for ease of identification that the fourteen traces are divided into six with rising trends after this tremendous event, and eight with falling. The six are also all of those in Yorkshire and the eight all of those in the East Midlands. It is quite needless to enter into any statistical examination of the fourteen trend lines to be able to assert with unqualified confidence that collective influences, very different in kind, were at work within the two sets of six and eight respectively, driving their averages so

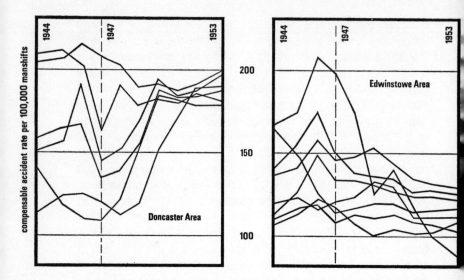

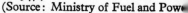

Figure 1: Trends of compensable accident rates for fourteen geologically and operationa[l] comparable collieries in adjacent areas of the Yorkshire (*left*) and East Midlands (*rig[ht]* divisions of the National Coal Board. (Vesting Day, Jan. 1947.)

(Source: Ministry of Fuel and Pow[er]

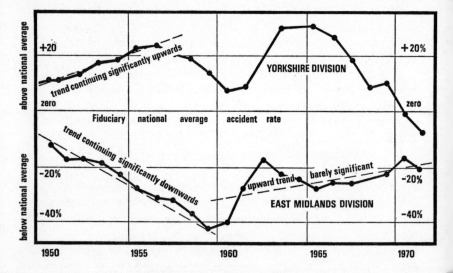

Figure 2: Later trends of accident rates in two adjacent and geologically compara[ble] divisions; entries in percentages of rates higher or lower than corresponding natio[nal] average.

(Source: NCB Repor[t]

112

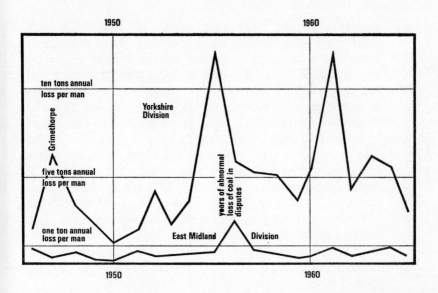

Figure 3: Annual average losses per man by disputes for two adjacent coal-field divisions.
(Source: National Coal Board Annual Reports)

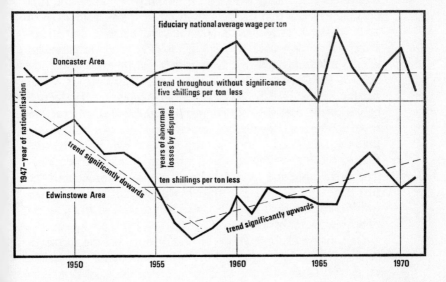

Figure 4: Average wages cost per ton of coal relative to corresponding national average two adjacent and comparable areas. Entries are made to the nearest half-shilling.
(Source: National Coal Board Annual Reports)

dramatically apart during those seven critical years that were the infancy of nationalization. Nor can the events recorded as compensable accidents be entirely accidental, since their short history manifests such evidence of assignable causes. As Freud suggests, accidents are the visible efforts of the subconscious to escape from the intolerable. To the ten thousand men who worked in the Barnsley seam in Yorkshire conditions had become worse than before the industry was taken over; to the matched sample in the same seam in the East Midlands, things had steadily improved. Figure 2 shows the same effect but for the two halves of the Midland coal-field forming the two divisions; the results displayed are for over two hundred collieries altogether, and are not confined to strictly matched units close together and working identical seams. We see that, until 1957, they tell the same story as the fourteen, after which managerial changes forced upon the Yorkshire division start to produce their benefits.

Figure 3 compares the losses of coal per man by disputes in the two divisions; there can be no doubt about Yorkshire getting off to a bad start with the Grimethorpe troubles, and it is possible to show that the decline in tonnage loss from 1946 to 1947 in the East Midlands is significant, namely, that it has some assignable cause. I believe this to have been the campaign of action learning that Sir Hubert was instrumental in getting started. Finally, in Figure 4 is shown the record of wages cost per ton of coal raised. Since the working conditions in the two halves of the coal-field are comparable, the wages cost per ton is an interesting measure of motivation. One can readily see that the miners of Yorkshire display no trend different from that of the industry as a whole, while those of the East Midlands give more and more for the same reward throughout the first decade of public ownership, but thereafter tend to regress towards the national trend because they have lost the inspiration from Sir Hubert to learn.

One may make a number of observations on the messages carried by our four figures. First, that it was quite impossible to discuss them with the senior officers of the Coal Board, to whom, it is to be supposed, the cost of mining coal or the rates of compensation to be paid to injured miners would have, from time to time, only distracted their attention from the political manoeuvre in which they were engaged to supply work for their administrative and clerical armies. But it would be unfair to censure those at Hobart House for their inabilities to grasp the significance of the facts, without pointing out that they are necessarily, like members of all large organizations, prevented by that membership from understanding the consequences, if any, of their daily efforts. One cannot expect to preach the gospel of *Small is Dutiful* to those who are themselves the innocent victims of administrative elephantiasis, and we see exactly the same anaesthesias in other large government departments. There are trends as different and opposed between the performances of otherwise comparable hospitals today as we saw between those of the Barnsley seam pits, but it is impossible to interest the officers of the Department of Health and Social Security in what they are and in how they may be caused. This is not because the higher civil service, being on inflation-proofed pensions and other cost-of-living guarantees, is totally indifferent to what may go on away from the bureaucratic battlefields; it is because the flower of their energy is consumed in the civil wars of their own internal systems. Like the Tower of Babel, the modern scientifically-administered organization does not lack working resources: there is no shortage of mines nor of hospitals; like the children of Noah, who also tried to reach to Heaven by the scale of their ambition, our contemporary bureaucracies also run into communication trouble: 'Go to, let us go down, and there confound their language, that they may not understand one another's speech' (Genesis XI, 7).

The second lesson to be drawn from the four figures follows immediately from the first. When Sir Hubert visited each of his mines in turn and suggested to their managers that, since they were responsible for drawing the coal every day up their shafts, they ought to have at least a few ideas about how to do so more effectively; and when he went on to say that he would like to know what those ideas were and what he might be able to do to help the operating managers put their ideas into effect, he not only advanced the thesis, *Small is Dutiful*, by settling upon his division the concentrated powers of intelligent localism: he introduced among his field officers the regenerative spirit of learning with and from each other during their attacks upon the very problems they had themselves been appointed to deal with. It was a novel experience, in an industry as traditionally authoritarian as coalmining, for the manager of a pit to find the chairman of his division knocking at the door and asking whether there was anything he might be able to help with. But the approach was not quite as ingenuous as it might appear to be at first sight; as soon as Sir Hubert had gone back to his office, the manager would be on the telephone to his colleagues at the adjacent pits, to find out if they had also been entertaining the divisional boss, and, if so, what had they had to say. He would then assemble his own officials and tell them of the unexpected interview. It would at once follow that the colliery team would make suggestions as to what improvements were possible to their existing methods, and, before long, most of those working in the pit would be discussing whether the chairman was serious and, if he were, what ideas he should be given to think about, to assess and to use. Within a month of the chairman's visit the pit would have become a learning community, and within a couple of months the senior members of its staff would be comparing their own proposals with those of their neighbours. Each would learn with and from the other, not only manager with undermanager and undermanager from manager in the same pit, but with and from those trying to make up their minds in other pits what they might reasonably put forward for consideration by Sir Hubert and his advisers. The future development of the East Midlands coal-field would therefore be based as much upon the ideas and experience of those called upon to take daily responsibility for running it, as upon the high-level expertise of the planning agents. To the benefits of easy communication by closeness of contact are added the incentives of comradeship in adversity free of all remote and imperious instruction.

The third lesson to be drawn from Sir Hubert's experience illustrates, alas, the infirmity of human nature. It is not only the traditions of coalmining that are authoritarian; so also are those of what passes for scholarship and professionalism. The idea that quite common persons, like the managers of collieries carrying the responsibility for the lives and efforts of a couple of thousand coalminers, might conceivably have something to suggest in a field normally reserved for experts is, the world over, invariably saluted with ferocious denunciation; when those who see themselves as the experts are high-ranking academics the responses are often laced with sarcasm and, occasionally, with malice. One does not spend five-and-twenty years in the footsteps of Hubert Houldsworth without recognizing how great is the fear among the half-clever and the too-clever-by-half that the ideas of tomorrow may also snatch the bread from the mouth tomorrow. The professional opposition to useful change that can be marshalled by the experts in yesterday's techniques offers a formidable testimony to social and economic inertia, and it may be of little use to protest that one is not attacking the tradition but only building upon it.

After this acknowledgement of the example set to me by Sir Hubert, I may review the further evidence, first published over twenty years ago, that only in organizations sufficiently compact to form learning communities are their members likely to be inspired by that sense of mutual responsibility necessary to achieving their ostensible aims. Since I have dwelt upon coal-mining for some pages, I will give as my first illustration the responses of student nurses to serving in hospitals of different sizes. In Fig. 5 are set out the average frequency of *absent sick* and the average duration of *absent sick* among six hundred or

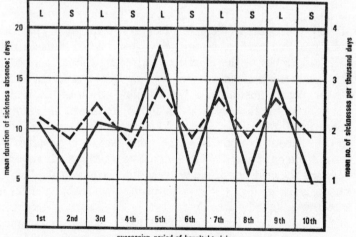

Figure 5: Mean incidence of sickness absence per thousand days (dotted lines) and mean duration of absences in days (solid lines) for 600 student nurses passing through one large hospital, L, and several small hospitals, S, in successive periods during their professional training.

so student nurses passing alternately between one large and several small hospitals in the course of their training for the professional register. All the hospitals were united in one training scheme, and all the girls moved around most of them in turn. We observe that whenever they returned to the one large hospital they were always more likely to fall sick and, having done so, to remain longer away from work. It is of no use to object that statistics of sickness absence are always misleading: one may be fully assured that the home sisters and others in charge of these particular student nurses would detect malingering almost before the girl herself might be rash enough to think of it. The records are of peculiar interest, because they suggested that the girls might be interviewed as they were ready to leave the large hospital for a small, and vice versa; without showing them the evidence set forth in the figure, we learned from them that they liked working in the smaller hospitals because it was there that, not only were their own questions more fully answered, but that they were helped to map their confusion by being encouraged to frame those enlightening questions that they would otherwise not have been able to put into words.

We develop elsewhere the thesis that action learning shows its strength, not in finding the answers to questions that have already been posed (the role of experts), but in finding the questions that need to be answered (the role of leaders); our early researches in the morale of nurses contributed much to this specification of what action learning can be expected to do.

Our second illustration of the disabling effects of size is also drawn from the hospital field. In Fig. 6 are shown (in a highly abbreviated form) the mean accident rates among all the workers, about 850,000 in all, at 4,680 American hospitals of four common classes. The marked upward trend strongly supports the evidence of the sickness absence among the British nurses given in Fig. 5; the range of the size-disabling effect is interesting, in addition, since it appears that the American nurse in the very large hospital is likely to sustain as much injury every day as the nurse in the smallest hospital will sustain in a week.

The next example of our thesis is drawn from the sickness records of the girl telephonists staffing exchanges of different sizes and locations. The data is given in Table 2, which was

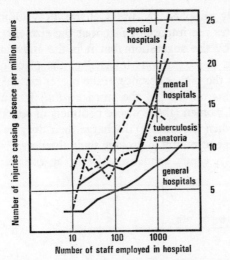

Figure 6: Distribution of accidents involving absence from work per million staff-hours 1953, for 4680 American hospitals, by size and type.

(Source: US Bureau of Labor Statistics)

(a)

Size of exchange by number of employees	Class of staff			
	Married established	Married non-established	Single established	Single non-established
Below 30	18.7	21.7	10.7	17.8
31–100	21.4	24.2	13.7	20.1
Above 100	21.5	29.2	14.3	25.5

(b)

Size and location of exchange	Class of staff	
	Married	Single
Small rural	21.7	17.8
Small London	22.4	16.2
Large urban	29.2	25.5

Table 2 (a): Average number of days per year absent sick (1952) by size of exchange and status of telephonist; (b) Average number of days per year absent sick among women telephonists (1952) by size and location of exchange.

very kindly supplied by the General Post Office. Table 2 demonstrates the important fact that the size-effect cannot be explained by the suggestion that it is the stress of urban life rather than the conditions internal to the place of work that determines the higher absence in the bigger exchanges. Table 2 also confirms our use of the word *dutiful*; it shows that the established women (those whose contracts of service guarantee their pay when absent sick) discharge their duty by not abusing this privilege wantonly to prolong their absences.

In Fig. 7, which condenses afresh the accident records of

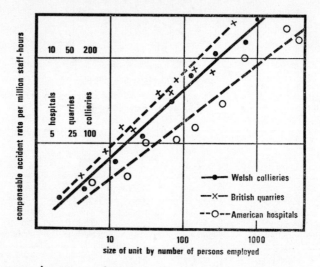

Figure 7: Average number of compensable accidents per million hours worked (1952) for 110,000 Welsh coalminers, 80,000 British quarrymen and 850,000 American hospital workers by size of working unit.

the American hospital workers, are also shown the same records for 110,000 Welsh miners and 80,000 British quarry workers (observing that the ordinates allow for the overall differences between the averages for the three communities of workers). The three trend lines shown all suggest that, were there such a place as a hospital, a colliery or a quarry employing only one person, he or she would be free of 'size-trend' accidents; such accidents, in other words, tend to be social events, staged by interactions with other persons. Some idea of the strength of these interactions in producing accidents can be gained by

120

calculating the correlation of the accident rate on size of under-taking, a statistic that cannot be estimated from Fig. 7, which shows only average rates within particular size-ranges of unit. This analysis suggests that about 40 per cent of whatever are the total causes of all accidents is associated with the size of the unit in which they occur. We find a result almost identical to this when we calculate the correlation between the attendance of coalminers at work with the size of the colliery at which they are employed; for example, there were 108 mines raising coal in the Yorkshire coal-field during the year 1957, and the co-efficient of correlation of absence on total annual tonnage raised was $+0.60$. The number of shifts lost per individual miner every year thus depends significantly upon the total magnitude of activity of the mine at which he works. A similar calculation for the total absences (from sickness, accidents and other causes) of the employees in the gas industry for the year 1954 gave a slightly higher correlation coefficient at $+0.70$; the same trends are visible in lateness to work, with a qualification for length of service. Even in very big units where lateness is on average higher than in small units, those longest on the books are least often late; it would be difficult to explain this except in terms of a higher sense of duty learned from ex-perience.

Another illustration of the thesis *Small is Dutiful*, is to be discovered in the Yorkshire coal-field during the early years of public ownership, using the statistics that have already gone into Figs. 1–4; from these we have prepared Table 3. This illustrates the reported causes (or occasions) of the 1,726 dis-putes of which notice had to be given jointly by the manager

Size-range of mines by num-ber on books	No. of mines	Total no. of men	No. of disputes by reported causes					
			W	P	O	C	B	All
Below 1250	67	42600	248	32	73	52	5	410
1251–2000	30	47500	262	24	144	95	17	542
Above 2000	18	45500	320	33	210	152	59	774

Table 3: Distribution of disputes by size of colliery and by cause as reported by colliery manager and miners' lodge officially to Minister of Fuel and Power for all collieries in Yorkshire and for four years, 1949–1952.

of the pit in which it occurred and the secretary of the local union branch; the disputes are those originating in the particular mines making the report, so that the table makes no reference to sympathetic strikes, such as that starting at Grimethorpe Colliery and spreading across the whole coal-field. For abbreviated presentation, the Yorkshire miners have been parttitioned into three families of virtually equal size, namely, those employed in the 67 smallest mines, those employed in the 30 mines of medium size and those employed in the 18 largest mines. The classification is not only by size as such, but also by the number of layers of supervision between the working miner and the manager of his pit. As a rough rule we may say that for the smallest mines there is generally one such intermediate layer, for the medium mines two, and for the largest mines three. The reported causes of the disputes are shown as follows:

(W) Arguments about wages, allowances and price lists.
(P) Personal disagreements with the management, including disputes over men being dismissed, reprimanded or suspended; objections to the remarks or attitudes of particular officials on particular occasions; grievances about personal allowances, such as for house rent or free coal, or about grading and promotion; friction over such miscellaneous matters as perquisites, loss of tools and breaches of the Fatal Accident Agreement.
(O) Criticism of the manner in which the working tasks are to be performed, about who is to perform them, and refusals to accept alternative work in emergency.
(C) Objections to environmental conditions, including refusals to complete work left over from the previous shift.
(B) Impatience at mechanical and similar breakdowns, followed by walking out from the place of work.

Our evidence suggests that, at least among the miners of Yorkshire at this highly critical time in their social history, it is not so much their wages nor any personal dislike of their managers that accounts for the disabling effects of size, since the men in the largest mines are but 20 per cent more ready than those in the medium and small to enter into disputes on these grounds. Their impatience with the factors of organization, however, is altogether greater; the scale of their irritation for causes to do with the organization of their work and the environment in which it is done rises by doubling and trebling as the two bigger size classifications are considered. Their impatience with what they take as management's inability to take corrective action seems to rise with the squares of these ratios, namely, as one is to four is to nine. It seems pretty clear that the Yorkshire miner feels little sense of duty to remain at work when the organization is so big as to put an unreasonable strain upon his manager in trying to keep it functioning. If action learning has any meaning whatever, it is here that we should try to exploit it.

Moreover, we may briefly explore the size-effect within the size-effect. Certainly in British coalmines (in which most of my personal experience of management research was first gained) there is an overwhelming tendency for morale, measured by the liability of men to go on strike, to stay away from work from time to time for their own reasons, and to injure themselves while at work, to decline as the scale of the manager's command is further and further extended. Does this effect apply also to the size of the working group within the mine to which the men are attached? The question is debated at length elsewhere, but we may present here sufficient evidence to suggest that there is a significant working group size-effect, in addition to that we have so far been illustrating. Table 4

Indicator of morale	Difference in morale indicator between small group and large group mines in same total size class by annual output				
	below 100	100–200	200–350	350–700	above 700
Attendance	+14	+2	+2	+3	+6
Accidents	−10	−16	−22	−7	−35
Disputes	−15	−10	−37	−22	−36

Table 4: Superiority of responses of miners in small group mines over responses of miners in large group mines for five size classes of all coalmines (by total tonnage annually raised in thousands); whether by coalface attendance (shifts worked per annum); by compensable accidents (number per 100,000 manshifts worked); or by disputes (percentage of pits involved in one or more). Year 1953.

presents that evidence in an abbreviated fashion; it gives the differences, in terms of the three operational indicators we have so far used, and by five size-classes of mines (very small, small, average, large and very large, using total tonnages raised), between the morale responses of the miners in those pits with working groups smaller than the size-class average and the responses of the miners in those pits with working groups larger than the size-class average. The size of the working group is estimated from the number of workers employed underground and the number of officials supervising them. We see that, for all three morale indicators across all five size-classes (fifteen entries in all) the mines with the more intensive supervision at the point of work return the more desirable experience. This suggests that the miners of Yorkshire are still more able to discharge their duties when there are sufficient supervisors to help with the organization of their tasks. The learning opportunities of the smaller group, as well as of the smaller mine, are evident from the observable performances of the miners.

A little more colour may be lent to the suggestion that the community of miners who make up any particular colliery might

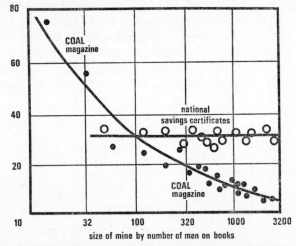

Figure 8: Percentages of miners subscribing for the year 1950 and for all mines in England and Wales selling *Coal* Magazine (450 in all), and for all mines with sales agencies for National Savings Certificates (531 in all). Note that, in contrast to the variation in magazine sales with size of mine, the sales of savings certificates is remarkably independent of the number of workers on the books.

be considered as a learning system by the evidence of Fig. 8. The Coal Board, in a praiseworthy effort to bring home to the miners as vividly as possible the tremendous task with which all in the industry were faced, produced an illustrated magazine in the genre of *Picture Post* for sale to the miners. It was called *Coal* and was designed as a forum for discussion; although it could not undertake to publicize such lively matter as dates, times and places of political demonstrations called to get rid of members of the administration, nor to print the speeches of those who saw nationalization as just one more prop to an ailing Western capitalism, it made a brave effort to explain the inevitable anomalies and incorrigible grievances that the new order could do little about. *Coal* magazine was an educational vehicle designed for the miners to use, so that its reception was some measure of the interest latent in the coal-fields, which, at its lowest, might measure the curiosity of those who must determine the future of the industry. Figure 8 shows how decisively that interest, that curiosity, fall off as the mines increase in size. In the small units over half the men bought the paper; in the large not so much as one man in ten. The evidence is crude, no doubt; there is, for example, nothing to tell us whether the miners of the East Midlands bought more copies per hundred employed than the miners of Yorkshire; there is nothing to discriminate, within Yorkshire, between individual pits with good, indifferent or bad indicators of morale. These omissions are not simple oversights; they are evidence of the resistances to all innovative approaches to the worries of Britannia: the Duke of Wellington would have had the idea if it were of any use. However this may be, Fig. 8, although confined to such data as was not refused its compiler, also shows the percentages of mines across a slightly narrower range of collieries by size who regularly bought National Savings Certificates. We observe that this figure is independent of the size of the unit; if men *want* to save through a colliery scheme they will do so irrespective of the intimacy or otherwise of their employing unit, an observable result suggesting that the saving certificate is a talisman of individual security immune against local and collective disaffection. It is not impossible to organize the sale of a thousand savings certificates a week in a three-thousand-man colliery if a thousand miners want to buy them, and presumably the same inference could be drawn about the sale of *Coal* magazine. As it is (but subject again to the same reservations about the withholding of data by the administration in order to promote confusion) we can only regard our hypothesis as not yet disproved: large organizations cannot readily learn and the nationalized industries are large organizations.

11.
Managers, Men and the Art of Listening

Even a fool, when he holdeth his peace, is counted wise: and he that shutteth his lips esteemed a man of understanding. (Prov. ch. 17, v. 28)

He that answereth a matter before he heareth it, it is a folly and shame unto him. (Prov. ch. 19, v. 13)

If a ruler hearken to lies, all his servants are wicked. (Prov. ch. 29, v. 12)

For if the trumpet give an uncertain sound, who shall prepare himself to the battle? So likewise ye, except ye utter by the tongue words easy to be understood, how shall it be known what is spoken? For ye shall speak into the air. There are, it may be, so many kinds of voices in the world, and none of them is without significance. Therefore if I know not the meaning of the voice, I shall be unto him that speaketh a barbarian, and he that speaketh shall be a barbarian unto me. (I Cor. ch. 14, vv. 8–11)

For if a man think himself to be something, when he is nothing, he deceiveth himself. But let every man prove his own work, and then shall he have rejoicing in himself alone, and not in another. (Gal. ch. 6, vv. 3 & 4)

Neither give heed to fables and endless genealogies, which minister questions, rather than godly edifying which is in faith: so do. Now the end of the commandment is charity out of a pure heart, and of a good conscience and of faith unfeigned. From which some having swerved have turned aside into vain jangling; desiring to be teachers of the law; understanding neither what they say nor whereof they affirm. (I Tim. ch. 1, vv. 4–7)

Since it is now more than twenty years since the *Political Quarterly* carried the opening statement of a proposition that contradicted the received wisdom of the contemporary economists – even if it has, in the long meantime, started to attract the attention of the more popular writers, and, in the last five years or so, of international lecturers and other trend-setting philosophers – there may be some virtue in recounting the arguments through which the original thesis has developed into the present theory and practice of action learning. It was one thing to sit in the miners' clubs of Cannock Chase and to notice that, whereas the men from Littleton pit (the largest in the coal-field) spoke of their managers as catalogues of depravity from which no single item was missing, those from Coppice (the smallest) occasionally remembered some act of charity that had been condoned there not so long ago. It was also interesting to demonstrate more generally the correlation between the numbers of men on the books of the sixteen pits on the Chase and their liability to stay away from work or even to produce coal. It became exciting to trace from these beginnings how the amount sold by a shop assistant falls off steadily as we examine the performances of the larger and ever larger shops, and to reflect upon the emphatic worsening of the lateness records of gasworkers as we move from small units, through those of medium size, to the large. Nevertheless, if the discovery were ever to be turned to useful effect – and in a technological society what can be more desirable than that we eliminate the disabling effects of largeness? – it is essential to understand more fully the causal dependence of morale upon size of working unit.

A chance to do so turned up at the Manchester College of Technology where, in 1955, I had become professor of industrial administration. This appointment I had accepted after agreeing with its Principal, the redoubtable Lord Bowden, that our contract committed neither the College nor myself to the view that there was (or could ever be) any such subject as 'industrial administration', at least in the sense that we understood the word *subject* from our having read physics together at Cambridge. But in 1955 British industry was much concerned with difficulties of renovation, and Lord Bowden had gone to help the College understand better what these difficulties might have been. All manner of ideas were in the air: automation was coming to spare us labour, computers were to abolish the drudgeries of thought. In such a climate we decided to ask what the factory workers of Manchester felt about the influences of change being brought to bear upon them, particularly as they were likely to affect life in the factory itself. We felt it might be useful to understand their points of view about the alarms of redundancy and the erosion of differentials likely to follow innovation, as well as any possible opposition to change *as such*, rooted not in any fear of unemployment nor of exploitation, but in the simple fact of variety itself.

We began by persuading fifteen Manchester firms of similar structure to let us interview a random sample of their workpeople. The firms were chosen because they had all sent some young managers to the College to be indoctrinated with the ideas of work study, a mixture said to be useful in bringing about change of manufacturing practice. The first encounters were with a young Pakistani, now professor at Lahore, a mechanical engineer of wide factory experience, sent by his government to find out about the responses of workers to the introduction of new methods of work. Mr Hussein spoke altogether to about 800 persons in the course of his researches, men and women, on day-wages and on piece-work, some skilled, others semi-skilled and unskilled; he interviewed managers and foremen, shop stewards and trade union officers. Some of the labourers had not by then learned to speak English, and Mr Hussein needed the help of other Indian students to understand what they were trying to tell him. The first 500 conversations, conducted in eight of the fifteen factories selected at random, were quite unstructured; at an introduction to the work force, made by the manager, our doctoral student simply explained who he was, that his country was intending to put up some large engineering factories, that he himself was an engineer and might have to run one of these, and that he had been sent by his government to Britain to find out what people over here felt about factory life. The message was so simple and yet so true that the workers had great difficulty at first in believing it; Mr Hussein, however, who arrived in Manchester a devout Muslim abstaining from all intoxicants, was able at the end of his three years to testify before his examiners as to the integrity of his field data by offering to produce local shop stewards and foremen of repute able to witness his convivial progress. At a farewell party, attended by many of the subjects whose opinions he had collected at the work benches of Manchester, a lot of beer was drunk, but none of it with a hand more firm than that of Dr Hussein, nor were any of the final valedictions uttered in a voice more clear than his. At his introductory meetings he mentioned especially his interest in how things are changed, since he was from a traditional culture; the aspect of factory life that therefore would occupy much of his attention in Manchester was work study, since it was through this that the British manufacturers were striving to innovate.

From the tape-recordings of the first 500 interviews, of which some lasted almost three hours, it was estimated that about 10,000 distinct particulars could be identified; these included verifiable reports about factory events, witnessed anecdotes, rumour and hearsay, moral precepts, wishful thoughts, exaggerated accounts of everyday trivia, fantasy and sheer rubbish. Mr Hussein was like a fisherman sweeping an unknown sea, and having to sort his 500 indescribable catches into some intelligible classification; he therefore spread the academic beach with an array of empty baskets, into which, helped by the staff and other research students, he proceeded to drop, not all his 10,000 fish, but a series of random samples drawn from the tapes. What fish joined which others in which baskets, so to speak, depended not upon any predetermined taxonomy of what factory workers ought to be talking about, but upon the apparent content of the particular thrown up by the random search of the day; the classification of these contents was less subjective than might be feared before starting on the sorting process. One basket was clearly to be reserved for those comments about the relation of reward to effort, such as: 'We do all the work and the managers take all the profit' (expressed by Aesop 2,500 years ago in *The Lion's Share* as 'You may share the labours of the great, but you will not share the spoil'). But the same basket also received the opposite expression of the same idea: 'Here we get as much out of work study as the management', together with many others touching upon the same relationship: 'The extra they pay you isn't worth the effort you have to make to get it'; 'Although we have to argue with the boss about our money, we have to admit he's fair in the end'; 'What I like about this place is that you can go for a bit extra any week you want it'; 'Here they make up your money to what you would have got if things hadn't gone wrong'.

Other headings – although we write of twenty years ago – covered fears of redundancy: 'Work study today; labour exchange tomorrow', and its opposite: 'Work study makes for a full order book and plenty of jobs'; the accuracy with which job times could be measured and the fairness of allowances; the attentiveness of supervisors to interruptions in the flow of work; pressures from the management to speed up output; working conditions and the state of machines; the readiness of managers to listen to complaints, or even to listen to anything at all; the undervaluation of slowly acquired skills in the face of 'reorganized' schedules of production; and many others. Yet, sorting and resorting the catch in this way, it was found that thirty-four baskets were sufficient to dispose of nearly all the fish. After deciding upon this variety, we felt that any not at home in some existing basket was unclassifiable. We did not, perhaps, make as much use of some of the more bizarre comments as we should have done; looking back nearly twenty years, into that heyday of full employment and Keynesian economics, I see that we ought to have given more attention to the openly-expressed fears of redundancy. Just as the scismologists are now hoping to predict the next Japanese earthquake by watching closely the movements of earthworms, so our econometricians might bring into their equations the anticipatory sensibilities of those who (unlike the econometricians) are likely to suffer most the consequences of recession. Action learning itself shows it to be a need of our times that we appreciate the subjective opinions of those who, unembarrassed by expert knowledge, still place their trust in common sense. For example, at the enquiry into the Aberfan disaster, in which the coal that had killed their ancestors suddenly turned upon the Welsh children and wiped out the whole school under an avalanche of mine rubbish, the resentment of the bereaved community was directed against those experts who had derided the views of the miners about the long-known instability of the fatal tip.

Once we had identified our thirty-four headings the task was to trace their interrelations and comparative importance. Merely to pick a few of them out and to try influencing them by managerial action would be like making up a medical prescription using any or all of thirty-four drugs at random. So our search for structure was pursued in a second study using the results of the first, and it was pursued in the remaining seven factories of the original fifteen. From each of the baskets still on the beach, two typical statements were selected, each characterizing to a high degree, either positive or negative, the fish in the particular basket. For example, the alertness of foremen to impending shortages or failures: 'If you tell the foreman, he'll soon do something about your trouble' is appreciative comment; 'You can talk to the foreman till you're blue in the face and he still does nothing about the mess you're in' puts the contrary view. The pairs, positive and negative, are then assembled, to form a master questionnaire of sixty-eight statements, every one originally drawn from the voluntary comment of anonymous workers willing for their opinions to be made available to whomever might care to listen to them – including their own bosses. Several entire samples of thirty-four items, positive and negative, were prepared; they were printed in random order and made up into survey instruments of half-a-dozen pages, to be scored by a 5 per cent sample, or by 266 workers altogether, of those on the floor of the seven residual factories. In scoring, the subjects were invited to record what they thought about the statements printed on the page before them; their responses could be any one of five: Strongly agree (SA); Agree or tend to agree (A); Uncertain, unknown or unintelligible (U); Disagree or tend to disagree (D); Strongly disagree (SD). Agreement with positive statements and disagreement with negatives scored plus; disagreement with positive statements and agreement with negatives scored minus; uncertainty scored nothing and strong opinions scored double. (In the treatment of the responses, care had to be taken to deal with ambiguity and acquiescence, or a tendency among some subjects happily to agree with both the positive and negative versions of the same statement; such instances occur but do not affect the final conclusions in so great a mass of numerical data, with 266 times 34 entries.) The resulting tables were then fed into a computer and factor-analysed; they revealed three main families of opinion, each of which may be read so as to suggest useful lines of action to be followed by the managements.

Before we discuss these, however, it is interesting to dwell upon a simple question. It is one that goes to the heart of action learning, the development of which has been powerfully influenced by the unsophisticated studies of Mr Hussein and his fellow doctoral candidates.

What is the single most-discriminating question that one ought to put to a shop-floor worker if, at one shot, one wants to know as much as possible about his feelings towards life in the factory?

The purpose of the question may be illustrated differently. Suppose you were to fall in by chance with a fellow-countryman on the airfield at, say, Benares and that, for any reason whatever, you had to decide whether or not *on the strength of his answering one question alone* you would want to meet him again three months later when you were both to be in London. What single question would, in your opinion, tell you most about him? Would it be what brought him to Benares? What firm he worked for? Whether he would lend you a couple of hundred rupees? Had he been to Katmandu after a load of cannabis? But there is a constraint. The question must be exactly the same as you would ask another chance acquaintance whom you see carrying an English newspaper in a Barcelona bullring, or in the foyer of the Automobile Club of Victoria in Melbourne. The conundrum is not exactly frivolous: to be able to spot the most discriminating question in conditions of ignorance, confusion or risk is a gift worth having. The most-discriminating question is that which attracts the most informative reply, that is, the message most useful in settling one's next moves. Such a question is, of course, strongly coloured by one's own value system and past experience; my own choice, in wishing to learn as much as possible about my fellow-countryman by his reply to one single question, would be to find out what school he had attended at the age of fourteen. Others ought to be able to identify their own choice of discriminating question.

But in the factories of Manchester we do not have to guess, nor even to search our subjective experience for the answer: the computer will find it for us from the mass of 266 times 34 responses, if we ask it the right question.

There are 34 columns of numbers, each with 266 entries ranging between $+2$ and -2, in this table. Which of these 34 columns is most like all the other 33?

This is a precise question to which the computer can give a precise answer. The column that enjoys the distinction contains all the entries about *the ability of management to listen to what the workpeople are trying to say to it*; closely related to this ability, whether to consider complaints about things as they are or suggestions for making them better, is the managerial disposition to settle issues by easy consultation. The willingness of management to be communicated with, or its sensitivity to the need for knowing the feelings of the shop floor, did not imply that it would agree to whatever the workers might ask or propose; its resolution in sticking to its point, even after discussion with the shop stewards, or even with the trade union, was seen by the respondents to the 500 primary interviews as something distinct from the simple capacity to listen. If management did not yield after argument, it was still seen as reasonable, or even as fair; what the shop floor could not stand was to be turned down without discussion. It is apparently less difficult to accept management's refusal ('being firm') after one's case has been thoroughly, even acrimoniously, debated ('being fair'). However this may be, the mass of the evidence from the 266 shop-floor workers in the seven Manchester factories is that the most sensitive indicator of what they feel about their factory experience remains their perception of the management's readiness to listen to what they have to say.

Before we enter into the significance of this simple conclusion to the effectiveness of action learning, we shall present the fuller results of the computer analysis. The 266 sets each of 34 responses revealed three evidences of internal relationships; the first of these was a family likeness between ten of the 34, the second was a family likeness between six others and the third a family likeness between another four. The first family of ten was composed of the following items:

(i)   management's capacity to listen
(ii)   management's essential fairness beneath its manifest toughness
(iii)   supervision's alertness to operational snags
(iv)   management's promptness in handling complaints

(v)   gearing of wages to output
(vi)   ease of taking over new tasks
(vii)   effort in gaining mastery of new tasks
(viii) belief that system values personal skills
(ix)   satisfaction with pay differentials
(x)   adequate consultation before changes of task

The first four are separated from the other six in the above list; they are essentially concerned with the worker's perception of the management, especially of his (her) communication with the management. The lower six are concerned with the worker's perception of the task itself, even if in some of the six items, notably (viii) and (x), the perception of the management must also enter. But the observational fact that, in the consciousness of any particular worker, these ten items attract the same kind of response, positive, indifferent or negative, is of the greatest interest. We may lump together the four scores of each worker under the first four items; the maximum score would be $+8$, the minimum -8. Those workers who score a total of $+5$ or more we may see as holding a high regard for the readiness of their managers to communicate; we therefore suggest that they see their managements as 'forthcoming', and there are 41 of them out of the 266. If, on the contrary, any worker scores -5 or less, we suggest that the management is seen as 'hostile'; similarly there turn out to be 41 of these. The remainder, according to whether their scores are positive or negative, are classified as 'aware' and 'indifferent'. We may repeat this process of classification into four main classes using the scores attracted by the other six items of the family; these will now range from $+12$ to -12; all those who aggregate $+6$ or more may be seen as 'highly satisfied' with the task and any with -6 or less as 'highly dissatisfied'; other positive totals indicate 'satisfaction', and other negative totals 'dissatisfaction'. We may classify the total scores of all 266 respondents to obtain Table 5.

Impression of management	Attitude to employment			
	High satisfaction	Satis- faction	Dissat- isfaction	High Dis- satisfaction
Forthcoming	29	9	2	1
Aware	11	67	10	2
Indifferent	5	6	73	10
Hostile	0	3	14	24

Table 5. Workers' impression of management responsiveness related to perceived level of task-satisfaction.

The distribution of the 266 sets of scores shown in Table 5 suggests that there is a highly significant association between what the workers see as the willingness of their managers and supervisors to listen to them, on the one hand, and, on the other, their perception of the worthwhileness of the tasks in which they are engaged. Without such an association the distribution of the entries in the above table, with 193 of the total of 266 falling on the diagonal, could occur by chance not once in a million trials. We have before us a striking illustration of the thesis on which action learning is designed: learning is a social process, in which the parties learn with and from each other as they tackle problems of common interest or concern. Where the managers are seen by the workers to listen to what the workers have to say about their troubles, these are soon dealt with, or so the workers seem to believe. For of the 131 workers who see their managers as either forthcoming or aware, that is, able to learn what the troubles on the shop floor may be, 15 workers only are negative in their attitudes to employment, suggesting that, in the view of the remaining 116, their troubles have been put right. But of the 135 who see their managers as indifferent or hostile, that is, incapable of knowing what the problems of the shop floor seen by the workers may be, only 14 have positive attitudes towards their employment, suggesting that their troubles are unalleviated. Where, in other words, for whatever reason management seems capable of learning, it may be capable of solving the problems that beset it; where it is incapable of doing so the problems will remain untreated and morale will suffer.

This study confirms an ancient truth, illustrated in the Apocrypha (Ecclesiasticus ch. 10, v. 2) 'As the judge of the people is himself, so are his officers; and what manner of man the ruler of the city is, such are all they that dwell therein'. I have referred to the same proposition as the *Principle of Insufficient Mandate*: 'Managers who cannot change their own perceptions of their problems cannot change the conditions that create those problems', or 'Without authority over one's own opinions one has no authority over one's surroundings'. As an operational device, action learning must select problems to work on in which management is already interested, that is, problems by which management is seriously embarrassed and of which it is already aware that its existing efforts are unavailing. Thus it is that in mounting any action learning programme the coalition of power must be deeply involved in the choice of projects; it is of no avail that they remit the selection of projects to subordinates, for only if the top management themselves are committed to learn will the existential conditions be improved. In the same way, managers who underrate the abilities of their juniors by dismissing their opinions, or who do not recognize their dependence upon those juniors, and are thereby seen as indifferent or hostile, will find themselves trying to command a dissatisfied work force.

Our second family of six items from the 34 suggests the exertion of pressure by the management to get things done; one indicator was the comment 'No matter how much you turn in, they keep on driving you!', of which the positive expression was 'Here we work with management as a team'. The six items may be listed as before, divided between attitudes to the management and attitudes towards the task:

(xi) no needling of diligent workers
(xii) no reneging on agreed rates if earnings mount
(xiii) adequate services to support determined effort

(xiv) repetitive work not monotonous if co-operatively planned

(xv)   all tasks objectively assessable if honestly approached
(xvi)   work efficiency need not imply redundancy

The first three above are all vital elements in the relations of management to its employees when there is a concern to increase the volume of production. Once agreement has been reached about the level of production to be aimed at and the rates at which it shall be paid for, the workers can express their views of how the management is keeping to its side of the agreement. The same scores, $+2$, $+1$, zero, -1 or -2, can be returned to the statements representing the six items above as were returned to the ten items falling into the family of managerial sensibility; a table similar to that used in presenting the results of that previous analysis can also be prepared. We do not give the precise figures here, but merely state that there is the same highly significant association between the two sides of the family of six set out above. Where the shop floor perceives the management as positive towards the raising of productivity – in not harassing its employees, in not trying to 'chisel' on the rates once the employees have shown that they can make a good thing out of them by working hard enough, and in supplying the services, such as machine maintenance, raw materials, transport and so forth, essential to keeping the work flow moving – the shop floor is also positive towards the speeded-up task itself. The work is not seen as monotonous, it is accepted as objectively measurable, and there is no fear that the increase of output will necessarily lead to workers being laid off.

We are, perhaps, stretching the results of Dr Hussein's work somewhat in identifying a third family within our 34 items. However this may be, four of them compose a little family among themselves; we have called it the resource recognition effect, from the identity of two of the four items. The first is the extent to which the management appear to recognize a useful role for the trade unions, and the second to which they appear to recognize the skill of the workpeople as such; both of these suggest the perceptions that the shop floor has of its standing in the eyes of the management. The other two members of the family are the belief that a good worker will never be laid off, and that work efficiency campaigns are no threat to the older employee. Hence, at the time when Dr Hussein's study was made, those workers who saw themselves as valued by their managements had no fear of redundancy, and vice versa.

It is many years since this elaborate study was made, and the economic condition of Britain, if it is not much changed in fact, certainly seems to have changed to those who are no longer in employment. This may not, all the same, invalidate our principal conclusion – that the relish shown by the shop floor to the tasks they are called upon to do is powerfully associated with their perceptions of the management, namely, with their beliefs whether or not it listens to them, whether or not it puts pressure upon them, and whether or not it is able to see merit among them. Action learning, designed as an exercise to improve relations between all who work in the enterprise by involving them together in the treatment of perceived problems, must inevitably clarify and strengthen these three categories of perception, at least if management sincerely wishes to do something about the troubles that torment it. And the original study itself can show how efforts to improve the total system of communication, incentive and resource are worth attempting. For even if we can do very little to change the personalities of either managers or men (and it may be a consoling truth to know that we cannot), the very differences in morale and motivation that Dr Hussein uncovered between the seven factories that participated in the second part of his study suggest that, even if we can do little to influence individuals, there are immense gains to be had by influencing the employing units as total organisms. His analysis showed that, using the scores that led to the classification of the 266 sets of opinions set out in Table 5, taking our sample as typical of British workers, total attitude (to management and to task combined) is far more strongly determined by the factory one happens to work in than it is determined by the person one happens to be away from the place of work. (In jargon, the analysis of variance of the 266 total scores shows that the variations *between* factories are many times greater than are those between individuals *within* factories.) In the following chapter we describe how studies of a similar kind were made, no longer on the shop floor, but among the foremen and supervisors, the engineers and the managers.

12.
The Morale of Supervisors and Managers

How long halt ye between two opinions? (I Kgs ch. 18, v. 21)

It is because people do not know each other that they hate each other so little. (Remy de Gourmont, *Decadence*)

We ought to do our neighbour all the good we can. If you do good, good will be done to you; but if you do evil, the same will be measured back to you again. (Bidpai, *Panchatantra* c. 326 BC)

The ancient Goths of Germany . . . had all of them a wise custom of debating everything of importance to their state, twice; that is – once drunk, once sober. Drunk – that their councils might not lack vigour; and sober – that they might not lack discretion. (Sterne, *Tristram Shandy*, Bk V, ch. 17)

We have been able to show that the attitudes of shop-floor workers towards life in the factory is powerfully influenced by the extent to which they believe themselves to be in touch with their managers, and their managers to be in touch with them. Since the communication between those at the opposite ends of the factory hierarchy is largely through a network of supervisors, we must try to find out how these intermediaries affect what management and men think of each other. I therefore describe very briefly some studies of the attitudes of foremen and of managers, and show how these studies have been exploited to develop the theory and practice of action learning. The methodologies used were much like those described in *Managers, Men and the Art of Listening* and nothing more will be said about them in detail.

Consider the following statement:

85. The higher management here rarely runs into trouble through being out of touch with shop-floor problems.

It was first made and recorded in the course of a series of interviews with foremen, lasting almost a thousand hours, on the floors of several factories in the north of England. This enquiry was the field work of Satish Kumar Sikka, an Indian doctoral student, who lived among the staff of one particular factory for over two years. He tells of a man there, once billeted as a soldier in his own Indian village, where (at very different times) both had been tattooed by the same artist with the same motifs upon their forearms. This extraordinary coincidence had opened all the doors of the community to Sikka, but led to a painful breach between the two comrades that eventually the works manager and I were called upon to heal. During an experiment to test his findings, it was essential for Sikka to draw a completely random sample of respondents to one of his survey instruments; in this sample the works number of his tattooed friend did not turn up. As soon as he heard that others were being asked to complete the questionnaire without him, he was apparently hurt beyond description. Backed by two mates he burst into Sikka's office, baring his forearm to reveal the talisman of brotherhood and demanding to be told by what lapse of integrity he had been struck from the register. The unfortunate Satish knew neither English nor statistics enough to convince the delegation about the impartiality of tables of random numbers, nor of the need to safeguard his researches by using them. The tattooed man remained unmollified and eventually we decided to exploit the incident, in the act of clearing it up, by calling a general meeting of the foremen to report progress on the study as a whole.

Statement 85 (there were 108 in the final editions of the survey instruments constructed from this interview series, of which a sample of forty is given at the end of this chapter) tempts any foremen to whom it is shown to declare their opinions of how they feel in touch with what is going on around them. There are advantages in any management knowing what its shop-floor problems are, even if it is unable to do much about them. Statement 85 seems to indicate clarity in the flow of operating information through the factory, and is thus called a K-statement (K for knowledge), along with nine others shown in the sample. It is possible to prove, by statistical analysis of the responses of large numbers of foremen, that all ten belong to the same K-family; any particular foreman, in other words, tends to have much the same opinion to give about any of the ten K-statements, and yet to give a series of responses that are different from those of any other foreman. The foremen within the same factory differ among themselves, therefore, in their overall views of the same factory communication system. This is no surprising result: first, the foremen differ among themselves as persons, with different senses of security, different sets of defence mechanisms and different attitudes to authority. Secondly, the jobs of the foremen are physically different and some may be more remote from the centres of decision. Thirdly, the managers may like some foremen more than others and thus be more willing to open their hearts to them. If we take the questionnaire to another factory, we find a similar result; the individual foremen responding to it are significantly consistent in what they have to say about the ten K-statements, but differ among themselves in the degree of approbation with which they say it. Since we find this same individual-consistency within the same group-dispersion at all factories, we may exploit the set of ten K-statements to make interesting comparisons between different factories, and even between different departments of the same factory. In the Inter-University Programme of the Fondation Industrie-Université of Belgium, sets of K-statements were used to identify the more obstinate supervisory opacities, and we give below an illustration of their use in the factory at which Dr Sikka first developed them.

We may, therefore, ask whether there are differences between the *average* levels of the foremen's responses at different factories. Do those at one particular factory, although differing among themselves significantly as individuals, express opinions about the same set of K-statements that are so much higher – or lower – than those expressed by the foremen at another that one must conclude the one information network to be much more transparent – or opaque – than the other? In Factory D, for example, the responses of nine foremen averaged -0.556

per response, suggesting them to be 'half-dissatisfied' with whatever it may be that the family of ten K-statements represents. The corresponding average for the fifty foremen at Factory B, on the other hand, was +0.218, showing them to have a slight but positive appreciation of the ten K-statements. The difference between the two means, of 0.774 of a 'satisfaction-point' is very highly significant; it could not possibly have occurred by random chance, and is therefore caused because the two sets of foremen hold beliefs of entirely different orders of confidence in the communication systems on which they depend. We note that it is in the smaller factory that the confidence is less, showing that 'small is dutiful' is not necessarily a universal thesis. Factory B was, in fact, one of the largest in the country, and I was particularly interested in it because, by the way in which it was organized, it had managed to overcome many of the disabling effects of size, and of poor communications, by which so much of British industry is bedevilled.

In our studies of the workers on the shop floor, we discovered that, to the extent to which the management seemed to them to be approachable, so were the workpeople satisfied with the rewards and conditions of their tasks. We proceed to examine the results of a similar search among the supervisors, and start by considering the following R-statement (R for rewards; nine others of the R-family are also given on p. 158):

25. Technical management in this firm tends to treat the suggestions of the foremen with less consideration than they deserve.

This negative statement suggests dissatisfaction with the task of foremanship; not to have one's abilities recognized by the boss is always humiliating, and where, in addition, one has little confidence in the boss himself, perhaps because one knows that he is not sufficiently aware of what is going on to be entitled to make a judgement of what is going on, the rejection of good suggestions may have disastrous effects upon morale. An early Belgian study revealed, for example, that the commonest reason for middle managers to seek jobs outside their existing enterprises was a belief that their talents were underemployed, not that they were underrewarded. We may well have succeeded in building an economic culture in which everybody today believes himself, or herself, to be underpaid, whatever the absolute level of their reward, but it may also be that, by depriving those who work for us of all opportunity to use their initiative, the management sciences have often prevented them from knowing themselves by their own fulfilments. Our unending scuffles about doctors' salaries and miners' wages are thus a search for identity, even although it may be presented as an insistence upon status.

Statement 25 reflects how the foreman feels his competence to be undervalued within his system of employment; it is a disturbing piece of feedback to him of his usefulness to the community in which he spends his life. Our measurements, like those made on the K-family, show that the individual foremen have their own characteristic responses to all members of the R-family, and that these characteristics differ significantly between different foremen within the same factory; there are also significant differences between the average values of the R-responses of the foremen in one factory and the average of those in another. In Factory B, for example, the mean value of R, taken over all fifty foremen was -0.016; over the nine foremen at Factory D it was -0.511. We take this to mean that, whereas the foremen at the first factory are neither one thing nor the other about their rewards, those at the second are about half a point dissatisfied. We know already that the foremen at Factory B feel themselves to get significantly more information (high K-scores) than do those at Factory D (low K-scores); we now see that they also express significantly more satisfaction with their work, or, what amounts to the same thing, less dissatisfaction.

Since this discovery seems to be repeating that made among the shop-floor workers, we at once demand if it is a personal effect as well as one visible across the two factories as a whole. The answer is that it is; the coefficient of correlation between the fifty pairs of scores of the foremen at Factory B is $+0.672$; this is so high as to suggest that K and R are two different aspects of the same parameter, so that *information* and *reward* are two verbally distinct descriptions of the same factory influence. This simple finding confirms the nature of information as 'the value to its recipient of the message that contains it'; reports, messages or data that are of no value to foremen or managers – in that they are of no use in dealing with perceived problems – have no information in them, however inflated they may be with precise facts. We may therefore add to the armouries of action learning the following proposition:

> Among factory foremen, the intelligibility of the communication system is strongly correlated with their sense of integration into the operational system; those who say they are adequately informed also feel that they are adequately rewarded.

It may be worth while to dwell upon this self-evident conclusion, for we shall come across it again in examining the morale of the managers senior to the foremen; in other words, we are able to show that, on the shop floor, among the supervisors and at the highest levels of the management, there exists a highly significant relation between the extent to which individuals believe themselves to know what is going on around them, on the one hand, and their sense, on the other, of being a respected member of the community in which those things are going on.

The first White Paper of the Conservative Government, on Company Law Reform (25 July 1973), which in a sense led to the setting up of the Bullock Committee to report on industrial democracy, contained the words: 'The more people can see what is actually happening the less likely they are to harbour general suspicions, and the less opportunity there is for concealing improper and even criminal activities. Openness in company affairs is the first principle in securing responsible behaviour.' Our need at the present moment is to build upon this principle some reliable forms of practice, and I believe action learning to be the simplest and most straightforward of those yet available to us for doing so. The task is not easy. To identify, as the studies of Hussein and Sikka have done, that there are particular blockages in factory communication systems is one thing; to remove them is another. Diagnosis is all very well, but however elegant and convincing it may be it is not therapy. And, faced with the intricate and uncertain demands of therapy, there are those managers, apparently reasonable men, who would sooner not know what is wrong than be led into having to do something about it. In can be very disturbing to discover that one's subordinates are unanimously critical of one's policies, or that the real problems of the enterprise are not what they have long been imagined to be. The evaluation of the action learning programmes of Belgium (see Chapter 19) shows that some managements not only resist the risks of therapy; they also reject the truths of diagnosis. To some extent, therefore, action learning can be a dangerous business; managers who refuse to follow the leads which it opens up may, by having revealed a condition that they deliberately ignore, find themselves in a second condition worse than that from which they started.

So far we have drawn from the studies of Dr Sikka only the joint KR-family of statements that suggest the foreman's job-intelligibility and job-satisfaction, corresponding to those of the shop-floor workers. But the analysis of the responses of about 180 foremen and assistant foremen to the questionnaire of 108 items that he had designed showed another family of statements bearing upon the major task of supervision. This family has no counterpart in the studies of Dr Hussein among the workpeople proper; it consists of the remaining 20 items of the lists on pp. 159–60, from which we have already drawn the 20 items of Family KR, and we shall designate it as Family PL. We do so because ten of the items are concerned, or seem to be concerned, with the foremen's perceptions of themselves as persons (P), while the other ten suggest their perceptions of themselves as leaders (L). We give a pair of them as illustrations:

32. Unquestioned obedience to a foreman is essential to the efficiency of a firm. (P)
75. There is nothing that a foreman can do to put interest into a workman's job if the job itself is uninteresting. (L)

We may test the internal homogeneity and the individual characteristics of the two families, P and L, respectively as we have done before, and show that the individual foreman who scores highly on P also does so on L, and vice versa. PL thus seems to be an individual trait. But it seems to have an invariant quality quite unknown to KR: although within any given factory there are significant variations between individual foremen in their total responses to the twenty statements of the

PL-family, there are no significant variations between the mean values of the PL-family totals at different factories. In other words, although the foremen differ among themselves as individuals in their PL-responses, on average those in any one factory measure the same as those in any other. This is in complete contrast with their KR-responses, where the variation between factories is significantly greater than that within factories (between individual foremen). PL thus seems to be a universal parameter, the value of which is not affected by the communication (intelligibility) patterns of the factories in which the foremen are engaged.

Whatever it may be that the P-family and the L-family stand for (if it is hard to accept the suggestion that they indicate the self-perception of the foremen as persons of status and as leaders), it is interesting to discover that their average values remain virtually constant from factory to factory; this suggests that they reveal aspects of the supervisory character that would be carried unchanged from one factory to another, while K and R vary greatly between one factory community and another. Hence job-intelligibility and job-satisfaction are institutional effects, while P and L seem to endure unchanged in the individual in whatsoever community of supervisors he may find himself. A most simple question therefore arises: can the management do anything to improve the intelligibility of the communication system (K), so allowing the junior officers to take better decisions, and the sense of their integration into the managerial team (R), so improving their motivation to work together? Action learning suggests that this is possible; by attacking those confusions in the operations of the factory that can be shown to arise from poor communications, as we show below (p. 150), it proved possible at Factory B to effect great savings of time and money, on the one hand, and to raise the morale of the staff, on the other. Such assumptions also underlay the Hospitals Internal Communications Project (p. 30), and several of the major exercises staged inside the Inter-University Programme of Belgium (p. 43). It is most important that the point is thoroughly grasped; action learning is not pretending to change the self-image that foremen have of themselves, either as persons or as leaders. It has no truck with academic psychotherapy, sensitivity training, non-directive counselling and so forth, although members of the same sets, working with each other on real-time problems, will not be slow to let their colleagues know whenever, in trying to deceive each other, they are deceiving only themselves. But action learning is trying to change both K and R, which are factory parameters independent of P and L. To emphasize this independence, we state that, for the fifty supervisors of Factory B seen in one of Dr Sikka's studies, the correlation between the totals, each of 20 statement-responses, of $(R + K)$ and of $(P + L)$ was -0.108; this is non-significant.

It is, in general, no easy matter to persuade an organization to take in hand the improvement of an opaque internal communication system. One of the reasons for setting up the Action Learning Trust is for the brave souls experimenting with this approach to keep in touch with each other sufficiently closely to learn with and from each other how to get started on missions so worth while. Our own experiments were simple and straightforward; alike at Factories B and D the senior managers were challenged to fill in the survey instruments designed by Dr Sikka for the foremen upon his interviews with the foremen. At each factory a number of managers, not very different from the number of foremen in each case drawn by Dr Sikka (48 managers at Factory B as contrasted with 50 supervisors; 11 managers at Factory D as contrasted with nine supervisors), were brought together at the same time, seated at tables. All were asked to write down in front of them the name of a foreman under their command whom they had known long enough to assert with confidence that they knew what he felt about the system in which he was working. Keeping the names in front of them, the parties of managers were then asked to complete the foreman's questionnaire as if they were the very foremen whose names were on the paper before them. When the exercise was completed all the names written down were destroyed and the questionnaires returned in such a way that it was impossible to identitfy which manager had filled in which paper. The results are of the greatest interest: in each factory (as in others in which the experiments have been repeated) the managers return the same average estimates of the PL-families as do the foremen (and all are invariant between factories), while the differences between the responses of the managers and their foremen in their returns of the KR-families are such as to suggest in the most unequivocal terms that the management is unlikely to have any working knowledge at all about how the foremen see the factory information system. While the 11 managers at Factory D grossly overestimate the confidence their foremen have in this, the very opposite is true about the responses of the 48 managers at Factory B compared with the responses of the 50 foremen. At Factory D the managers *over*estimate by 0.647 of a satisfaction point; at Factory B they *under*estimate by 0.615. This contrast in differential perceptions is profoundly significant, and was used to persuade the management at Factory B to undertake a successful action learning exercise.

The managers who contributed to the survey at Factory B were all university graduates, and well able to grasp the significance of the finding that there was so great a difference between the two perceptions, managerial and supervisory, of KR and none between those of PL. Their gratification to discover that the foremen had more confidence in the way the factory was organized than they (the managers) believed led at once to discussions about how the finding could be used. Two suggestions were made and followed up.

The first proposal was to build on this confidence a detailed study of those aspects of the organization about which the foremen had complained in their original interviews with Dr Sikka. This was found to be the supply and spare-parts system (which had recently been reorganized at considerable expense by a firm of experts); the management, fortified by the support they felt themselves to be getting from their foremen, decided to invite them to make suggestions about improving the system. A working party, under the chairmanship of a senior engineer from another section of the factory altogether, of six permanent members and of six others changed after a couple of attendances, was set up from foremen representing the main user and supplier departments; it met once a week for three months and worked out recommendations for reorganizing the system. Its ideas were constantly checked by individual members in the field between meetings, and all its recommendations were finally accepted. These were naturally all specifically situational, more so, indeed, than had been those of the experts who had set the new system up several months before. It would be out of place to describe them here in detail, but they ranged from re-siting the first line holding depots, redesigning the forms for ordering spares, tightening the procedures for turning in surplus stock to specifying a radio-controlled van for use in extreme emergency. The most interesting outcome of the exercise was not the estimated annual saving to be secured in running the supply system – although this was put at an annual sum of six figures – but the enthusiasm of the supply manager, whose own new plans had been turned inside out by the foreman-users. He was so impressed with the improvement in the relations between his own storekeepers and supply foremen, on the one hand, and the line and engineering departments out in the field, on the other, that he personally wrote a 2000-word memorandum on the origins, design, conduct and outcome of the exercise. This he then posted to his dozen colleagues elsewhere in the same company, advising them to initiate similar experiments in co-operation. He was dissenter, apostate and evangelist, all in three months.

The second proposal to emerge from involving the managers in an effort to estimate the attitudes of the foremen on whom they necessarily relied to run the factory (employing 2,000 men and more) might, at the time, have produced less effect than the reorganization of the local supply system. Its consequences for the development of action learning have, however, been profound. For the sixty-five senior men at the works posed themselves a simple question:

If we can be so inaccurate in our views of what the foremen think about the system we all work in, how well do we communicate among ourselves? Of what value is the information we think we are getting, and on which we base our decisions, if we so underrate the reliability of what, to our supervisors, seems a more adequate and trustworthy communication system than it does to us? Do we also underrate what we tell each other? Are we trying to run this factory only half-believing what our own colleagues have to say? If so, why is this? And what are we going to do about it?

In such a frame of mind, progress through action learning may be possible. We note, however, from Chapter 19 that studies prove such frames of mind are not common; it remains a challenge to action learning to bring them about.

The significant differences that were discovered between what the supervisors themselves thought of their communication system and the opinions of it attributed to them by their managers naturally suggested that we should try to measure what the different senior managers had to say about their experiences of life in the factory. Since statistically consistent measures could be secured of the impressions made on the managers by their supervisors, it was obviously possible to assess their impressions of other things as well. In particular, might the levels of managerial satisfaction – indeed, of their motivation – be linked to the confidence they had in the works information system, as it was with the shop-floor workers and the foremen? If so, how might the total communication system itself be improved, alike to raise the quality of information that went into the managers' decisions and to enhance the satisfaction they got out of their tasks?

Another survey instrument was therefore constructed at Factory B, using to the maximum extent the ideas of the managers themselves about the relevance of particular factory topics to successful plant operations. These ideas had, naturally enough, been stimulated by the participation of the managers in the supervisor study, and it was difficult to resist the overloading of the survey instruments that they set out to help construct. That finally adopted had 112 items, and was prepared, tested and scored by fifty senior managers with responsibilities in the factory itself, and in the higher administration that was responsible for a number of other factories in the same company. The analysis of the 112 times 50 numerically assessed responses shows that 16 of these 112 form a close family with the same logical structure as the KR-set among the foremen. They are listed under two headings; eight K-statements touch upon the managerial perception of organizational structure and of information channels, and eight R-statements touch upon the managerial perception of personal tasks and their rewards (see p. 160). The figures in brackets against each item measure the mean strength of feeling, positive or negative, among the 50 managers; these figures are the simple averages of the 50 entries against each statement, $+2$, $+1$, zero, -1

or -2 as the opinion is expressed. Sceptical readers are re-assured to observe that among the 16 responses the two most negative are Nos. 38 and 64, both of which touch upon the salaries of the responding managers; it is highly improbable that these two low rankings could have occurred by chance, and the hypothesis that they have thus been caused may in-crease our confidence in the findings. There are, of course, internal checks to the consistency of the responses that are not given here, but that are available to any who might wish to pursue the results further.[8]

Since the responses were discovered by the computer analysis to be loaded with a common factor, it is clear that the score of any individual among the fifty managers to the eight K-statements must be correlated with the same individual's response to the eight R-statements, with all members of the two families highly consistent among themselves. Indeed, the separation of the 16 items into two distinct sets of eight each is a highly artificial business; it is made merely to re-emphasize the point that intelligibility and satisfaction are again correlated among the senior management. Even so, it is not usual for managers, any more than it is for shop-floor workers or fore-men, to think of rewards and communications as other than two separate work parameters not likely to have much effect upon each other, except when important news is deliberately sup-pressed, or, as the Conservative Government feared in its White Paper, 'employees do not have an appropriate opportunity of influencing decisions which can closely affect their own in-terest'. To put the relationship beyond all doubt, we show in Fig. 9 the fifty totals of managerial responses set out diagram-matically; the coefficient of correlation of R on K is $+0.753$, suggesting that easily the most important single factor in deter-mining job-satisfaction among managers is their confidence in the sources of information upon which they need to rely. The diagram enables us to assert with confidence the following proposition:

In this sample of fifty managers, those who suggest they understand the information channels of the organization also suggest satisfaction in their work; and vice-versa.

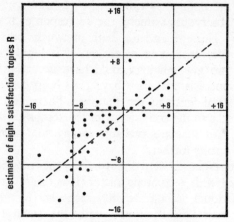

estimate of eight information topics K

Figure 9: Relation between sense of satisfaction or reward at work R, and perception of quality of information available to carry out that work K, for fifty graduate managers at the same factory. Both R and K are indicated as the sum of eight responses, so that a score of +8 suggests average satisfaction. We note that, even in this well-run factory, both grand averages are negative; the managers themselves were concerned to find this result.

It does not, however, enable us to answer the question:

> Does any particular manager imply that he likes (or dislikes) his personal job because he understands (or does not understand) the operating organization; or does he imply the converse, namely, that he understands (or does not understand) the operating organization because he likes (or dislikes) his personal job?

We have a clue to seeking the answer to this question, although it is not conclusive, in identifying the most discriminating question in the set of 16 statements. Just as, in the study of shop-floor opinion, the computer told us that the item most like all the others that went to determine the profile of worker-response was the extent to which management was felt to listen to what the shop floor was trying to say to it (p. 134), so the statement to which the senior manager's response was most indicative of his view of the factory culture as a whole was

No. 53: 'Managers in this works are in no doubt about how their objectives are set.' Those, in other words, who know this are most likely to have positive views of the other 15 KR-items; those who feel that they do not know this are most likely to have negative views throughout. We still cannot be sure, however, whether it is the satisfaction with the task that leads managers to feel that they know how their task is determined (and, it seems, who are the directors above them who determine it), or whether those who know the agents of their fate above them are most likely to be content in enduring that fate. At this chicken-and-egg ambiguity the statistician must stand aside and offer the study to the managers in the field; their immediate impulse is to determine whether the average levels of K and R alike can be raised, since it is clear from Fig. 9 that, averaged over the 50 managers who responded to the questionnaire at Factory B, both management parameters are significantly negative; their balance of opinion is towards opacity and discontent, and the question they asked themselves was 'Can, and should, the two values be changed, to suggest instead clarity and satisfaction?' As the distribution of Fig. 9 shows, there are 36 managers whose KR scores are negative and but 14 whose views are non-negative; the recognition of this by the managers themselves led to a series of arguments that have made considerable additions to our understanding of action learning. These arguments, turning upon the felicity of communication between different members of the senior management, might have led to acrimony had it not also been revealed by the analysis of the 112 times 50 statement-responses that another factor, similar to the PL-family of the foremen, revealed a highly positive spirit of self-awareness and group-morale among the 50 respondents. A fuller reference to this factor can be found in the literature;[9] it is unnecessary for our present purpose to describe it more fully here. It is sufficient to identify the most discriminating item among the 16 selected by the computer as most representative of the quasi-PL-family. It was No. 75: 'In spite of the pressure upon us to see that our plants are working efficiently, it is essential to keep our people in the picture.' Since this statement contains one element of personal status (awareness of key role in maintaining output) and another of leadership (necessity to act as source of inspiration to subordinates), it is clearly indicative of social relations at the factory. KR, on the other hand, suggests information about the work and one's inner satisfactions for getting that work done. At Factory B the average value, taken over all 16 statements and all 50 managers, of the PL-equivalent was +0.795, suggesting a high degree of personal security and of social stability. The mean value of KR, on the other hand, was −0.336.

These two contrasting figures, the one highly positive, the other significantly negative, exemplify two sets of ideas, or perceptual syndromes, strongly colouring the approach of these 50 managers to the total mission of the factory. The practical question is whether the security of the 'human relations' suggested by the high PL-syndrome could be exploited to try to raise the level of the KR-syndrome? Could a programme of activities, through action learning, be devised *by the very managers* whose previous curiosity had led to these evaluations, a programme aimed at both making more clear how objectives are set and at *involving subordinates* in studies of how the system functions under the increasing pressure of demand made on those who work in it? This is a typical specification of an action learning assignment, with the generalization that increasing pressure of demand is not always that for increased physical output from a manufacturing plant. It might as well be increasing load upon a hospital or, even more important, the increasing demand among unemployed adolescents for useful work.

The immemorial contribution made by the involvement of these fifty graduate engineering managers was to their further analysis of the KR-syndrome. If, they asked, by collectively examining our *problems* in order to raise among ourselves the quality of our information system, how do we select the most economical problems on which to work? (Economical, in this sense, implies two criteria; first, if successfully treated, most likely to advance our interests; second, if properly attacked, most likely to yield useful results. Difficult problems promising little return are to be avoided.) The longer we debated the nature of managerial problem solving, the more the analysis tended to take up the engineering parallels with which these men were professionally familiar; the one-to-one correspondence of management and engineering soon emerged, both being activities to create order out of disorder, or to assemble resources so as felicitously to overcome the obstructions to achievement. Since the general theory of engineering postulates an organizing agent, the engineer himself, who must command three flows or sources – of information, of energy and of materials – it was soon established that any manager, or organizing agent, must also command the same three sources or their analogues in the field he is endeavouring to improve. First, he needs information about his mission; second, he needs energy to move towards its fulfilment; third, he must have the sinews of effective execution. In more familiar terms he must know what he is trying to get done, he must command the motivation to get it done, and he must have the necessary facilities to do it. In a community in which he is the organizing agent, he must be able to find those who know what is to be done, those who want to get it done, and those able to do it.

From these arguments at Factory B emerged the trio of questions that every action learning project must attack from its outset: 'Who knows? Who cares? Who can?' To form a working team of such as these is the constant aim of any action learning project, as we describe elsewhere in this book (see p. 44); it was the debate among the self-motivated engineers at Factory B that first identified the importance of these simple questions. Our attempts to see the problems of Factory B in terms of them also heightened our skills in diagnosing the problems worth attack; we remember that the most discriminating question in the KR-syndrome turned upon knowing how one's objectives were set. 'What *are* the objectives? And if we agree that these are realistic, what is *hindering* our achievement of them? And if we can go on to agree what this may be, how do we *overcome* it?' These three diagnostic questions, like the three engineering – or therapeutic – questions above, can also be shortened: 'What are we trying to do? What is stopping us? What can we do about it?' The victory of the fifty engineers at Factory B was to condense the whole theory of organized effort into these two sets each of three questions; they are unlikely to be displaced from the first page of any future manual about action learning.

List K for supervisors; statements mainly about knowledge of works information systems.

11. In this firm the management clearly explains to all its employees the purpose of what they are doing.
13. If the decision of a foreman on a matter of works discipline is reversed by the management, the reasons for it are always made clear to those concerned.
44. In this firm the foreman has very few complaints about getting all the information he needs to run his department properly.
49. The foreman finds life easier if he tells the management what they would like to hear, whatever the truth may be.
53. Agreements with the trade union at this firm make quite clear the foreman's disciplinary powers.
69. Mistakes and misunderstandings are kept down when our management put all the instructions they can into writing.
71. In this firm, if any change is ever proposed in conditions of service of the men (whether the proposal comes from the trade union or from the management), the foremen are made fully aware of it before the change is brought about.
84. Foremen in this firm are satisfied that their duties have been made perfectly clear to them.
85. The higher management here rarely runs into difficulty through being out of touch with shop-floor problems.
89. When management has had to put some exceptional interpretation upon an agreement with the trade union, all foremen in this firm are told why the management has done so.

List R for supervisors; statements mainly about satisfaction with the supervisory tasks.

9. The management of this company encourages the foreman to show his initiative and forethought in dealing with the shop steward over any matter likely to cause future trouble.
24. A foreman in this company is easily able to get the help of other departments he needs for doing his own job.
25. Technical management in this firm tends to treat the

suggestions of the foremen with less consideration than they deserve.

36. Departments such as maintenance and stores do not seem to realize that they are there primarily to service the production departments.

39. In this firm the co-operation between departments that can help each other is very good.

43. In this firm the management will, under pressure of work, usually give authority to the foremen to settle problems that they normally settle themselves.

52. Friendly personal relations between foremen and their shop stewards are unnecessarily strained because the higher management insists upon keeping too closely to the works rules.

64. Foremen and assistant foremen frequently feel that too many people above them have a hand in the same piece of business.

90. In our firm, the management attends to the foreman's problems so promptly that he has no cause for complaint.

92. In this firm the foreman is confident that the higher management would never go back on a foreman's decision.

List P for supervisors; statements mainly about the supervisor's view of his personal influence upon the system.

3. A good incentive scheme makes supervision easier.

5. A foreman likely to be involved in future trouble should keep hopefully quiet rather than consult his manager.

8. A factory cannot run smoothly unless the foreman believes that the senior staff are genuinely open to be persuaded that they may sometimes be mistaken.

21. A good foreman should be judged by the extent to which he persuades his men to accept a management decision that he personally believes to be mistaken.

23. A training department should save the foreman having to explain to the men how to do any part of their work.

29. A foreman who keeps news of impending change under his hat is putting himself in a strong position for dealing with his men.

30. The foreman who expects obedience from his men must, in turn, believe that his own superior is always right.

31. However busy he is, a good foreman should not ask his subordinates to do any part of his work.

32. Unquestioned obedience to foremen is essential to the efficiency of any firm.
46. A good foreman will not admit to his men that he has made a mistake.

List L for supervisors; statements mainly about the supervisor's view of his leadership.

1. A good foreman will go to great trouble to bring home to his men how they fit into the work of the factory as a whole.
6. If management asks a foreman to make a change in the distribution of duties among his men, it is unnecessary for the foreman to discuss it with them before putting the change into practice.
19. An efficient foreman will discourage his men from using their own time as well as his in discussing trivial complaints.
28. It does not matter what a worker thinks and feels so long as he is getting on with the job.
35. The leader who always tells his men precisely what to do, and how to do it, leaving nothing to their imagination, secures the best work.
40. So long as he is doing well on the job in front of him, a workman does not need to know much about what he will be doing next.
51. If discipline is to be maintained, the foreman should never adjust the works rules to fit special cases.
56. It is no concern of the foreman if a worker on bonus scheme chooses to stop work before the end of the shift.
66. If they are going to keep up with technical change, most foremen just have not got the time to listen to suggestions and criticisms from their own men.
75. There is nothing that a foreman can do to put interest into a workman's job if that job is in itself uninteresting.

List K for managers; statements mainly about knowledge of works information systems.

9. The long-term strategies and tactics employed by this enterprise are clear to all who have to implement them (-0.44).
46. Most managers on this works clearly understand what the various departments headed by our divisional directors are intended to do (-0.72).

53. Managers in this works are in no doubt about how their objectives are set (−0.30).

61. The distance between those who settle the policies of this enterprise and those charged with their execution can sometimes lead to serious problems and misunderstandings (−0.54).

62. Any allocation of management responsibilities between line management and advisory staff in this enterprise is so rooted in common sense that it cannot create confusion or delay (−0.54).

69. Management in this enterprise goes to great lengths in keeping its foremen up to date on all trade union matters affecting the foremen's tasks (−0.44).

81. Recent research in a major engineering firm has shown that no single member of the top management of a particular department could, even after consulting his colleagues, draw a flow process chart of its principal product; further study showed that no single member of the top management was even aware that no comprehensive description of this process existed. Neither of these findings could have any parallel in this enterprise (+0.10).

110. The main components of our objectives (specifications, supply of raw materials, technology, development, distribution, consumers, and so forth) are already known to, or can at once be made known to, any manager who wants to know them (+0.10).

List R for managers; statements mainly about satisfactions with the managerial task.

38. In this enterprise the future rewards of management have been thought through no less carefully than the future return on capital (−1.02).

54. Modern automatically controlled plants demonstrate the principles of measurement, feedback and corrective action. Management performance here is judged by the same impartial processes (−0.14).

59. Managers in this works are confident that their seniors are ready to give them all reasonable backing in the event of conflict (+0.20).

64. The company pays as much attention to good relations with its staff as it does to those with the payroll (−0.80).

67. A majority of managers in this works genuinely believe

that much of our human resources are still underused (−0.72).

68. First-hand experience of management in this enterprise soon shows that the encouragement and reward of individual initiative are among our greatest sources of strength (−0.16).

70. In passing through the profound changes now being faced by this enterprise, the collective diagnosis and treatment of unexpected problems has done much to strengthen relations between top and middle management (−0.24).

72. However often he may be shuffled from one post to another in this enterprise, any manager can soon find out where his new task fits into the organization as a whole (+0.28).

List P for managers; statements mainly about the manager's view of his personal influence upon the system.

3. In this enterprise the detailed specification of a manager's task is communicated to him more effectively than is any sense of his personal commitment to do it.

57. If a manager sees clearly the nature of his task, he will see no less clearly his dependence upon his subordinates at all levels.

58. In the adaptation to change that is now one of the nation's greatest needs, most managers have as much to learn about other people as they have about science or technology.

66. In a situation of change, the real test of a manager is not so much his knowledge as the use he makes of it in securing change.

76. Although trends in modern management practice, aided by electronic data processing and mathematical analysis, demand the approach of the scientist, the successful top manager in this firm will always need to understand men no less than methods.

77. Technologists, on the whole, do not reflect sufficiently upon what others think about them.

99. The authority of a manager depends upon his skill in concealing his hand whenever he is not sure of himself.

102. Every discussion that he starts with his subordinates should also be seen by the manager as a lesson for learning a little about himself.

List L for managers; statements mainly about the manager's view of his leadership.

42. Before taking action upon any issue, I invariably make use of whatever advice my supervisors have to offer.

56. Good relations with the men depend, not only upon the clear presentation of plans and policies, but also upon consultation so genuine that it may lead to their constructive modification.

71. I am sure that my foremen have to spend too much of their time on getting the co-operation of other departments.

75. In spite of the pressures upon us to see that our plants are working efficiently, it is essential to find the time to keep our people in the picture.

85. There is little I can do to put interest into the work of any man whose work is in itself uninteresting.

92. One of my main tasks is to ensure that my supervisors make clear to their men how they help the works to meet its targets.

105. The future success of this works will depend, among other things, upon our ability to develop supervisors able to handle mixed teams of tradesmen and process-workers.

112. We have not taken enough trouble in the past to ensure that exceptional interpretations of agreements with the men have been as widely understood as they ought to have been.

13.
The School as a Community

Aristippus being asked what were the most necessary things for well-born boys to learn, said 'Those things that they will put into practice when they become men.' (Diogenes Laertius, *Aristippus*, 4)

A teacher who can arouse a feeling for one single good action accomplishes more than he who fills our memory with rows and rows of natural objects, classified with name and form. (Goethe, *Elective Affinities*)

There is no absurdity so palpable but that it may be firmly planted in the human head, if only you start before the age of five and constantly repeat it with an air of great solemnity. (Schopenhauer, *Psychological Observations*)

'What single question would, in your opinion, tell you most about your fellow-countryman? . . . Such a question is, of course, strongly coloured by one's own value system and past experience; my own choice, in wishing to learn as much as possible by his reply to one single question, would be to find out what school he had attended at the age of fourteen.' (p. 133)

Our studies of morale, effort and communication in factories and in hospitals led to the suggestion that every organization is, or could become, a learning system. Some groups, some units or even some whole enterprises seemed to learn from their experience to do better; others of all descriptions seemed to learn from similar experience to do worse. For this reason we decided to see what happens in those institutions that are supposed to be set up mainly, or even solely, so that those who attend them are able to learn. For whereas it seemed very strange to suggest that the patient in hospital needed to learn how to get better – and that if he had no wish to do so he would remain sick – nobody could be found (at least in 1960) to dispute the proposition that schools were there to help their pupils to learn. This does not imply, of course, that the children were also to become aware of their own learning talents and of how more effectively to deploy them; 'learning Pythagoras' was one thing, and many thousands could be observed in the act of going through it, while 'learning how to learn' was something else and was rarely a topic of collective attention.

But we may ask even simpler questions about learning Pythagoras. What, for example, are we driving at when we teach children his theorem? Is it other than to follow another geometry lesson? Why need anybody be able to follow geometry lessons? If the ability to do so is not an end in itself, but a step towards some goal more remote, what is this further goal? Since nobody seemed either able or willing to discuss these simple questions, we thought it might be worth while to document what went on in a sample of classroom lessons, merely to find out if the record of observable activity might itself suggest the outcome of the communal effort, and if we could relate that outcome to what the children thought about their teachers, and even, perhaps, to what the teachers thought of one another. And, in accordance with our emerging conviction that, were anything amiss with the schools, only those working in them could do much about it, we decided to plan our studies in close co-operation with the teachers themselves.

Our base of operations was the Manchester College of Science and Technology. Such was its reputation that we had no difficulty in persuading ten headmasters of local secondary modern schools (for it was in days before women's liberation and comprehensives) to work together on recording what can be seen to be going on in a typical classroom, namely, one in which an average lesson is being conducted much as it would be conducted in another school in the consortium. It was agreed that such uniformity between schools could be secured by all of them choosing the same items in the mathematics syllabus, and working through them with children of the same age group and of roughly the same attainment. Ten courageous teachers

in ten different secondary modern schools in and around
Manchester thus volunteered each to give five lessons of forty
minutes to their classes of 35 or so B-stream children of 13
years of age; the teachers decided, after several private meetings among themselves, to build the exercise around the use of
logarithm tables. They agreed that all 50 lessons should be
tape-recorded and that two cameras should be set up, one facing
the class from the front of the room, the other facing the
teacher from the back; these cameras photographed what was
going on once every three seconds, giving us 800 shots per
camera per lesson.

The classification of the pictures gave us plenty to think
about; we were never short of suggestions about criteria to
judge what the children might be doing. Apart from doubt as
to what the child might be up to (was she sharpening a pencil
or unwrapping a sweet?); if she sat with her eyes fixed upon
the teacher, was she listening to what he was saying?; or trying
to remember what had been said last lesson?; or working out a
question to put to the teacher in a few moments' time?; or was
she thinking about what she did last night?; or was her mind a
complete blank? All these and more were suggested as the
necessary material for tracing structure in the lessons. But it
would have been wasting our time to pursue them; we simply
could not enter into the consciousness of a single child, let alone
350 every three seconds for 200 minutes. So we showed the
pictures, frame by frame, to the children themselves and merely
asked them to tell us what they saw. This exercise the children
found of the greatest interest, and one class of boys gave up
their Whitsun holiday to help us classify the activities we had
recorded. Given ingenuity enough, there is no difficulty in
exploring the mind of the school child and the culture of the
classroom.

After listening to the taxonomic ideas of the children, we
settled upon seven criteria for partitioning the visible records
we had managed to take. Firstly, listening to the teacher, or
appearing to do so; secondly, asking or answering a question
or, judged by being seen holding up the hand, attempting to
ask or answer a question; thirdly, referring to or reading from
a document (other than a comic below the desk) or from the
board, other than while the teacher is speaking; fourthly, writing

on a paper or in a book before him; fifthly, not attending to what is going on, in accordance with a long list of alternatives supplied by the children; sixthly, settling down at the start of the lesson or making to go at the end; and, seventhly, being unobservable, as when eclipsed by the teacher or by another child. With practice, a pair of observers, one to watch the screen and to advance the film, calling the activity of any particular child frame by frame, and the second to write it down in a special seven-line code, could scan the records at twice the rate they had been taken.

Not all ten sets of lessons have been scanned in this way; the first two were used for developments in lighting and recording, and are therefore incomplete. For the other eight sets of five lessons, however, we can give a pretty accurate analysis of how the active lesson time is consumed; a summary is presented in Table 6. It is based upon a 20-per-cent sample of the children in each class, so that, of the 35 whose names were on the

Identity of school	Listening	Asking Answering	Reading Referring	Writing	Not attending
1	30.4	5.8	36.2	17.0	10.6
2	28.0	3.8	30.8	30.8	6.5
3	32.1	9.6	37.6	18.4	2.2
4	51.8	11.4	24.1	10.9	1.5
5	43.0	4.0	37.1	11.4	4.3
6	38.6	2.5	34.6	21.8	2.5
7	50.2	3.6	29.7	13.6	3.0
8	37.3	4.2	38.3	15.8	4.5

Table 6: Showing, for 13-year-old B-stream children at eight secondary modern schools in and around Manchester, distribution of lesson time between observable behaviour. (Entries: percentages by rows.)

register, seven were continuously observed over the whole 200 minutes. The results show great variations between classes (teachers, schools) in the patterns of average class activity. Learning theory, especially that on which action learning relies, suggests the cardinal role of feedback (asking or answering questions), and we see that some teachers get very much more than others. We were unable to continue the experiments, as we had been able to continue them in the factories, to determine whether the teachers who excited the greatest responses from the children were perceived as the most agreeable; this had to be left to a further study. Nevertheless, these searches with camera and tape-recorder showed the pattern of behaviour of any particular child, lesson by lesson, to be marked by a consistency characteristic of that child and distinguishing it from any other child in the same class; the great differences between classes is evident at a glance from Table 6. We therefore shifted the object of our studies from the observable behaviour of the children to an assessment of their attitudes towards being in the schools at all.

We may review what has so far been said about the classroom. An observational study of the children in eight different schools shows beyond doubt that, even when comparing like with like at like activities, some exhibit much richer communication with their teachers than do others. Statistical analysis shows that in tracing the differences among all the children in the eight schools, the school (or class or teacher) contributes more to spreading them out than do the children themselves. In jargon, variations *between* classes (or schools or teachers) are significantly greater than variations between individual children *within* any of the eight classes; although the children under any given teacher (or in any given school or class) show a measurable range in ability to respond to that teacher, that range is small compared with the range of the average ability to respond from one school to another (or from one teacher or class to another). There are marked differences in overall attitudes from one class (or school or teacher) to another. Since the concept of the 'tone' of a school is traditional and may be important to understand in operational terms, namely, to find ways of improving, it might be of interest to find out whether the discriminating influence is the school as an organism, the teacher as an individual or even the accidental sample of children that happened to be formed into what is called the class.

To answer this question demanded a different approach. If the school were to have an appreciable influence upon the attitude of the children towards their teachers, it would be necessary to show that, at any given school, those in different classes, whether boys or girls, showed a common attitude on average different from another common attitude among the boys and girls in the different classes at some other school. It might also be found that, irrespective of individual variations between the attitudes of the teachers *within* any one school, there were also observable differences in average teacher attitudes *between* schools. We thus needed to find out, in a number of schools, among even more classes and therefore a lot of children, as well as among their class-teachers, what they all seemed to think about communicating with each other. What is more, if the results of our searchings were to be of any use we had to involve the teachers and the children in the planning of them. But this did not prove to be difficult. The time we had given to the recordings of the mathematics lessons put the staff and research students from the College on easy terms with many of the local headmasters, and they looked forward to the results of our further studies of the perceptions that those, whether pupils or teachers, within the school community held of its human climate. This enthusiasm we decided to exploit, and we therefore set about designing, with the co-operation of the staffs of 27 senior modern schools a major survey of how life in the educational world was seen. If our ideas upon the factory as a system in which all might learn had any meaning, they should to an observable degree be reflected in the schools themselves. To make the parallel as instructive as possible, we chose to study the attitudes, not of the 13-year-olds whose classroom behaviour we had observed during the lessons on the use of logarithms, but of the 15-year-olds who would soon be leaving to earn their livings in the industrial and commercial excitements of Manchester; since there were 2,265 of these in the 27 schools, looked after by 475 teachers, we had our work cut out.

The recording of what had gone on in the mathematics lessons had given us opportunity enough to reflect upon the seamier side of school life. Our tapes, if not our films, had harvested a splendiferous crop of impertinent weeds. Taken off their guards the teachers and the pupils had disclosed their feelings about the earnest and lofty mission to which they had been called and, following the example of Dr Hussein in the factories, we were able to use what had been garnered as a statistically reliable guide to their deeper sentiments. The remark, an amiable flourish, perhaps, but so good for a laugh in every senior common room: 'There is no other institution, not even perhaps a gaol, in which the wrong person in charge can exert so great a tyranny upon the lives of others, as a school!', is not of much use for quantitative analysis; it is merely a verbal cartoon, illuminating the darker caverns of the mind with a solitary flash of humorous malice. It suggests, all the same, that the relation of the head to the assistant staff may be worth exploring, and for this such comments as the following were plucked from the tapes and used, after the manner of Dr Hussein in the factories, to estimate how authoritarian the heads were seen to be by the class-teachers:

> In this school the assistant staff are expected to take the view that their seniors are always right.
> Teachers are given every encouragement to contribute suggestions about the running of this school.
> Teachers here are confident that any solutions to their problems proposed at their own meetings will always be given serious consideration.
> The headmaster receives too much, the staff too little, of the credit for the success of our school.

When, using methods such as those developed by Dr Hussein, to measure what the teachers of the 27 schools feel about these topics, we discover great and significant differences between schools. In the most positive school (the staff feeling close and concerned) the mean item score among the class teachers was +0.656 and in the most negative (the staff feeling remote and alienated) the mean item score was −0.542. In the scales we have used +1 represents normal satisfaction, zero indifference and −1 active hostility. Our results suggest that *between* these two schools there is a difference in the perceptions of the assistant staff of about 1.2 units of satisfaction. We do not need much further proof of the proposition that each school has its own characteristics, but, even if we did, this would not be the place to elaborate it; our purpose is merely to point out that within a short distance of the Manchester College of Science and Technology there were schools that differed in their staff relationships by so vast an amount. Nevertheless, although our talents as quantitative research workers were much admired, the suggestion that the staffs of the schools themselves should set up their own action learning programme, to do something that might help to understand (by changing) those staff relationships, encountered much resistance.

It was not only the attitudes of the assistant staff towards their heads that were revealed in the harvest of seditious comment; they had a lot to say about the external administration of the school:

The governors are not as closely in touch with classroom problems as they should be.
School problems which concern both the headmaster and the education committee, such as finance and supplies, are generally dealt with quickly and sensibly.
Inspectors, on the whole, seem able to treat the assistant staff here without condescension or patronage.
Not a few of our troubles here arise because the local education office is thought to be out of touch with the affairs of the school.

These statements, offered at the same time as the four set out above, enticed the 475 class-teachers who were shown them to express their view of how they saw the authority outside the walls of their playgrounds. Again there are very significant differences between the 27 schools, although they are not as marked as those between schools in the attitudes of the assistants to the heads. A moment's reflection would suggest this to be no more than to be expected, since the external authority is more remote than the heads and so apparently to all observers toned down by the distance. And, although our study was made so long ago, the chance remarks of the teachers had much to tell us about how they saw the parents:

A teacher should use his own judgement and need not consult the head about what information to give parents on the progress of their children.
Parent-teacher associations are all very well in their way, but it is no part of a school's task to re-educate grown-ups.
A teacher can always be judged by the tone in which he speaks about parents as a whole.
No staff, other than the head, should discuss a weaker pupil's prospects with the parents.

172

It turns out that the responses of the 475 teachers to these four statements suggesting what they might feel about parents are strongly correlated with their feelings about the external authority; if the staff dislike the parents, they dislike the education office and vice versa. But there is nothing in the study to suggest which is cause and which effect, namely, whether disliking the one makes them dislike the other or whether disliking the other makes them dislike the one, or whether their disliking of both reflects some other effect altogether. However this may be, the three sets of opinion may be taken together to express a composite staff attitude – towards the head, towards the external authority and towards the parents – and these composite staff attitudes vary sharply from one school to another. The three components tend to be positive or negative school by school, so that each is an expression of the innate character of the school. Using our quantitative methods we can assert with confidence that the responses of the 475 teachers, taken school by school over the 27 altogether, strongly suggest that what might appear to be three separate objects of perception – the head, the education authority and the parents – have much the same tint at any one school but that the tint of that school is significantly different from those of the other 26. We may make the point simply: the 27 schools are ranked by each set of teacher-responses, most positive at the top scoring 1, most negative at the foot scoring 27; thus each of the 27 schools has three entries against it, from 1 to 27, according to the strength of the three opinions among the teachers who serve it. When this is done, one particular school scores respectively 1, 2 and $1\frac{1}{2}$ (tying for first place on the third ranking); another scores respectively 26, 27 and 24. In which of these schools are the pupils likely to feel ready to ask their teachers that manner of question helpful to their learning? Alas, we cannot yet predict with confidence.

The 27 schools had well over two thousand 15-year-old children whose opinions of the staff we also set out to measure, starting with the range of comment that had been passed during our tape and film recording sessions and the subsequent interpretation of what had been gathered. For dealing with the perceptions of the children we used a rather more complex method than the five-point scales of Dr Hussein, by enticing each child to complete 60 sentences that were offered in a small and attractively printed booklet; their tasks were done together in the classroom under examination conditions but anonymously. A typical incomplete sentence was: 'If I heard our teacher was moving to another school, I . . .' and another 'If our teacher had to go to hospital, we . . .', leaving it to the children to express thought or proposed action as they wished. The task of the marker scanning the responses was to gauge the direction and strength of the feeling by the form of the reply; joy, relief, indifference, sadness, despair; exultation, thankfulness, unconcern, regret, sorrow. Responses to indicate these might be:

> should arrange a celebration for the whole class as soon as we were sure he had really gone.
> should think what a good thing it was.
> ought to get a new teacher.
> might feel sorry.
> would get the class to buy her a present or else arrange a bit of a party for her.

Where the sense is highly negative, so much so as to suggest not only feeling but also to propose action, the score is −2; and so forth, scoring on the same five-point scale as Dr Hussein.

With 60 returns from 2,265 children we had a considerable amount of data, of which some was unintelligible; for all that we were able to get the bulk of it into a computer and make all manner of interesting analyses of it. Again there emerged great differences between schools in the attitudes of the children towards their class-teachers, whether these attitudes judged the teachers as persons or as teachers. These attitudes are, in fact, so closely correlated that, if the children do not like the teachers as persons, they have no regard for their teaching skills; among the 27 pairs of average attitudes, towards teachers as human beings and as professional instructors of the syllabus, the co-efficient of correlation was +0.872. This is so high that no other factor (apart, that is, from being liked by the children) can have any significant influence upon the children's estimate of their teachers' competence (see Fig. 10.)

Having used the five-point scale to verify this proposition, we can now ask, as we did with the teachers, how much the

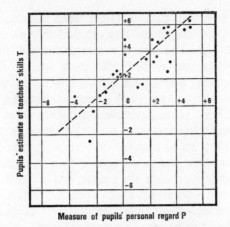

Figure 10: Showing, for 2,265 children of 15 years of age, and in 27 secondary modern schools in and around Manchester (1964) averages by schools of estimates (a) horizontally, of personal regard for teachers and (b) vertically, of their perceived teaching ability. While, over all, the grand means are both positive, many of the schools have marked negative characteristics. The correlation by schools between the two variates is +0.872. Variance analysis shows that it is the school rather than the individual children that determines these attitudes.

children differ *between* schools. For reasons pointed out to us by the computer, we are able to take 14 of the completable sentences as an indication of attitude of child to teacher. In the most positive school, in which the children seem to like the teachers most and to have the highest regard for them as teachers, the mean item score was +0.819, averaged over more than thirty 15-year-old children; in the school where there was least regard, or even none at all, it was −0.356, averaged over more than fifty. The first school was mixed, the second was of boys only. We can show, by tests similar to those used by Dr Hussein, that, as with the attitudes of the teachers towards their heads, the external authority and the parents, the differences in attitudes of the children towards their teachers vary very greatly between schools. Without doubt, between adjacent and apparently comparable schools, there are the widest differences in the outlook of the pupils upon the staff who have the task of looking after them. These differences can, it seems, be measured. It is not so easy to understand in what the differences consist nor how they arise; youth and age make odd alliance.

Our lack of insight becomes yet greater when further calculation shows that there is but a weak positive correlation between the culture of the teachers and that of the children in the same school. There is a measurable tendency for the children to like the teachers who think well of those under whom they work, and for the children to dislike the teachers who, in their turn and school by school, are hostile to the school as an institution. There is always a danger in expecting simple and significant correlations, since a school is a complex organism and its social relations must depend upon many other factors, such as the size of the school – which tends to depress the attitudes of everybody the greater it is – and the condition of the premises – which have the opposite effect the worse they are; in conversation with the staff this was explained by the efforts that need to be made together if limited accommodation has constantly to be used for different purposes by different groups. Elaborate buildings tend to keep staff to themselves; it just does not seem to be true that to reduce staff friction necessarily improves over-all morale. On the contrary, the unremitting need to work out among themselves who is going to use what room for doing what task between what hours seems, at least in the opinion of the staff, to contribute to their good temper rather than to detract from it.

I cannot claim that our excursion into the schools advanced very far our mastery of action learning, although it showed clearly that the staff and the pupils alike can soon be inspired to help in the design of enquiries that might eventually lead us all to understand, by efforts at improvement, what goes on in a classroom and what may be expected to influence the attitudes of those who spend so many laborious years giving and receiving education. The studies were never continued. For reasons that had nothing to do with these particular efforts to get the teaching profession, as well as its training colleges and education officers, interested in the notion of self-examination by action learning, I left the University of Manchester and found myself for the next twelve years in Belgium. Yet of all the people who should be asking themselves what education means and how it may be more effectively provided, those who are trying to run the schools should be foremost among them. If, as we show, the attitudes of children towards those set over them depend more upon the particular school they happen to

176

be in than upon all other factors put together, ought not those in charge of the schools be trying to find out *for themselves* why this is so? For it is certain that those in charge of the schools are the only agents who can do much to change whatever within them needs changing.

If, as I suspect, the attitudes of the pupils towards authority are formed within the schools before they leave at 16 years of age, who is to tell us how those attitudes are formed, why some schools seem havens of peace and others a few blocks away, drawing pupils from the same neighbourhoods and similar families living in similar houses and pursuing the same trades and amusements, seem the academies of Satan? Is it not the school rather than the home that determines the attitude of the child to those in authority? And if, as the evidence suggests, it is, what are the teachers and their employers going to do about it? There is no alternative to action learning, and, happily, action learning may well be given a chance to exhibit its powers (as we saw in Chapter 6) in the ancient city of Lincoln. There, the local education authority has joined with the most powerful local employer (GEC, represented by Ruston Gas Turbines and English Electric Valve) and with the police authority, to examine the relation between school and industry. The first six months of their joint programme has revealed how great an interest can be aroused by the involvement of the responsible officers of the organizations in the study of their own problems. If the study, with the police as an observer deeply concerned with its own integration into the wider society, can advance to the comparison of factory with factory and of school with school, then action learning may not only correct some of the contradictions between schooling and employment (as well, with the help of the police, throw a little light upon the origins of adolescent disaffection); it may lead to a keener and more operational understanding of the differences between otherwise comparable school cultures.

Who but the teachers concerned, we should ask, ought to be tracing and treating whatever it is that leaves the adolescents of one Lancashire school more than one whole point unhappier with their teachers than are the adolescents at another? And, should it turn out that the resentment of those adolescents to their teachers is carried, after leaving school, into society as a whole, finding expression in violence and vandalism and providing unwanted work for the police, who but the teachers themselves can take the first steps towards reducing the classroom resentment? And, finally, if it must be the teachers to make the first moves, how, other than by action learning, are they to make them?

PART III

The four chapters of the third part of this book attempt to show action learning in its cultural, social and historical settings. In the first chapter we trace the long-established tradition of the superiority of the clerical professions over the manual trades and show with what tenacity the nurseries of scribes will fight to preserve their privileges. We infer that, in a country dominated by the Oxbridge cult of scholarship as the mark of social prestige, action learning will make a reluctant start. In the second and third chapters we trace the developments in the rift between scribe and artisan since the Industrial Revolution, always in the hope, however feeble, that action learning may do something to bring their talents together in the quest for national salvation. Both chapters can draw upon a wealth of historical and contemporary fact to suggest that the present tribulations of our country may be traced to a violent readjustment in the ancient relation between scholar and smith. We believe that action learning will prove to be an effective medium of employee participation; in the joint attack upon widespread problems that is the operational essence of action learning, scribe and artisan alike can play their own constructive parts, and in the fourth chapter we treat of the future of action learning as worker participation. This is no easy subject of which to treat, since it demands that very co-operation between the book and the tool which it is the mission of the Oxbridge cult to discountenance; those whom you despise on Monday, Wednesday and Friday cannot reasonably be expected to co-operate with you on Tuesday, Thursday and Saturday. Nevertheless, action learning, when things get bad enough for the British to recognize, offers us the chance of taking ourselves in hand; if it is accepted we shall soon discover a lot about action learning. Then, but not sooner, we shall be able to rewrite this chapter, if not the whole book.

14.
The Book and the Tool

The British are the sick persons of Europe. (Anon 1978)

But in 293 Carausius was murdered, and Constantius, evading the British fleet in a fog, soon recovered Britain; he repaired Hadrian's Wall and rebuilt York. The mother of his son Constantine, Helena, was converted to Christianity by her son; she was really an inn-keeper's daughter, but legend made her a British princess and the discoverer of the True Cross. (The European Inheritance, ed. Sir Ernest Barker *et al,* OUP, 1954, vol. I, p. 244)

. . . at the Council of Ariminum held in the year AD *359, the British bishops were the only bishops who accepted the allowance for expenses offered by the emperor. (History of the Church of England,* H. O. Wakeman, Rivington Percival, London, 1897, p. 2)

The greater part of the fourteenth and fifteenth centuries may be considered as a period dominated by the phenomena of economic depression. This is particularly striking in Western Europe, properly so called: England, France, the Low Countries and Western Germany. The Hundred Years' War, and the taxation and the monopolies – in particular that of English wool – to which it gave rise, had the effect of discouraging production in France and England and among their neighbours. The continual alterations in the coinage, which were carried out with the object of increasing the financial resources of states, had a profoundly disturbing effect upon the exchanges. [And] when the two greatest Florentine banks failed, in 1343 and 1346, it was because the king of England, whom they provided with currency for his military expenses, did not fulfil his obligations. (The European Inheritance, vol. I, p. 426)

From this time forward foreigners complained of the insular and surly exclusiveness of the English common people. In Henry VII's reign the Venetian envoy noted that: They think that there are no other men than themselves, and no other world but England; and whenever they see a handsome foreigner they say 'he looks like an Englishman' and that 'it is a great pity that he should not be an Englishman'; and when they partake of any delicacy with a foreigner they ask him 'whether such a thing is made in his country?' (Illustrated History of England, G. M. Trevelyan, Longmans, London, 1956, p. 233)

British belief in the superiority of the British nation knew no bounds. It was an article of faith that one Englishman could beat six Frenchmen, more than six of any other foreign nation, and it was an almost religious conviction that the British possessed a sense of justice and fair play to be found nowhere else. An Englishman stood up for the weak, faced disaster without losing his head, kept his word and never kicked a man when he was down. (Cecil Woodham-Smith, *Queen Victoria,* Hamish Hamilton, London, 1973, vol. I, p. 2)

The rest of the world does not owe Britain a living. (Anon 1973)

In his recent book, *The Rise and Fall of the British Manager,* Mr Alistair Mant has this to say about management education:

What then of management education, one of the very few areas in and about British industry to show a substantial growth pattern since the war? I mentioned before that the Continental Europeans have managed with rather less of this particular commodity although it seems to have done them little harm. What they do have in abundance are educational institutions designed to prepare people for *doing* certain kinds of work and, what's more, they are institutions of high status. What Britain has is a small network of extremely powerful educational institutions which, while providing some guidance about doing preponderantly teach how to *be* a certain kind of person. It has always been true of Oxbridge and it was probably expecting too much of the new management education Establishment that it would entirely avoid the same trap – that is, becoming dominated by acculturisation for social roles at the expense of work itself.

The origins of British management education are deeply rooted in British Binary Thinking. Since 1946 there had been Henley, the archetypal country house, modelled on the very big companies' similar establishments. The head of one of these establishments once reflected to me, 'We are really in the civilising business here' as though the sons of toil he dealt with were Hottentots fresh off the veldt. But when the 'white heat' era came in the late fifties and early sixties and real money began to be spent on management education, the obvious influences were Harvard, MIT and urban America rather than pastoral Britain . . . London and Manchester were the outcomes of an argument, and a traditional one at that, around the old north-south split: should the business schools' primary task be to spend a longish time nurturing a 'seedcorn' of bright young men for a brighter future, or should they quickly get to work on the old lags who, like it or not, were in charge of ailing manufacturing enterprises up and down the country, mostly up. Not surprisingly, it was the hard men from the Midlands espousing the latter view. Whatever the outcome, it was assumed at the time that what came to pass would be unequivocally about *doing* and, more important, doing in the key jobs.

But the British social structure is not outflanked so easily. Ten years later almost the most important man in the London Business School remains John Nash, the creator of its magnificent home . . . if you missed university of any kind, not to mention Oxbridge, then to pass through this building is to press a little closer to the extreme centre of concentric British society. It is not a process to be despised; it is a matter of no little import to British businessmen to be made whole again, to re-enter society more fully from the social outskirts of trade and commerce. It is no surprise, in such circumstances, to find the central problems of manufacturing management and the legitimacy of work taking a back seat.

The pen may now be that of Mr Alistair Mant, writing in London during 1977, but the same ideas were expressed over four thousand years ago, as we saw in the first chapter of this book. The Instruction of Duauf, son of Khety, was then laid down 'for his son named Pepi, when he voyages up to the

Residence, in order to put him into the School of Books, among the children of the magistrates'. Five times as long ago as the origins of Oxbridge, Duauf instructs his little boy about the values of the world: the very dawn of human history illuminates the synthesis of gentlemen, so that the civilizing business of the modern staff college may well share with another (if more popular) profession the claim to be the oldest of all:

I have seen him that is beaten, him that is beaten; *thou* art to set thine heart on books. I have beheld him that is set free from forced labour: behold, nothing surpasseth books. Every artisan that wieldeth the chisel, he is wearier than him that delveth . . . Let me tell thee, further, how it fareth with the fisherman. Is not his work upon the river, where it is mixed with the crocodiles? Behold, there is no calling without a director, except that of the scribe, and he *is* the director.

It is in remembering Duauf, of worldly understanding (and his reinterpretation today by Mr Mant), that we appreciate the formidable obstructions lying across the path of action learning. At the very moment when Britain needs most desperately to close the gap between the symbolic culture of her management and the mechanic aggressiveness of her working class, we call again upon our educational establishment to divide the book still further from the tool. Of what appeal to the sons of scholarship can be the shifting uncertainties and uneasy threats of industrial life, compared with the immemorial changelessness and reassuring predictability of the printed page? The book of tradition remains itself for ever, so that its message, once pronounced, steadily gains in scholastic veneration and aristocratic prestige. But may it not be, on the contrary, that recorded knowledge and transmitted learning are also used defensively, to avoid the pain of reappraisal in the face of change? Is it unrealistic to suggest that Britain's perpetual failure to come to terms with tomorrow's world may partly be encouraged by what Mr Mant describes as the 'acculturisation for social roles at the expense of work itself'? Thus it is that the social aspirant, seeking to enter some profession that, unlike his dad's, does not demand that he must wash himself all over at the end of every shift, is obliged to know his books. It is no longer the real-time activity of the pit and of the factory that we are supposed to study and to value, but what the books have to say about it.

Lord Keynes gives us a hint of how this can be at the very end of his monumental work:

> Madmen in authority, who hear voices in the air, are distilling their frenzy from some academic scribbler of a few years back. I am sure that the power of vested interests is vastly exaggerated compared with the gradual encroachment of ideas. Not, indeed, immediately, but after a certain interval; for in the field of economic and political philosophy there are not many who are influenced after they are twenty-five or thirty years of age, so that the ideas which civil servants and politicians and even agitators apply to current events are not likely to be the newest. (*The General Theory of Employment, Interest and Money*, Macmillan, London, 1954, p. 383)

There may be some who feel that Keynes himself has now been promoted to the very scribbler against whom he warns his readers: it may remain his own theories (of government expenditure to stimulate demand) by which our economic salvation will long be vainly sought. Having known the great man half a century ago at Cambridge, I feel sure that he would be among the first to recognize the ebb of the Keynesian tide, and to assert that Britain should now treat all abstract general theories of management – whether peddled by frenzied madmen or by the staff of business schools trying to imitate them – with reserve. I also feel that he would advise the country to put her faith in, and her resources behind, enterprising parties eager to seek out what the world really wants, and then to supply it at an acceptable quality and price; it would not be necessary for such adventurers to read many books. Indeed, there is and can be no *a priori* theory of commercial innovation, and if Britain is to survive – if only as the ghost of what she was as the Workshop of the World – it will be by the hard work of manufacture and trade alone; she does not need academic scribblers to take her attention from this simple truth. The lure of investment, the courage to back subjective judgement, the spirited response to risk, challenge and opportunity do not distil from the pages of books nor from the print-outs of computers; they are the personal qualities of resourceful men and women, and it is my thesis that assets so precious may be discounted – if, indeed, not finally written off – by the lofty self-assurance, authoritarian dogma and unquestioned sophistry of our academic establishment. The indelible countermarchings up and down the pages of our doctoral dissertations may well imprint a maze upon the mind from which our genius of invention struggles to escape in vain.

But Mr Mant may begin to take fresh heart. The unreality of management education has now reached levels at which even a few of its practitioners are themselves expressing doubt:

> The accumulated evidence suggests that management education is in trouble. The following are some possible causes:
>
> Management education is largely based on theoretical, neat and unrealistic models of administrative behaviour. It does not deal with the realities of organisational life. Management graduates, as a result, are mired in the code of rationality ... The point is that value systems, which partly constitute the basis of rationality, in the management school and in the real world are simply not the same ...
>
> Another reason is that there is no other discipline in which practice seems so unaffected by its own principles. There is, for instance, no other intellectual area in which the practitioners contribute less to knowledge than management ... This is an unhealthy sign that the gap between the theory and practice is widening, hardly a condition for a professional discipline to mature and grow.
>
> ... assumptions concerning the missions of schools of management, the general orientation and structure of curricula, admission criteria and student-faculty relations are faulty and should be re-examined.
>
> Management educational programmes have failed partly because management is one of the few academic areas that does not have an 'internal' foundation ... Medicine and other established disciplines have all along had a common internal base, strong internal foundations and well recognised boundaries ... this has not been the case in management; the proper study for managers is management itself ...
>
> ... management education, as discussed above, is knowledge-oriented but not skill-oriented. It overdevelops the individual's analytical skills but underdevelops his adminis-

trative and interpersonal skills. Despite attempts to develop 'problem-finding' skills through role-playing, simulation techniques, the case method and so on, the student's diagnostic skill remains highly underdeveloped, simply because the data and the problems are given to him, not found . . . management education, mistakenly, provides students with a 'top-management' skill orientation, so by the time they graduate 'they are all set to be presidents'.

The learning process is faulty for several reasons . . . it does not encourage or provide adequate opportunity to explore individual interests and to identify one's own needs, capabilities and potential. The student, hence, plays a very passive role in the learning process.

. . . differences in value systems and cultures between the schools and the business community are enormous. Learning has to take place in one environment and be put to work in another . . . the student has to realise that, trained in analysis, he must spend his time on data collection, and adjust from a world where analysis is highly regarded, to a world where that sort of perfection is far too costly and thus is justly condemned. After lengthy instruction in problem solving, he must turn problem finder . . . (M. K. Badawy, 'Design & Content of Management Education: American Style', *Management International*, p. 75, No. 3, 1978)

Although we cannot expect all management professors to agree in detail with these disturbing observations (written in 1978 by a professor at Cleveland State University and published in the leading management journal of Europe), especially the members of the staff of British business schools who are said to ask four hundred pounds a day for their services, they accord with my own experience. Others also concerned with the fantasy world that education (not for management alone) now inspires in this country might well start to do something about it by tracing the arguments of this present book against the background of Professor Badawy's diatribe-vignette; our evidence suggests that it might be an exercise worth doing.

The divergence between hope and fulfilment, between anticipation and experience, between theory and practice, between promise and performance, that is now so characteristic of Britannia – even to the point of a television interview suggesting to Cardinal Hume that he was about to be elected Pope, let alone the national press encouraging the Scots to imagine that they were bound to win the World Cup – is, in my view, a constant and emphatic testimonial to the abundant and untestable confusions of the new half-sciences. The innuendoes of sociology and economics now pervade the whole of our education system and are writ large upon the pages of our popular newspapers. Our victories, so complete in prediction, so convincing and unanswerable in the arguments of the analyst, so obviously deserved during the chat-show of the telly-tots, so weighty and yet so reasonable in the leading article of the financial magazine, not seldom display an unhappy diffidence at the striking of the hour. The Union Jack at the mast head, that streamed with such Cockney defiance *into* the tempests of adversity until the very crack of the starting pistol, has again, to our utter stupefaction, been replaced by the ensign of some obscure and devious foreigner. Our boastful assurance does not seem to survive its encounters with a contemptuous world, whether directed at economic growth, administrative reorganization, technological investment, agricultural reconstruction, social reform, the control of large-scale enterprise, or even our quest for a non-stick frying pan that, we were persuaded, lay at the heart of the Concorde programme. I must forgive the constant doubts of the politicians and businessmen whom I meet across the world: 'Are you sure, professor, that your schools in Britain are using the right books?' . . . For it is the world itself that we need to study in greater depth, not the books of imagination that purport to describe that world.

It is the culture of the tool rather than that of the book which now offers Britain its rewards; it is the workshop and the market-place rather than the library and the scriptorium that, should we accept their risks, might pour their hoarded jackpots into our weary laps. We note, nevertheless, that of recent years our education system has been turning out more graduates in Welsh literature than in production engineering and that, in general, the university departments that prepare for careers in technology measure their deficient recruitment by the thousand. This is merely the latest witness of the Instruction of Duauf, since it has long been our practice, on spotting the bright apprentice, to take him away from the factory bench or the market stall into the drawing office or the counting house. As a result, we have plenty of designers and architects to suggest what ought to be made, but few general foremen or site managers to ensure it is made; nor do we lack bookkeepers and forecasters to tell us all about that second conversion process on the road to salvation, namely, finding and persuading enough customers to buy what has been made at a price that makes our efforts worth our while. No less than skilled craftsmen, we need adventurous salesmen, willing to face the risks and endure the disappointments of a relentless and competitive market-place.

But it is no longer by doing such things that one acquires prestige in Britain but by *writing and talking* about doing them, just as Duauf was aware four thousand years ago and more. Perhaps the most whimsical of this theory-before-practice, words-above-deeds dichotomy was related by the South Korean doctoral student (Chapter 19) who studied the comportment of European managers: after observing that they seemed to have but two amusements, vice and education courses, he added that, whereas the Continentals pursued each with wholehearted personal involvement, the British were more theoretical, in-clining both to the case study and to artistic pornography, but giving the essential touch of practice through jigsaw puzzles of ladies' backsides. We do not, of course, need to invoke our knowledge of foreign parts: that most masculine of our fellow-countrymen, Mr Bill Shankly, on the occasion of his retire-ment from the arduous task of managing Liverpool Football Club, remarked: 'Never had any education myself; had to use my own bloody brains.' As his creative genius implies, the absence of preconception may be essential to fresh advance. Action learning, indeed, goes even further: each individual conspires, through his own freedom from inhibiting tradition and prefabricated model, to release his colleagues from the bondage of their own past experience. In our programmed quest for booklearning, on the other hand, we crowd shoulder to shoulder down the same beaten path as the students of yester-day, to finish at the same point – even, perhaps, at where we started.

Since we now see Duauf to have been the precursor of so much that is thought to be so modern, we should ask ourselves precisely what his message was. We note that nothing he told Pepi was about *conserving* (much less abolishing) the curse of Adam; Duauf had not the slightest concern for the condition of humanity at large. His advice was about *avoiding* hard work, by judiciously leaving it to others; Pepi was to cultivate his books as the talisman of work-evasion. 'I have beheld him that is set free from forced labour: behold, nothing surpasseth books.' But a question remains: When all are become scribes, who brings home the bacon? Six centuries after the Peasants' Revolt we must re-phrase John Ball's immortal doubt:

> When each was thanne the gentilman;
> Which Adam dalf and which Eve span?

Now that the civilizing business can turn us all into gentlemen overnight, if not, indeed, into scholars as well, who is to provide our food and clothing?

From the Egypt of antiquity we move forward two thousand years, to the Book of Ecclesiasticus, written about 600 BC:

The wisdom of a learned man cometh by opportunity of leisure and he that hath little business shall become wise. How can he get wisdom that holdeth the plough, that driveth oxen and whose talk is of bullocks? He giveth his mind to make furrows and is diligent to see that the animals get their food. So every carpenter and workmaster that laboureth night and day and watcheth to finish their work. The smith also sitting by the anvil and considering the iron, the vapour of the fire wasteth his flesh and he fighteth with the heat of the furnace; the noise of the hammer and the anvil is ever in his ears and his eyes look still upon the thing he maketh. So doth the potter sitting at his work and turning the wheel about with his feet. He fashioneth the clay with his arm and is diligent to make clean the furnace. All these trust to their hands and every one is wise in his work; without these cannot a city be inhabited. They shall not be sought in public counsel, nor sit high in the congregation; they shall not sit in the judge's seat nor understand the sentence of the judgement, and they shall not be found where parables are spoken. But they will maintain the state of the world and all their desire is in the work of their craft.

But he that giveth his mind to the law of the most High and is occupied in the meditation thereof, will seek out the wisdom of all the ancient, and be occupied in prophecies. He will keep the sayings of renowned men, and where subtle parables are he will be there also. He will seek out the secrets of grave sentences and be conversant in dark allusion. He shall serve among great men and appear before princes; he will travel through strange countries, for he hath tried the good and evil among men. He shall direct his counsel and knowledge and in his secrets shall he meditate. He shall show forth that which he has learned and shall glory in the covenant of the Lord. Many shall commend his understanding and so long as the world endureth it shall not be blotted out. Nations shall show forth his wisdom and the congregations shall declare his praise. (Ecclesiasticus ch. 38, v. 44 to ch. 39 v. 10.)

Even although the author of these lines seems a little more sympathetic himself to the sons of toil than was Duauf so long before, he still discriminates clearly between those condemned by their servitude to the tools of productive labour and those privileged to command the books of power and authority. It was a distinction often dwelt upon by the miners of Cannock, who saw themselves striving for their livelihoods with the stroke of the pick, while the bureaucracy above them increased their own salaries with the stroke of the pen.

The historical ascendancy of booklearning, such as is now the foundation of the business schools, owes much to the classical tradition of Oxbridge, and the path of its development is not hard to trace. Aristotle, too, had a hand in the civilizing trade:

There are many sorts of slaves, for their employments are various. Of these the handicraftsmen are ones who, as their name implies, get their living by the labour of their hands, and among all these mechanics are included, for which reason such workmen in some states were not formerly included into any share in the government, until at length democracies were established. It is therefore not proper for any man of honour or any citizen or any one who engages in public affairs to learn these servile employments, for, without this were observed, the distinction between a master and a slave would be lost. (*Treatise on Government*, Bk III, ch. iv)

The celebrated philosopher seems to have had a particular down on mechanics and peddlers, for not only does he justify their lowly station but he goes out of his way to insult them. So does the classical syllabus of our ancient seats of learning cast before it the shadow of today's industrial relations:

> . . . a democracy may be framed where the majority live by tillage or pasturage; for, as their property is but small, they will not be at leisure perpetually to hold public assemblies, but will be continually employed in following their own business, rather than meddling with state affairs and accepting the offices of government, which would be attended with no great profit. The generality of the people of whom other democracies are composed are much worse than these, for their lives are wretched, nor have they business with virtue in anything they do; these are your mechanics, your peddlers, and your hired servants. All these sorts of men frequent the market place and the citadel, so that they can readily attend the public assembly, whereas the husbandmen, being more dispersed in the country, cannot so easily meet together, nor are they equally desirous of doing it with these others.' (*Ibid*, Bk VI, ch. vi)

These are old tributaries to the idea that those who make (the mechanics) and those who trade (the peddlers) are in occupations bereft of virtue. As we have already suggested, there are those who, contemplating our economic and social miseries, might see in them more clearly than do others our failure to make more profitable sales of our produce abroad. May it not be that the immemorial attitudes of Duauf, seconded by those of Aristotle, turning our children from the arduous endeavours of the factory and the market-place, are now being accorded the accolades of what is called management education? It is interesting to observe that neither Germany nor Japan have any counterparts to the business schools of Britain, which have been copied (if not in detail) from that other great economic invalid, the United States of America.

Any Grade II management teacher can now (autumn 1978) draw £6,500 a year for chatting, 20 hours a week and 36 weeks annually, about what the books say on industrial relations or production control; the real manager, trying to run the factory across the street, with 500 robust and mettlesome workers struggling to produce goods for commercial sale, may get less in salary, invariably put in more than 60 hours a week, and consider himself lucky to take the whole of his month's annual leave. Who can possibly defend such inequality other than the teachers' trade unions? Nor does this tell the whole story, since the same academics are constantly assembled, not without their fees, to explain to us on the telly what is wrong with the British economy, and, with particular emphasis, wherein lie the managerial shortcomings of our trade and manufacture.

It is not Professor Badawy alone (and I know nothing of him otherwise) who now seems to be disturbed about the present condition of American management education; others are also becoming aware, even if slowly, that questions are being asked about costs and benefits, and that there may soon be no such thing as free lunches for the teaching profession.

The historical account starts around 1964, when the top businessmen of Britain began to suspect that all was not well with the management of their affairs. There was a steady accumulation of disquieting evidence that our industry was falling behind that of our competitors; although British science was, we were assured, still the finest in the world, and had even won the war for the allied cause, we were unable to translate our scientific ingenuity into commercial value. Although we had committed ourselves to become the first welfare state even before the war was over, our trade unions were said to be bleeding the country to death by their unappeasable clamour for more money; although proud to be described by Adam Smith as a nation governed by shopkeepers, we were failing miserably in the sale of our products overseas. Report after report dwelt upon the details of these shortcomings: missions by productivity teams to America, to Japan by employers, to Sweden by econometricians, to Germany by trade unionists, to Switzerland by bankers, to Rhodesia by mining engineers, to the Middle East by politicians, to Iran by armourers, and to the residues of the Commonwealth by members of the Royal Family – all returned with the same message, that Britain ought to do something about its management. What that something was, or where it might be found, nobody seemed either to know or to care. The responsibility to provide it was, self-evidently, one for the educational establishment. A brief review of possibilities was scurried through, a lot of money put up by the shareholders and, overnight, Britain was provisioned with its business schools. At least, it was possible to point to a number of buildings in which it was said that management courses were to be run. It was difficult to specify what these courses were to be; all that was sure was that those in charge of the schools found themselves with vast sums of money before they were ready to spend it. They were the innocent victims of a cultural landslide, an economic avalanche, a national panic, prematurely forced to dispose of assets immeasurably greater than they had ever handled before. Like others called upon suddenly to do what was beyond them, they did what they had always done *but at a quicker tempo*.

There is a tale of a huckstering acrobat, an entertainer of the village market-place, who turns up, hungry and penniless, at some little town on the day of its patron saint; the locals had been to the thanksgiving service at the church and had left their gifts to the saint before her shrine. The priest, noticing the mountebank creep into the building after the others had gone home, followed him back in, imagining that he planned to help himself from what had been offered to the saintly image. To his relief and astonishment, he found the furtive pilgrim moving aside some of the oblations, but only to clear space enough for him to perform his somersaults in front of her altar. For, having nothing else to give the saint on the occasion of her anniversary, he exhibited to her the full range of his contortions, with a vigour that would have brought down upon him a shower of coins from even the poorest of spectators.

Thus, too, it was with the business professors, suddenly caught short by the artless optimism of their industrial and commercial patrons; knowing little of business reality, uncurious as to what might form an effective experimental syllabus, and fearful of the responsibilities of whatever real world action might have helped them to discover it, they simply carried on doing what they always had done, and even what their own teachers had done before them. When they filled up the time-table with lectures upon economics, sociology and mathematical bric-à-brac, it was not because these subjects had been proved essential to the prosecution of better management: they offered them because, like the mountebank in front of the shrine, *it was all they had to offer*. There simply was nothing else they could do. And, when it was discovered that none of it seemed – at least in the short run – to do any observable harm, and there were inexhaustible funds available for paying those ready to do it, most exponents of these particular half-sciences, not intellectually crippled, got in among the tumblers; those not so agile bravely struggled against their natural handicaps and organized remedial exercises known as 'refresher courses for teachers of management subjects'.

It must not be imagined that I regarded the events of these early years with detachment. Had I not been led by them to resign my professorship at the University of Manchester and to seek in Belgium some support for my ideas, it is unlikely that action learning would have developed – at least in the forms described in the first part of this book – for many years yet. It would most emphatically not have reached those countries, like India and Australia, whose distances from Manchester seem so critical to the encouragement of educational novelty. The University of Manchester is a living embodiment of the Instruction of Duauf, for it is, like Janus, a two-faced organism. One head, the Manchester College of Technology (as it was in my time, now the Manchester University Institute of Science and Technology) represented the tool; the other head, Owens College (generally known as the University of Manchester) represented the book. In so far as industrial administration could be studied at all (and this admittedly was not far), its students were to be found in my department at the College of Technology. Before 1964, the attitude of the economic and social philosophers at the University towards management education was a mixture of sarcastic blarney and amused contempt. But in 1964 things suddenly began to change. Rumours of vast wealth becoming available from businessmen and from the Treasury were brought back to Manchester by travellers who had got as far from home as

London. It was reported that the managing director of one world-wide corporation was devoting himself fully to raising millions of pounds from his business colleagues, in the conviction that the whole future of the British nation lay in salvation by management, and that the path to that salvation was through a circle of elite business schools to be seen as centres of excellence. The senior common rooms of Manchester palpitated with excitement, as must have done the taverns of Genoa when fables of Peruvian gold reached them at the time of Pizarro.

In due course an invitation came from London to our Vice-Chancellor, soliciting proposals for management education programmes to be offered in Manchester, the very cradle of the industrial revolution. Since I was the official professor (although I had already made known my conviction that there is, and can be, no such subject as 'management science') I was perforce consulted in the matter and put up a few suggestions. (Some of my contemporary papers are referred to at the end of this chapter, since, even then, I had been on for more than a decade about the need for action learning.) I saw in that short-lived quickening of interest an opportunity to try out, on a modest scale, what I still believe to be the essence of management development, namely, managerial *self*-development, supported by the encouragement of other *self*-developing managers. I was particularly concerned not to be associated with any assumption that managers can be taught *managerial operations* (as distinct, for example, from how to read books about management) by schools of the half-sciences. What I was looking for in this promise of the New Jerusalem was the support, not necessarily in money, of the businessmen in getting *managers themselves to influence their own development in the course of their ordinary work*. I was thus strongly opposed to proposals from Manchester that our joint team should spend any of the money, should it come our way, on elaborate bills of professorial acrobatics. As President of the European Association of Management Centres – a federation of over forty schools of university rank in fourteen countries, struggling with different depths of conviction to discriminate between the activities of managers *as managers* and the textbooks of the half-sciences – I had made it my principal office to discourage the jumbling together of our different academic ragbags, to give all teachers on any local payroll their turn on the 'middle management course', with their cut of the money provided for it. But my position was precarious, for, in suggesting that whatever the University of Manchester might offer should mainly be conditioned by the untidy and fitful demands of industry and commerce, I was sharply reminded, even by the Vice-Chancellor himself, that, although it was entirely proper that the businessmen should give their money to the University, they must do so unconditionally: it was not for them to suggest what its professors should teach in return. Academic freedom is the right of professors to pursue their private hobbies at the expense of society, and businessmen had better not interfere with it. Nonetheless, I persisted to the best of my ability. I wanted us from the outset to enlist our prospective students, all mature managers, in the sober and realistic solution of their own problems, and was, indeed, led to believe by the eventual silence of my colleagues from Owens that I had their agreement to my real-time and participative suggestions. When the Manchester delegation finally assembled in London to meet the committee of award, I was even more firmly under this impression, having heard that the managing director behind the public subscription was particularly interested in my ideas about action learning.

Before we entered the interview there was a short discussion as to whether the Manchester case should be presented by a spokesman from the Tech (the tool-school) or from Owens (the book-school); in this I acknowledged my inferior status. The committee of award was forthwith confronted by the Owens professor with such a mish-mash of an Alhambra as (so I thought) we had agreed never to touch; it was evident that he had combed his local warrens of scholarship to flush out the bulk of his faculty: within a few minutes we were out of the room with the promise of a terrifying sum of money to sign up the most indiscriminate volley of academic mountebanks ever to cartwheel one behind another across any ballroom floor.

Although this interview was the first step towards a Manchester business school, I was left no choice but to hand in my resignation and to seek a post out of the country; it took over ten years of exile to assure me that the businessmen of Britain were at last repentant about their academic advances. On my return one of them observed that, in appointing an industrial figure to strengthen the faculty of the new business schools, the committee were aware that he had been a trader in vacuum cleaners. It had, however, not occurred to them that in his new post the real professors were to get him to trade in the very vacuum itself.

In recounting this incident, so characteristic of the history of management education in Britain, I do not wish to impute to my former colleagues any deliberate equivocation. There was nothing calculated or underhand in their behaviour, either in the preparation of their razzle-dazzle spectacular or in the committee tactics by which it was approved. I now recognize that they simply could not imagine that *the managers themselves* might have ideas of any kind about their own needs, much less that they might have interpretations of their own lived experience to support or deploy those ideas. My colleagues had studied under other professors, and they saw what they imagined life to be only as it had been recorded by generations of scribes. It could never occur to them, with the privileged concretions of five millennia of book-learning settled upon their ancestry, that others than themselves might know anything of value.

Looking back upon my experience of the University of Manchester in 1965, I admit that my departure had become inevitable before then. The long ascendancy of the school of economic theory associated with the town was a sure defence against any true innovation, as I should have recognized while I was still there, and as the record of management education in Manchester has now shown. But, like the economists themselves (who, as Keynes himself suggests, being all over thirty years of age were immune to innovation) so had I become incapable of learning from purely intellectualistic argument. I needed the frustration of the incident at the interview to be finally assured that nothing could ever emerge from our endless academic countermarches. Only by a total change of setting, and newly striving to purge myself of the predisposing notions that I had about the possible role of the university in our economic recovery, was I able, with the help of Gaston Deurinck, to develop the Inter-University Programme of Belgium, and thus to set action learning on the road to successful practice. Moving out of the comfort and security of an

English professorship enabled me to exchange top-level managers between totally different enterprises in totally different industries, and thereby to open up for them (and for us all) opportunities and advantages incomprehensible to the traditional university box-office.

Action learning has now taken off, and is rapidly diffusing, in many different cultures; such advances would have been impossible had I remained surrounded by the books and imprisoned by the rituals of Manchester. We may judge from the comments of Professor Badawy the condition of much management education even in America, and there is little to assure us that it is any different in Britain; indeed, there is reason to believe that our diminishing resources are expended upon techniques calculated to strengthen management education as a brake upon our economic recovery. One ingenious project, for example, subsidized with government money, is now advertised to assess the subjective judgements of managers, not under real conditions that quicken the heart and stir the adrenalin by exacting penalties for actions ignorantly misconceived, but by comparing them with the models in some computer, themselves the fabric of doctrinal ratiocination. It is like training commandos under the poppings of paper bags inflated and burst by some tremendous machine programmed with the theories of a deaf-mute; anything to escape reality, to put words before deeds, books before tools, scribes before artisans. Human experience holds nothing as tenacious as the self-deception of very clever men.

POSTSCRIPT

I am very happy to say that some of the present staff of the Manchester Business School, notably Professor John Morris and Miss Jean Lawrence, are proving redoubtable supporters of action learning. They are now embarked upon a campaign, not only to spread this educational approach throughout the North West, but to carry the school officially with them. It may call for greater moral courage than one imagines to stay among the unregenerate in the hope that they too may, one day, see the new light; perhaps it is only cowards who seek the protective exile of a foreign shore. Or may it even be that new ideas are entering the universities?

APPENDIX TO CHAPTER 14

Some of my earlier publications on the inadequacy of traditional approaches to the development of managers:

1962   *The Theory of Practice*, Universities Quarterly, September issue.

1963   *Management Education and the University Tradition*; Comité International de l'Organisation Scientifique: NEW YORK Conference.

1964   *The Design of Management Courses*, Management International Magazine, vol. IV, no. 4.
       The Development of Research into Management and its Problems; OECD Conference on Management Education, Paris; December.

1965   *Our Educational System and the Development of Qualified Personnel*; Conseil Européen de CIOS; MUNICH Conference.

Most of the reservations now (December 1979) being expressed by businessmen and academics (including the President of Harvard University, questioning the value of the celebrated 'case method') are exhibited and confirmed in the above small sample of my contemporary works. It cannot now be said that I, too, have been able to recognize the impostures only by having long practised them.

15.
The Industrial Revolution and Culture M

In the eighteenth century the English working man – then called the jolly yeoman or industrious 'prentice – was intensely British, boasted himself a free-born Briton, and had no use for the frog-eating, priest-ridden Frenchman of his imagination . . . There was therefore in eighteenth-century England, prior to the changes gradually made manifest by the Industrial Revolution, a national solidarity and unity of idea which bound all Englishmen of all classes together and separated them from foreigners. Power, as we think looking back, was unduly concentrated into the hands of one class, the country gentry, but their monopoly was not popularly regarded as a grievance . . . But there was little or no discontent, and the national idea made every one proud of being a free-born Englishman. (*Johnson's England*, OUP, 1933, vol. I, pp. 6–7)

Let us for a moment consider the state of the two great divisions of the labouring order. The manufacturers, at present in comparative comfort, are experienced in organisation and assured of their strength. The agricultural labourers are sunk in the last depth of misery and are breaking into desultory violence. Whenever these two extremes meet – and extremes they are – the one class resorting to force from the extreme of misery and degradation, and the other in an extreme condition of power, from the best management of their means of strength – what will be the state of society, tossed upon these vast and furious elements? (*Westminster Review*, 1831)

We live in a deeply irrational society if only prolonged strikes and widespread industrial damage can ensure that the felt injustices which a group of workers experience are carefully considered and recognised. A society of this kind is dangerous if it succeeds in repression and dangerous if its repression breaks down. (Sidney Webb, Royal Commission on Trade Unions, 1906)

Undoubtedly the miners' strike and the militancy with which it was run had a profound effect upon the Government. One senior minister after another now says that 'We mishandled it', although it is less easy for them to admit that they suffered a serious defeat. The outcome of the strike and the settlement was that the Government decided to lift the pressure on the trade unions that unavoidably had to be applied during the passage through Parliament of the Industrial Relations Bill. With the miners back at work, the Government tried a new tack. TUC leaders were invited to 10 Downing Street in an attempt to win by persuasion the recognition of common national interest that could now demonstrably not be won by confrontation. (*The Times*, 27 March, 1972)

The four references are to epochs equally spaced. The first tells our 'national solidarity and unity of idea'; a life-time later we read of the same nation, but of 'society tossed upon these vast and furious elements'; 75 years on and the chaos is seen to be polarized, for the workers are organized and the state is asking what should be its policies towards them; finally, we are told the result of one such policy – to open once more the quest for the 'common national interest' so manifest in the first reference to 1760. We believe that action learning has a part in that investigation.

It is hardly sufficient to describe, however honestly, however accurately and however convincingly, the circumstances of the birth of the British business schools and thereby to explain the tenacity of the opposition to the spread of action learning in the country of its origins, unless one is also prepared to examine the conditions in which the haughty ethic of the universities themselves was brought into being. For this we must return to the Industrial Revolution, and trace the impact of that tremendous invasion of novelty upon the ancient stability of the ruling establishment. When we do so, we discover that the barbarian hordes, emerging out of the unknown darkness of capitalist technology, were the true ancestors of the Manchester College of Technology, and that the ruling establishment, called suddenly upon to withstand the uncivilized assaults, is perpetuated in the true sons of 'The University'. To some extent the new forces of the revolution have reinvigorated the custom and the practice of the past, just as the civilizing influences of polite scholarship are invoked to fettle the latter-day proletariat. Nevertheless, the professional training of the engineer and of the technologist, let alone of the commercial traveller and of the merchant, is still respectful of the Instruction of Duauf. Our books are for the directors and for the nourishment of the higher faculties, and action learning, eager to challenge the here-and-now of operational necessity, has no place in the same syllabus. It is this argument that must be traced to its roots.

We shall note in the next chapter that the teaching profession, faced with a need to defend their own interests, have now, exactly like the miners, admitted that it is not their books, but their physical actions – such as refusing to see that the children got their lunches, or that their students had their examination papers marked – that has brought them victory. This admission (that the society they profess to educate rejects their claim for more money when argued in scholastic terms, but at once accepts it when backed by threats to those unable to defend themselves) is evidence of the changes by which our world is overtaken. Nevertheless, although when securing the benefits that enter their own pockets the teachers are ready to resort to intimidation, industrial action, withdrawal of labour or whatsoever else is obviously so much more effective than negotiation between gentlemen, when they continue to act as teachers, as the custodians of the Instruction of Duauf, they display the most profound contempt for action learning. Never in 25 years, even when I was President of the European Association of Management Centres, was I asked by any teachers' association to contribute to their literature or to their professional conferences. So tenacious an opposition to what is new, fixed like a rock in an ocean boiling with change, must be explained; the manifold crises through which our education system will for long continue to struggle, and which some insightful observers fear that it may not survive, must force us to seek their origins.

We must first touch briefly upon the record of change in recent times. In the year 1700 the population of Europe has been estimated at 152 millions, in 1789 at 173 millions and in 1935 at 525 millions. Thus, during the comparatively stable eighteenth century the annual increment of population was about one part in seven hundred, or 0.145 per cent. Since 1789 the figures become one part in one hundred and thirty, or 0.763 per cent. Throughout the nineteenth century, therefore, the rate of population growth advanced about five-fold, using figures that have already been depleted by copious emigrations to America and other distant lands, outpourings from Europe that continued in spate until the First World War. It is likely that, were these emigrants included as further evidence of the changes in Europe, we should be able to estimate the rate of growth as advancing seven-fold. It is an impressive ratio. We are not, of course, committed to the date of 1789; the fact is that, after the political revolution in France, or the industrial revolution in Britain, things started to alter; a leisured tranquillity began to give way before influences previously unknown. In the imagery of the Chinese, a long reign of Yin was coming to an end and the disruptive forces of Yang were making known their arrival.

There are many ways in which the rate of innovation may be estimated, other than by counting how many persons lived in Europe, such as advances in the maximum velocity of human travel, or the speed at which we can perform arithmetical calculation, or the total volume of artificial fertilizer by which the nitrogen of the atmosphere can be more intensively brought to the production of food, or the complexity of the task of the nurse on the floor of a general hospital, or the ratio of persons taking their holidays abroad to the numbers taking them at home. Those with a mathematical turn of mind may care to look up such crude figures as are available and to plot them on a simple graph back to the time of the crusades; it will be found that all the traces are much the same in shape, keeping close to the axis until we approach our own times, when they suddenly turn upwards, like a flock of starlings that were at one instant on one course and have suddenly made a unanimous departure upon another.

The predisposing reasons for the upward turn that set in

towards the end of the eighteenth century and the opening of the nineteenth were many, and Britain's contribution to them was greatly magnified by the wars with France. Industry had made a start in the middle of the eighteenth century, with iron-making, the steam engine and an astonishing range of textile machinery. Nearly all manufacture was stimulated by the wars, since they cut off our supply of high-grade ores from Sweden and Russia, forcing Britain to improve its armaments technology at the very time when the sinews of war were most needed. The response was spectacular: abundant ores, cheap coal, cheap money, accumulated capital, good transport, an expanding foreign trade and, above all, an immense fertility of sound mechanical ideas – protected (until an act of 1825 repealed it) by legislation forbidding the English artisan to emigrate, and so take with him to the Continent the technical secrets that lay at the very foot of the precipice the nation had begun to climb. Inventiveness, energy and raw materials are the ingredients of all achievement and this country had them in abundance. Within a couple of decades she also produced the agents who understood their application to practice; these were the new captains of industry, and it was they who set off the industrial explosion:

> It is admitted on all hands that the first and chief feature distinctive of this revolution was the appearance of a new class – the captains of industry. The modern capitalist was no longer a member of a corporation, binding him by its strict regulations. He was no longer content merely to supply the demands of trade. He had won his own independence, and was himself his own merchant. He systematically forced the rate of production, anticipated the demand for his goods, and was aiming at the conquest not only of the national markets but of the markets of the entire world. (Elie Halévy, *England in 1815*, Ernest Benn, London, 1949, p. 258)

This account of the men who transformed the face of Britain rings with evangelical fervour; their mission of conquest, of converting the whole world to the use of our manufactures, seemed to offer an achievable satisfaction to a religious need. They gave themselves to a purpose that transcended any immediate personal gain and that brought them no social honour nor even recognition. No avenues of preferment opened up in front of them; enlistments by marriage into the ranks of the aristocracy were unlikely; the circles of the gentry, if they referred to them at all, did so only in terms of derision, with jokes about their daughters learning to play the pianoforte. For them, their new activity was sufficient unto itself, a relentless drive into an ever-expanding market. Their vitality sprang from this very rootlessness, as had that of the Jews in the Middle Ages and of the Chinese shoemakers today in the bazaars of Calcutta; their enterprise was not inhibited by what at times is even now mistaken for the instincts of a gentleman, nor was their freedom impaired by any respect for ancient regulations and abuses reaching forth from such-and-such a guild or corporation. It was as if, in the timeless chronology of their unresting imaginations, they had seen the precipice of the nineteenth century looming up ahead of them and were determined upon ascending it.

Far different was the condition of the established nobility. Whereas the governing classes of Britain were enjoying a political liberty guaranteed them by the Glorious Revolution of 1688 and lately confirmed by the defeat of Napoleon, they were hopelessly entangled in a net of social convention and of aristocratic privilege, deliberately maintained – or so it now seems – to throttle not only any change or initiative from below, but any initiative whatever. George III had mounted his throne declaring that he would have no innovations in his time; in the last years of his reign the notorious 'Six Acts' of Lord Sidmouth, to curb the liberties of ordinary people, enthroned reaction. Despite the insanity of the monarch, the profligacy of the Regent and the opinion of the Duke of Wellington of the next three royal princes – 'They are the damnedest millstones about the necks of any Government that can be imagined' – the Royal Family was universally held in reverential awe; the preservation of the orders of precedence that cemented the aristocracy beneath it had become, as Jane Austen tells us, a moral duty, calling for a vigilant assumption of superiority among all levels such as is today found only in our classier business schools. A bizarre illustration of this hierachical pursuit is offered by the vast dinner service made by Josiah Wedgwood for the Empress of Russia; the decoration of its many hundreds of pieces, according to their size, with the views of the palaces, mansions and other seats of the nobility, exactly replicated the order of precedence among their owners: the higher the rank the bigger the crock, so that by knowing the size of the piece on which the residence was painted one could estimate the standing of who lived there. Many landowners were able, like the Thornes of *Barchester Towers*, to count back their ancestors to some period long antecedent to the Norman Conquest, so that twenty generations on the same estate had settled upon them the cycle of Nature; the business of government and such other urban entertainments as the gaming-house, the theatre and the university were reserved for the winter – the closed season, as it still is called – while the summer was given over to life out of doors.

In so natural and pre-ordained a repetition of events there could be no place for such contrivances as might depend upon mechanical power, surging relentlessly on, day and night alike, winter and summer, indifferent to the influences of sun, wind and rain. If these new monsters were to call for unceasing attention, they would have to find their own dedicated servants far from the inviolable routines and insolent ceremonials of country house and parliamentary session; it was the upstart industrial captains, of untraceable origins and hotch-potch vitality, who supplied them. And if the warnings of Nature had been insufficient to keep the nobility clear of the factory smoke, there was always the tutelage of Aristotle: 'It is not therefore proper for any man of honour or any citizen or anyone who engages in public affairs to learn these servile employments, for, without this were observed, the distinction between a master and a slave would be lost.' So far, indeed, from the souls of the true-born Englishman was the notion of industrial and commercial initiative that the language of Shakespeare has no word for those who display it; a nation of imperialists must still draw the name of those upon whom they now most depend from the language of their traditional enemies, the French: *entrepreneur*, sobriquet of contemptuous abuse, much as action learning is today. Those other relics of our expansive past, moreover, the legal, parliamentary and university calendars, still remind us of the seedtime and the harvest, when the landed classes were too preoccupied to attend to the affairs of the nation; nor were their sons able to take up again the study of the classics until the crops were safe in the barn and the sheep provisioned with their turnips.

The emergence of the new race of energetic mongrels, the architects and builders of the industrial precipice up which they were to struggle in uneasy partnership with the established aristocracy, has not yet run its term. There are still clear divisions within our education system between those professions concerned with maintaining a status quo, on the one hand, and those, on the other, primarily interested in helping Britain to make a living in the modern world. Our wealth-creating sources are the trades that make and sell, particularly those that make and sell for the overseas markets, and it is still the case in 1979 that the professions concerned with invigorating these vital exercises are the least attractive to the young persons of brains. Thousands of places, since the Second World War, have remained unoccupied in the university schools of engineering, the largest and most technically advanced firms in the country cannot find instrument mechanics, and there is a national dearth of managers qualified to run practically any system of production handling physical outputs. In the very business schools themselves the popular choice is to become an accountant or a lawyer, rather than a manufacturer or a salesman. This is not to say that the pursuit of commercial advantage is being entirely overlooked within the professions – as the doctors, for example, threaten to force up their market value by withdrawing their services to the sick – but the fact remains that the Briton, once fully civilized, seems to lose interest in the sharp end of our economy; the vigorous example set by the industrial captains of the Napoleonic age seems temporarily to have lost its appeal. Action learning may yet prove to be a vehicle for its restoration.

The aristocratic pauperage that still masquerades under the name of Great Britain thus continues, in its emaciated fashion, the struggles between the gentleman and the engineer that began at the foot of the precipice and that have persisted throughout its giddy ascent. We may seek in the top businessmen of today the ghosts of those tenacious and self-sufficient pioneers, of whom some believed that by their personal fortunes they might redeem the entire national debt, and we may read in the marmoreal complacency of our governing bureaucracies the very disdain which their landed predecessors had reserved for such vulgarity as getting hard cash for hard work. For the conflict has more than one dimension; it is not only, as Duauf makes clear, that labour tires the arms and threatens one with the crocodiles – thus encouraging the smart lad to leave the physical effort to the others – but that those who direct the others to perform the labours are in turn inferior to those in charge of the smarter lads who have managed to avoid it. In the university itself, therefore, the professor of economics or accountancy takes precedence before those of mining engineering or textile chemistry; at Manchester the cleavage kept apart two entire institutions, 'The University' and 'The Tech'. Our top businessmen, distracted by the future uncertainties of investments, of home demands for products with a fifty-fifty chance of selling abroad, of tariffs and of subsidies, and by a hundred other risks of trade, must still contrive a synoptic vision of their world; every single action reaches out into the irreversible future, every mistake must be paid for in full, every concession to one party may make an enemy of another, every invention saluted as a benefit may turn out as a treachery, and every promise a calamity. The world of business reality is tough, and there are those who would avoid it. But those who struggle within it must, not seldom, take their problems of supervising those who produce the nation's bread and butter for discussion with those who have come out on the sunnier side of the Instruction of Duauf. There, in the corridors of Whitehall, built with the amplitude that enables drunken aristocrats supported by their bodyguards peaceably to pass each other, are re-enacted the cultural feuds of the industrial revolution, the clash of landed noble and of rootless huckster. It is true that one party no longer reposes securely in the ownership of land, but in these iron times the inflation-proof pension is a pretty acceptable substitute; it is no less true that among the others there are none who might aspire to repay from their personal fortunes the whole of our national debt, but they are still treated by the civil servants as if they were expected to.

The new captains of industry and their factory chimneys may well have provided the outward visible signs of the industrial revolution; its inward spiritual grace was to be found in Adam Smith's essay in political economy, *The Wealth of Nations*, described by Burke as the most important book ever written and appearing in the same year as the American Declaration of Independence and James Watt's first commercially constructed steam engine. The tract made four points: freedom of enterprise, division of labour, standardization of task, and machine pacing of human work. Nevertheless, the bland ratiocinations of the Glasgow professor and the fitful melancholy of the instrument maker working close beside him would not have got far without the exploiting genius of Richard Arkwright, the barber's apprentice from Preston, and we may summarize the essential messages of the trio in such a way as to identify what it was that they created for the world:

'Machinery, multiplying manual movements, makes millionaires most money.' (Adam Smith)
'Mill marries mine.' (James Watt)
'Management manipulates muted men.' (Richard Arkwright)

and since the headquarters of the culture was Manchester itself we may safely describe it as Culture M.

The legacy of Culture M is with us today, amplified by the passage of six generations, and lurking in many unexpected quarters. First, we glory in success; the acknowledged prerogative is of those supreme in the exploitation of circumstances, whether through their personal efforts, gifts or opportunities, or by turning to their own advantage the conditions of others; those who draw the lucky number now command the admiration and esteem of the neighbours rather than their envy or commiseration. In the rat race it is the winner who makes the rules for next time. Thus the unimpeded exercise of individual liberty so seductively extolled by Adam Smith was soon admitted and long protected because those who lost were ready to grant the victor not only the prize, but also the morality of his style. Their readiness to do so expressed their own undefeated cupidity, in the hope that all could make the fortune of an Arkwright. Such optimism must accept the mere facts of success, however arbitrary or accidental, as the final justification of all ambition, all endeavour and all entitlement. Second, so intensive has become our attachment to a particular profession or calling that the way in which we make a living is alike the first entry upon our passports and the first means of our identification when facing a criminal prosecution. It is by their deeds that men shall now be known, and in reporting who scored the goal in the football match or who won the race at the Crystal Palace, it is not enough that he be named as Jones or Robinson: it must be Jones the schoolmaster or Robinson the second-hand car dealer. And, to help in the identification of the wanted man should his trade be unknown, the ignorance is admitted and John Brown, occupation unknown, is advertised for by the police. Third, the progressive simplification of tasks carried out within particular cultures, whether farm or factory, mine or office, has made possible, by the endless repetition of simple motions, the mass production of most goods now in common use. (The modern production line, bringing the job to the worker rather than the worker dodging from place to place assembling the job, is not the essence of mass production, for this had been achieved by Josiah Wedgwood through the standardization of process and of part over two hundred years ago, let alone by the Romans with their standardized brick.) The most powerful illustration of the continued division of task, all the same, is given by Adam Smith himself at the opening of his immortal treatise and showing, from this third factor alone, a multiplication of output by 240-fold. Fourth, now become as fruitful a source of conflict as it was once of profit, is the machine pacing of productive work, and to determine the maximum acceptable speed has become a branch of the management sciences, so-called. It is not that speeding-up is itself new; the slave-masters of the Roman Empire, as of the Egyptians before them, would have had little to learn from the certificated work-study engineer. But it was still men who set the pace for other men; now it is often the machines who set the pace for the men who mind them.

It might well be expected that, since Culture M is the true expression of all that the new captains of industry were up to, as opposed to what the landed aristocracy continued to observe and to respect, it would have little impact on education as the apprenticeship of the governing classes. At first sight Culture M would appear to be just the very thing to give to the scribe for getting just that extra bit out of the muscles of the stonemason, off the loom of the weaver or out of the net of the fisherman. This was certainly one objective of Adam Smith himself, toiling so long over the great masterpiece. But Culture M has had an unexpected effect upon the education system itself. An inspection of the typical university, conducted with that degree of particularity essential to understanding how to change it, reveals that, not only is it now the true child of Culture M; it is, perhaps, that culture's most faithful and abiding image.

For the unimpeded exercise of individual liberty by university staff is now expressed as their unquestioned right to dispose of their time and effort as they themselves think fit. The cry so often on their lips, for academic freedom and the need to preserve it, is nothing more than the reiteration of their claim to pursue their private hobbies at the expense of the rest of society. A recent study of the distribution of public funds for 'research' shows that the bulk was intercepted for the projects being supervised by the members of the allocating committee; the only consolation that the public could derive from this discovery was that, the projects being in the social and behavioural sciences, their outcome could have been of no possible use and hence brought no dangers to the socially disadvantaged in the way of new therapies. As was mentioned in the last chapter, the tumblers on the stages of the business schools offer the performances they are able to get through with the least effort, not what might be needed to bring out to the greatest extent the unused abilities of the managers.

We have identified as the second element of Culture M the division of labour, leading to the segregation of trades, the jealousies of professions, the idolization of acquired skills and, eventually, the setting of each man's hand against that of his neighbour. But it is at once apparent that no institution, save perhaps a zoo, depends more for its very existence upon the isolation of souls and the separation of minds than does the true university. The statement is not inconsistent with much talk about 'the communion of intellects', 'a fellowship of scholars', 'the advance of knowledge across a broad front', 'the essential integrity of learning', 'the university as an academic organism', and much other rhetoric of the same nature. Such expressions ante-date by many years the jargon of the public relations man.

212

Here we run against the barriers, cultural, administrative and personal, set up at great expense by a multiplication of officers, to segregate those who, in the culture of action learning as a challenge to the ills of the external community, might well act as eager and co-operating colleagues.

Our third element in Culture M is the standardization of task, the insistence upon uniformity, its idolization of the original text, its emphasis upon the inviolability of each particular truth. Agreement upon the evidence is, of course, essential to all scholarship; the printed book must, as far as possible, compare what it has to say with what is known to have occurred. The tradition of the one and only true message, delivered from the lips of The Prophet himself, can be traced back more than a thousand years, when in the mosques of Cairo the teachers began to recite to their students the revealed and unchangeable words of the divine inspiration; it was for each of them to learn by heart and to repeat by rote to each succeeding generation. Other books, with other texts, have been admitted to the syllabus with the passage of time. But the stereotypes remain and the media of diffusion do not change. The professors still sit in front of their disciples and intone with soporiferous monotony the rigid formulas of the dead and of the past. It is true that the system is under attack, but not from those in charge of it; in action learning, most of this would be swept away, for the working material would be drawn, no longer from the standard inventory, but from the exercises of the students in trying to understand the real world by changing it. Real people challenging real trouble in real time, rather than examination hands counting paper puzzles until the end of term.

Our identification of Culture M was completed by its fourth element, the machine-paced task, the predetermined schedule, the index of assignments and the mortgaging of the future to the Examinations Board. Here the arm of authority reaches forward, not only to order what must be done and in what conditions, but by what hour and in readiness for what is to follow next. Here, in the academic calendar, half steeplechase, half treadmill, So-and-so must be listened to on Monday, Such-and-such must be done on Tuesday, and, continuing in this way, we account for every hour of our lives long before

213

that hour is ours to live. We reach this staging post by Christmas and that by Easter, with some maze of minor and distracting exercises to be traced – all on their appointed days and in their appointed ways. Here is the relentless echo, down fifteen centuries, of the monastery bell, compulsive with canonical duty. Again we see how action learning will make the school more creative, challenging each and every student, to form with others his own set, to design their own projects, to discover their own learning needs and interests; each will go ahead in his own time, at his own depth and in as many or as few dimensions as he may please. And if it is objected that he will not know whether what he is learning is of any use, he can respond with two replies: first, that he is learning how to learn-by-doing, which is the ultimate in the processes of human perfectability; second, whether or not what he learns is of any use is settled, not by any teacher, but by the outcome of the activity by which he discovers it.

The contrasts of this chapter are caricature, but the caricature has been chosen to emphasize what those contrasts consist in. The first is that between the Yin and the Yang; between those who look backward and below as the cultural precipice is climbed, upon what has already been experienced and esteemed, recorded and ritualized, on the one hand, and those who look upward and ahead, solving their own problems, making their own judgements and setting their own standards, on the other. It is the contrast between the establishment, that decides what must not be done, and the entrepreneur, who takes the risk of doing something; it is the contrast between those who answer questions in the light of yesterday and those who pose questions in the darkness of tomorrow; it is the contrast between the expert who can read with facility what the book already has to tell us and the leader who has to decide what must be entered upon its still blank pages. It is the contrast between those who teach management from books that are supposed to record what happened to other managers, and those who expect their managers to learn through the confirmation or rejection of their own devices. Caricature it may be, but not without a purpose.

Our second contrast is between the education system that has evolved out of Culture M and the approach of action learning. The curriculum, the syllabus and the examination schedule of the academy have become the assembly line for the education industry; however liberal might once have been the studies preparatory to the station of a gentleman, something has managed to turn the tables: the narrow-minded inflexibility of mass production now cramps the university imagination and what was once seen – even if through a haze of romantic conceit – as a vigorous tradition of creative scholarship, is become, like all factory production, merely the expression of Culture M. But the factory now has the advantage over the academy: it is constantly forced off its programmes by the unforeseeable changes in the world around it, and at each of these departures those who run the factory are obliged to think. The manufacturing culture has become the arena of spontaneous adjustment, even if unwillingly, while the academic culture has degenerated into an illiberal stagnation, even if unknowingly. No longer is the spirit of production stifled beneath a deadening routine, no longer does the flower of scholarship bloom in smug Arcadia. It is now the artisan who must play the genius, while the scribe may rest content to be the slave. So it is that the miner will now defeat the bureaucrat, and that the teacher-as-scholar must give way before the teacher-as-intimidator. The very changes forcing the artificer to think may free the modern pedagogue from further need to do so. Certainly, there is little inclination among the business professors to cast aside their hallowed texts one day sooner than they are obliged to. And there is certainly no evidence that, given the adversity of change enough, Britannia's rude mechanics will fail to cope with it. In a leisurely and spacious world it is, perhaps, a leisurely and spacious scholarship that will prevail. But when that world has gone, perhaps for ever, to be replaced by one of risk and rivalry, it is to the shrewd importunate that fortune calls.

Such was the reversal of tradition. These momentous changes were reflected in educational policy; a dual system appeared, in which the polytechnics – in so far as they had not already been turned into universities in name – were given the same status as the ancient seats of learning. In the hope that talent would now flow into the streams of manufacture and of trade, the schools that professed to teach these useful arts were suitably tarted up; the technical instructors became the new elite, and many a donnish pastime soon got the Whitehall chop. Nothing like this had ever been known before, and for several months there was genuine fear that the new institutions would set a scorching pace. But normalcy was got back to; the *parvenues* used their windfalls to buy the second-hand raiment of the classics, and trained their sights upon the old objectives of parable and allusion. If engineer or merchant call for help, from whence will it arrive?

16.

Miners and Teachers; Labourers and Scribes

When in the darkest depths the miner striving,
Feels in his arms the vigour of the Lord,
Strikes for a Kingdom and his King's arriving,
Holding his pick more splendid than the sword.
  (G. A. Studdert-Kennedy, *Songs of Faith and Doubt,* 1922)

Don poor at Bed and worse at Table,
Don pinched, Don starved, Don miserable,
Don stuttering, Don with roving eyes,
Don nervous, Don of crudities;
Don clerical, Don ordinary,
Don self-absorbed and solitary;
Don here-and-there, Don epileptic;
Don puffed and empty, Don dyspeptic;
Don middle-class, Don sycophantic,
Don dull, Don brutish, Don pedantic;
Don hypocritical, Don bad,
Don furtive, Don three-quarters mad;
Don (since a man must make an end)
Don that shall never be my friend.
                    (Hilaire Belloc, *Lines to a Don*)

On the evening of 11 February 1972, I telephoned my wife
from my office in Brussels, where, since my departure from the
University of Manchester, I had been living, surrounded by the
opportunities and moved by the encouragement offered by the
Belgians, businessmen and professors alike, to develop my ideas
on action learning. My wife, in a singularly unaccustomed way,
urged me not to waste time on the telephone, since she was

trying both to handle an invasion of neighbours and to keep an eye on our son, who had been sent into the cellar to chop up the furniture. I was able to talk for long enough to learn that, because of the coalminers' strike, already in its fifth week, Manchester was suffering a severe and protracted electricity cut. Since our house, in what has since become a conservation area as well as a smokeless zone, was the only one widely known in the locality to have preserved all of its Victorian firegrates, and since I had recently carried there an ample provision of Belgian candles, our neighbours had taken possession of the ground floor for the evening, alike to keep themselves warm at, and to cook their suppers over, the miserable fires smouldering so reluctantly in the crowded hearths. Our own stock of smokeless fuel had been used up only a few days before, and the older children had been detailed to scour the local parks for fallen branches; they were forbidden to use their cycle lamps, since these would be wanted by their parents for getting upstairs to bed. 'Next week,' my wife told me, 'according to the Prime Minister, who has just been on the telly, there will be millions out of work.'

Since I had spent ten years in the coal industry, both at its London headquarters and out in the pits themselves, working on their problems of management, I found a lot of interest in what my wife had to say. I read next day in the Belgian press about the state of emergency that the government had declared. Among the welter of comments the most outspoken (after the event) were those about how unexpected it had all been. The Ministry of Energy, in particular, had been taken utterly by surprise; it had not believed that the miners could have stuck things out for so long, nor that they could have recruited so many partisans to hinder the movement of coal and other commodities so vital to the electricity supply. None of the television personalities had anticipated with what facetiousness the miners' leaders were to reject the government's offer of a settlement: a minimum wage of £22.00 a week for underground workers.

Their refusal had left Whitehall in disarray, for, like Napoleon on the way to Moscow, Mr Heath had no strategy alternative to his own total victory. He had forgotten the thesis of his illustrious predecessor, Mr Lloyd George, who also owed more of his further education to the grandfathers of Mr Heath's formidable adversaries than he did to any books he might have studied: 'There are,' he had observed, 'three institutions that shall never disappear: the British Empire, the Catholic Church and the Mineworkers' Federation of Great Britain.' Events may have shown him inaccurate in detail; Empire has become Commonwealth, but the spirit of colonialism has long survived the farewell of the last British uniform and of the last British desk-worker; the Roman Church may well be up against some spirited internal challenges, but out of their responses the Church will emerge a more convincing fellowship as a whole; the Mineworkers' Federation has changed its name and its membership has fallen to a quarter of what once it was. All these modifications to Mr Lloyd George's forecast we admit. But he was still essentially right, and all British Prime Ministers likely to have any business with coalminers ought to read carefully what Mr Lloyd George had to say, since he spoke always in prophecies.

We are now only too painfully aware that, after all the confident promise of nuclear physics to have every British home, however humble, glowing in the white heat of atomic power; after all the assurances of the patriots that the Suez Canal was no loss since we should henceforth be building tankers too big to get through it; after all our half-hearted smirkings over the inexhaustible energies of the North Sea: after all this (and who but a Cambridge man also remembers Zeta?) my unfortunate wife, in the once-richest suburb of the once-greatest industrial city of the world, was on her knees at the fire-grate, struggling to warm her shivering neighbours. Whatever other misfortunes the housewives of Bowdon imagine themselves to suffer, they surely cannot complain of monotony: *that* the miners will look after, exactly as Mr Lloyd George said they would. These *enfants terribles* of industrial reality will always be here to keep us on our knees: in the very hour when we can at last see that the theoretical physicists had grossly overcalled their hand; when the governments of the oil-producing nations had at last defied the political scientists by starting to bargain with their collective strength; and when the true costs, as distinct from the estimates of the economists, of working the North Sea reserves have at last become apparent; then, in this very hour, the miners demand that they shall be paid half as much per week (the time is 1972) as other men get for fixing parts of motor cars together or half as much as any professor of industrial relations would demand, over and above his regular salary, for a public lecture to explain exactly how many unemployed are best for British industry as a whole.

It is instructive to compare the miners' strike of 1972 with that of 1926. No two national events within living memory illustrate more vividly the contrast: scribe versus artisan, director versus labourer, book versus tool, word versus deed; no two national events chronicle so clearly the cultural change that overtakes the nation. For the 1926 strike was won by the scribe–director–book–word faction, and that of 1972 by their artisan–labourer–tool–deed counterparts. The 1926 struggle was with the weapons of bureaucracy: propaganda, emergency legislation, alarmist rumour, newsroom vilification, poster slogans, patriotic appeal, a campaign of words and insinuation fired twenty-four hours a day from the paper popguns of the administrative yeomanry. The miners' stand against cuts in wages so savage that some of their wives and children died of starvation, or were still in debt to the local co-operative societies at the end of the Second World War, was represented to the middle classes as the opening moves in a Russian invasion. Mr Winston Churchill was manipulated, not unwillingly, by the Prime Minister to produce an official broadsheet, the *British Gazette*, which denounced the strikers as 'the enemy' from whom Mr Churchill demanded 'unconditional surrender'. The nurseries for scribes, our universities (I was myself an undergraduate at the time) strongly supported their own class, by providing volunteers to drive lorries and even underground trains, as well as special constables and other officials to supervise the emergency legislation. But there was no action. The conflict remained a frenzied argument, with each side attributing extremist policies to the other, without believing a single word of their denunciations in private. Mr Arthur Cook, the miners' leader, was typical of the fracas, and more so than Mr Churchill; to begin with, he was a better speaker, the finest I have ever heard, for what he said came not so much from him as it came from every man who heard him. Many audiences, no doubt, have found the orators to tell them what they want to hear; Mr Cook had the singular gift of making men listen with enthusiasm to all that they did not want to hear, so that they might still find hope in the blackest misery. Mr Churchill, on the other hand, who has also won transitory fame as a speaker, did not quite fit the vituperative campaign of his colleagues, despite his control of the *British Gazette*; as always, he wanted to turn the war of words into a war of weapons, but, although he tried to provoke the strikers by parading armoured cars in the streets, he was not taken seriously. The prevailing climate was not for action, but for talk; the culture of scribe–director–book–word was still in the ascendant, and action learning still lay in the future.

But things had changed by 1972. After forty-six years the miners' leaders were not, in the slightest degree, intimidated by the warnings of the government about breaking the law; the miners themselves could all now read and write, and they were well represented in the House of Commons – even in the House of Lords; the newspapers, now nervous about the effect of falling sales upon their advertising revenues, thought twice before slandering their own readers. The miners took on the government, not with the weapons of scribe and legislator, as they had been obliged to do in 1926, but with those of artisan and labourer; they simply used the tools they had to stop the supplies vital to the nation's services, and that was the end of the business. They had no speaker to compare with Mr Arthur Cook, and those of their leaders who did appear on the television screen conveyed nothing except that they looked like coalminers. Nor did the government produce any man of action who might dare outflank the miners' tactical dispositions. Perhaps Mr Heath, although forgetting the words of Mr Lloyd George in allowing himself to be drawn into the battle, was old enough to remember that even Mr Churchill had been defeated by the miners when the thunder of the *British Gazette* had sunk away:

When the miners of Kent came out in 1941 and resisted arbitration recommendations, the Government (of Mr Churchill) found nothing better than to arrest the lot of them. But then it chickened out of facing a procession of 4,000 'Not Guilty' pleas, and served summonses on a mere 1,000 underground workers. The NUM advised them all to plead guilty: and they all turned up with their families on trial day, accompanied by music from several bands. The court gave three NUM officials sentences of hard labour and the rest of the 1,000 were fined £1 each (except for 35, who were fined £3 each), with the option of prison. It was a bluff, which failed. With the country's need for coal, no room in the prisons to take 1,000 men, and the miners refusing to work without their leaders' release, the Government had no option but to release them and waive the fines. In a week after reopening, the miners' output trebled. (Miscellany, *The Guardian*, 22 February 1972)

It is not hard to see that the Kentish strike of 1941 occupies a place between that of 1926, fought with the brow-beating vituperation of the scribe, and those of 1972 and 1974, conducted as exercises for the picket and deploying all the threat of artful confrontation. Indeed, we may take the exact turning point from the very extract itself: 'It was a bluff, which failed.' The shift in battlefields over the past half century deserves our close attention, for it is symptomatic of a trend in Western society, that I believe to be historically and culturally determined, and that we ought to understand more clearly than we do. It seems at first sight to be little more than the collapse of law and order, to be treated by condign, or even retaliatory, countermeasures, deploying the same weapons as those of the revolutionaries themselves. It is as well, however, not to confuse the growth of criminal violence succumbing to the temptations of modern technology, on the one hand, with the more effective application of industrial muscle, on the other.

It may well be that several years have now passed without our having to chop up the furniture to keep ourselves warm and to cook our evening meal. But we have now seen the schoolteachers refusing to look after the serving of their pupils' lunches, seconded by the university lecturers who refuse to mark the examination scripts of their own degree students. Such examples suggest that, while the tactics of the miners might be such as to provoke violence – for how, without the physical backing of those on the picket lines, could the movement of the vital coal have been so successfully impeded? – the teachers and lecturers have exhibited their higher standards of social protest and, so far from precipitating conflict, have sought that genteel preservation of the peace so essential to all scholarly pursuits and to the cultivation of the mind so appreciative of them. Does not the difference between their form of denial, all peace and withdrawal, and that of the miners, brutal with shovings and bawlings, emphasize what Duauf was on about when he wanted his little boy to acquire the manners of the magistrate's son? A moment's reflection, however, may suggest that the behaviour of the academics is merely a more subtle expression of violence, so contrived that the victims, being in no condition to retaliate, cannot kick up the row that rises from the picket line, much as they might like to do so. How one chooses to regard it seems to me a highly personal business; there are many who would prefer the teachers to deprive the kids of their food and the lecturers to walk out on their students rather than to have either of them setting fire to the local nursery school – even when there were no children in it – or laying about them with a few crowbars on the personal records stored in the university computer.

Yet, if the tactics of the academics do not directly offend public order, they may, nevertheless, relinquish any claim to moral integrity. The argument appears to be that, since the British economy is undoubtedly on the decline and others are out to snatch all they can while the going is still good, it would be foolish of the teachers to lose out by being polite beyond the calls of duty. I have never had the experience, but I should imagine that those aboard a sinking liner might not care, in its final minutes, whether the passengers, or the crew, started to rob each other. All the same, I think that the majority of them would draw the line at robbing the children. For all these instructors of scribes, deliberating to advance their own interests, have suddenly cast their books aside, closed their lips upon the grave sentences and subtle parables and other degrees of ancient wisdom, given up judging the good and evil among men and have displayed their industrial muscle by abandoning the infants' dining hall and sending back unmarked the examination scripts of their own disciples. 'If you, the government, so behave as to deprive our children of their food, not only shall we, their friends the teachers, be robbed by your short-sighted callousness of our own rightful rewards, but our hearts will be forced to bleed for the tiny tots as they weep around the neighbourhood for a spare crust.' This may not be the language of the moralist, but it is logically unassailable. The scribal resource is not wisdom but power, for while awkward and unlettered persons might endlessly argue the nature of wisdom, power will get what one wants when it is used against those with lesser power, like children and candidates for their final degrees. Hence, a vast cloud of academic humbug has suddenly been blown away; in walking out on their charges the teachers have openly announced that they resign their traditional claim to intellectual and moral dominance.

It would be foolish to attempt too firm a forecast of what is likely to follow from the uncompromising behaviour of the teaching profession. But now it is become so clear that the polarizations, alike of Duauf and of Ecclesiasticus, have been repudiated by the scribes themselves, there is hope for action learning. For our thesis is that the trials of the academy teach us little, and that not much worth knowing; it is the comradeship of adversity that truly tells us who we are and what, if anything, we believe. Now that the teachers are beginning to grasp their affinity with the miners there is hope that scribe and artisan may join forces on the battlefields of action learning.

This conversion of talkers to doers, even although it has come so late, may have consequences for action learning so positive that I may be allowed to recapitulate the argument. We have compared the miners' defeat in 1926 with their triumph in 1972. The campaign of 1926 was conducted in the media of the scribe: propaganda, the *British Gazette*, patriotic appeals; that of 1972 entered the culture of the labourer: the picket, the sympathetic but practical support of other labourers not immediately caught up in the issues under dispute, the work-to-rule and even, alas, threats of sabotage. The first was a war of ideas, the second of actions, mostly, it is true, passive, but actions in the here-and-now, nonetheless. Ideas are to be found in books, actions in the muscles of men; ideas may be spread rapidly and multiplied even more rapidly, by newspaper, by broadcast and by rumour; they lend themselves to analogy, to comparison and to contrast; they are shaped and perverted by the interest of those who transmit them, often unknowingly; they may be catalogued, stored, retrieved, blended, allowing the imagination of those who work with them whatever licence they choose; they may be sent to third parties in order to create impressions totally unknown to others. The scope, richness and mobility of these manipulative processes is such that those who learn to master them come, in the end, to believe that they are masters of the reality from which the original idea has sprung; in particular, the university mind ends by convincing itself that some intellectual process that obeys the laws of logic and syntax is, or can be, a reflection of Nature herself; since these processes are fast and inexpensive, they have become the foundations of our education system, enabling those in charge of it to judge whether others within it are able to conduct the manipulative processes in accordance with the canonical rules. So long as the whole world accepts these rules, those better at applying them must be pronounced the winners; thus the government won the 1926 strike, since the ideas which they manipulated were accepted by the majority of the nation, and thus action learning has so far always lost because it does not accept (at least in the university world) that the ideas and the manipulative processes bear any relation to the real world in which managers have to struggle.

Action cannot be described in words, except in the obvious sense of naming the person who took it, the objects affected by it, and so forth; even at such primitive levels, however, those making the description may give so personally selective an account of the action that witnesses to it, and perhaps other participants, such as the man whose kneecaps were blown off, honestly contradict every single statement in the narratives. A full specification of action must therefore be highly detailed in many different dimensions; every action is a unique event and therefore impossible to classify in every imaginable particular. Some of the more important of these particulars may be the consequences at some much later time, and these consequences might be totally unforeseeable for those trying to give an account of the action, at least, up to the moment when they ceased personally to be receiving messages about it. Beyond some point of convenient generality, therefore, we cease going into the specific details of particular actions in our efforts to communicate with others about those actions; we are, at times, not aware of how little of the totality of the action is accounted for up to that limiting point, with disastrous effects upon our understanding of the real world in which the action has occurred. We say we *know* something, when, in fact, all we have in our memory are a few symbols that refer us to that something; only if we can significantly replicate the action can we be said truly to *know* it. For me to say that I *know* a leap of seven metres will win me the next Olympic pole-vault is one thing; to go out on the stadium and leap seven metres is another. Knowledge by words and knowledge by achievement are totally different, and it is a reproach to the whole of the management education culture that it does not sufficiently stress the difference between taking action and *talking about* taking action. Only the taking of the action, such as walking out on the children and the examination candidates, brings people to realize who they are, what they *actually* believe in and why they do the things they do; they may well talk about who they believe themselves to be, what they persuade themselves and others that they believe in and what they wish to perceive as their motives for their actions. Not until they see the consequences of their actions, however, have they learned in the sense that their behaviour may now be changed.

In short, action learning is a subjective expression for the verifiable postulate in cybernetics: 'Systems that are to change their responses in a specified direction must receive inputs about their own outputs in that specified direction.' There is no effective learning except by (and after) observing the results of attempting to learn; *a fortiori*, there is no effective learning of a specific task except by (and after) observing the results of attempting to learn that specific task. All those teachers who deny this proposition by assuming that to *talk about* such-and-such a class of tasks enables others to learn to fulfil such tasks must now recognize that the way to get more money (i.e. all those teachers who have learned how to get more money) is not by argument, but by action. The hope is that they may transfer this shift of perspective to their teaching and other professional duties; if so, they will be taking the first steps along the road to action learning.

17.
Worker Participation as Action Learning

Matters concerning all should be agreed by all. (Emperor Justinian, AD 530)

No sort of scientific teaching, no kind of common interest, will ever lead men to share property and privileges with equal consideration for all. Every one will think his share too small, and they will always be envying, accusing and attacking each other . . . True security is to be found in social solidarity rather than in isolated individual effort. (Dostoyevsky, *The Brothers Karamazov*, Pt II, Bk VI, ch. 2)

The most crying need in the humbler ranks of life is that they should be allowed some part in the direction of public affairs. That is what will develop their faculties and intelligence and self-respect. (Ibsen, *An Enemy of the People*, Act II)

When the rich get together and concern themselves with the affairs of the poor, we call it government. When the poor get together and take a hand in the affairs of the rich, we call it anarchy. (Paul Richard, *The Scourge of Christ*, misquoted)

You may judge a clever man by his choice of influential friends, but a wise one by his choice of influential enemies. (Machiavelli, misquoted)

If you feel like a fight, make sure you attack the proper foe: you have three choices, the man you can see, the man you cannot – and yourself. Think hard before you strike; think harder still, and keep your peace. (Indian analect)

Our interpretation of the authority of the book over the tool must not run away with us; even in the slave societies of the Hellenistic world the revolt of the labourer was not unknown, for genuine strikes broke out in Asia Minor during Roman times, among those who were no longer serfs, and passive resistance, or folded hands, became commonplace in Egypt under the Roman protectorate.[10] The ascendancy of the litterati had its uneasy moments, and it is nearly fifteen hundred years since Justinian announced his celebrated maxim 'Matters concerning all should be agreed by all'. The significance of this statement for what might be called industrial democracy should not be ignored simply because the imperial law-giver so frequently ignored the maxim himself.

There were sceptics enough about the wizardry of scribes, well over two thousand years ago, to put heart into the action learners of today.

To do a little good is better than to write difficult books. The perfect man is nothing if he does not confer benefits on others, if he does not console the lonely. The way of salvation is open to all, but know that a man deceives himself if he thinks he can escape his conscience by taking refuge in a monastery. The only remedy for evil is healthy reality. (Buddha, addressing his disciples in the deer park of Benares, 518 BC)

One must learn by doing the thing; for though you think you know it, you have no certainty until you try. (Sophocles, *Trachiniae, c.* 417 BC)

But be ye doers of the word, and not hearers only, deceiving your own selves. For if any be a hearer of the word and not a doer, he is like unto a man beholding his natural face in a glass: for he beholdeth himself and goeth his way, and straightway forgetteth what manner of man he was. But whoso looketh into the perfect law of liberty, and continueth therein, he being not a forgetful hearer, but a doer of the work, this man shall be blessed in his deed. (St James ch. I, v. 22 ff)

Each of these references brings in the need for action as a quality of truth or of integrity; unless whatever is claimed as knowledge can be tested in its effects there is no means of judging its truth.

A distinction begins to emerge between the ability to command words and the power to control the environment, or, as Buddha calls it, healthy reality. Sophocles stresses the need for action explicitly; knowledge is the ability to act, since to prove that one has learned, namely, increased one's stock of knowledge, one must demonstrate one's use of it, or by 'doing the thing'. St James backs this proposition up, by suggesting that what may be discussed may not be knowledge at all, but self-deception. His reference to the man beholding his natural face in a glass, going away and forgetting himself, may be taken to illustrate a conversation with a like-minded acquaintance from which nothing is expected to follow; it is an interesting social occasion and an end in itself.

I have engaged in many in my time, and would agree with St James that I remember nothing of them, except on the two occasions when I was obliged to verify what had been asserted. My obligation was onerous, for as junior fellow of my college I had to find the evidence for settling two bets made in the senior common room. The first was as to whether so-and-so had ever been a fellow of King's College; my researches disclosed that he had in fact once been an assistant teacher in an elementary school in King's Road, Chelsea. The second was as to a remarkable dog owned by a long-defunct classical fellow of another college; the beast had been taught to speak Latin and conversed in the most agreeable fashion with any superior person who would open the conversation by enquiring after the animal's health. My researches showed that there was such a classical fellow, attended in his old age by a servant called Airedale, who had picked up a few tags of dog-latin which, for the price of half-a-pint of beer, he would recite. I believe the anecdotes demonstrate at least two of the truths of antiquity set out above: first, that simply talking about things, whether fellows of King's College or dogs that converse in Latin, may lead us into a willing self-deception; second, that there is nothing like having to act upon a message if it is also to be remembered.

It was not for twenty more years that my tasks at the Coal Board, of trying to train managers, led me to question still further those recondite powers of rumour and hearsay on which so much of our higher education seems to be established. Only when, in the action-oriented culture of drawing coal up colliery shafts, I tried for results expressed as better performance, did I start to ask what we meant by 'educating managers'. Much of our university system seemed little more than a socio-commercial contrivance, indifferently conducted, to fulfil two related aims: the distribution of testimonials for directors and scribes as their qualifications to manage, and the perpetuation among the less literate of a respect for those to whom the certificates had been distributed. I had already seen, in a decade of service with the Essex County Council, how the lower-middle-class officials would brandish their diplomas in the faces of their artisan-councillors, and do so with a confidence that would have won the approval of Duauf himself. It was becoming apparent to me that education, such as it was, so far from nourishing the brotherhood of man, was still the prime agent of social divisiveness fashioned over four thousand years ago for the children of the Egyptian magistrates. But since some things had changed in the meantime – the miners, for example, were now winning their strikes hands down – it seemed useful to examine the Instruction of Duauf from the lower side; we might also ask, of the opposing schools of antiquity, Duauf, Ecclesiasticus and Aristotle, on the one hand, Buddha, Sophocles and St James, on the other, which is to prevail in our own future?

We may approach our enquiry in several ways. How have the artisans responded to Culture M? Since this has taken over education, it must also have infected the early idealism of the trade unions. Or how have the artisans encouraged the growth of democracy, from protest to defence, from defence to attack, from attack to government? Or, to be highly specific, how are the artisans helping to restore the National Health Service?

We begin with the artisans of antiquity. According to Ecclesiasticus, there were those who trusted to their hands, who were neither sought in public counsel nor were to be found where parables were spoken, but without whom the city could not be inhabited nor the state of the world maintained. The mechanics and their acquaintances, according to Aristotle, hung about the market place, led wretched lives and had to be shunned by men of honour. Things are no longer quite what they used to be in the Ancient World, at least in the City of New York, where about a quarter of a million employees are for ever threatening the municipal fathers to strike for more wages. Although the courts of law have forbidden the transport workers to walk out, the unions have merely reiterated their policy: 'No contract, no work.' They were pressing (during summer 1978) for a rise in pay of 'at least 17 per cent to put them back on the living standards they had four years ago'. The police, teachers and social workers were awaiting the outcome of the transport dispute before declaring their own tactics of aggression against their employers but, although these may differ in detail, their strategies were the same. By making life hard, if not impossible, for those who, in addition to themselves, also inhabit the city, they expect to see their employers capitulate and yield up the money for which they ask. The mayor observes: 'It will be a time to test us, to test the people of this city, to see if they are able to take the inconvenience, and sometimes more than inconvenience, to keep the city going.'

The cost of running New York City, of providing it with schools, transport services, a police force, new housing and a score of other classes of social necessity has been mounting steadily for many years. This can be said of most large towns. But the wealth-creating activities of New York have also been rapidly shrinking. Indeed, large sections of the suburbs, like Bedford-Stuyvesant, and even parts of Manhattan, formerly given over to busy and profitable manufactures, are now utterly derelict. Far from being a source of income from which the municipal employees might reasonably expect part of their increases in pay to be met, these districts are now become a deadening burden upon the declining total revenues of the city administration. It is not only that those who just about manage to hang on in these desolated slums produce no wealth and pay no taxes; they are also a lifeless debt for the falling numbers of citizens who still keep solvent despite the soaring exactions of the municipal treasurer. Sooner or later each of these survivors will have to decide whether or not he can afford to remain in the city that has been, if not his home, at least his place of work, perhaps for half a century, or whether, like the corporate officers of Shell and IBM, they will move elsewhere, either just beyond the city limits or a thousand miles away. If and when they do so, they must inevitably still further reduce the total of taxable property as well as create more burdens for those who remain and for the social service departments who must aid them.

The civil management of New York City would have broken down long ago, were it not that the city is in the state of the same name; this, in turn, is but one of the states in the Union, so that we may see the financially unsound edifice of the great municipality being shored up by two adventitious props. But the reliability of these external aids depends upon forces not always at the command of those who (however well disposed themselves to the employees of New York City) run the affairs of the state from Albany and of the nation from Washington. The decline of municipal income following the retreat of wealth-creating businesses from inside the city's own boundaries has an exact counterpart in the persisting trade deficits of the United States as a whole, now at record levels following a severe devaluation of the dollar.

We may also ask, by interpreting the city's ordeal as a rehearsal for America as a nation, if it may also foretell the fate of Britain? Although her own powers of wealth-creation are much enfeebled, her shrinking exchequer must still fulfil the swelling hopes of those creating wealth, and sustain the growing armies of unemployed and other victims of national insufficiency. But, while New York has but 5 per cent of all Americans, each one of us is in retreat. Nor have we the counterparts of state or federal aid, even if our cosy chauvinism still persuades full-corseted Britannia, bouncing in undiminished majesty upon the economic trampoline, that beneath her stretch the safety nets of Brussels and of Washington. Whatever miracles may yet postpone disaster in New York we cannot count upon in London. Our path back to solvency we have to find for ourselves.

None knows where that path may lead; we must explore it on our own with action learning as our faithful guide. How do all who share the adversity learn with and from each other? If managers do so among other tormented managers, doctors among their nurses, bankers among steelmasters, why not bosses among workers and trade unions among employers? In the GEC programme a trade union officer tackled his problem in the austere company of five line managers, all with their own;

in the HIC project laundry-workers and consultant physicians were fellow participants in helping their own hospital. But is this not blatant collaborationism, a fraud to bolster up an economic system in decay? Why should the worker help the boss out of his mess? That question is not for me to answer. All I know is that those who serve that system now need constantly to learn: whether to replace that system or to restore it they must start from where that system now is, and learn to achieve in practice what they desire in theory. What may be feasible lies solely in the organic here-and-now: to achieve this is the participative end, but action learning offers us the means.

The New Yorkers had the same idea. Besides attacking each other, ought not their different interests to unite against the encircling menace of the times? They had no choice of enemies as such, only of their priorities. Thus the City Council undertook to study its difficulties with the help of the new profession of operational research. The hideous exercise in mastering reality long known as war had now brought the scribal classes face to face with those violent tasks generally prosecuted by labourers and artisans on remote battlefields; the time had come to experiment with novel forms of reasoning long familiar to the seminar, laboratory and computing room, by applying them to the logistical exigencies of moving fleets at sea and armies on land. The Rand Corporation, by the subtlety of its approach, had created for itself an international reputation in operational research, and was invited by the City Council to recommend what ought to be done about the mounting embarrassments of the municipality. An account of their joint efforts with the Office of the Controller of the Budget appears in *The Analysis of Public Systems*,[11] and it has this to say about the relations between the scribes and the artisans in trying to help the stricken city:

Crime, drug use, fire alarms, solid wastes, automobile traffic, under-privileged children in the schools, housing deterioration are all outrunning the services designed to deal with them. The continuing need to run twice as fast to stay in the same place buries the successes from improvements in the system, and obscures their impact. The research effort worked well in some departments and abysmally in others.

The sine qua non was an administrator both interested in analysing his own services and able to attract the staff to do the job. Consultants, in the main, were useful in those agencies with staff sufficiently competent to manage the consultants' efforts.

There can be, it seems, no salvation by experts trying to advise those heads of departments unwilling, or unable, to involve their own field workers; complex systems already in trouble need for their recovery more than sound advice offered to the directorate in charge.

The report continues:

More and more our society is coming to regard interest groups – ethnic and racial associations, labour organisations and neighbourhood communities – as legitimate participants in local decision making. Over the long run, policy research may well depend upon the ability of our society to provide those groups with the means of participating in public debate in a more informed and more rational way. We will then find that the quality and usefulness of the analyses carried out for governments will improve towards a competence, relevance and comprehension rarely seen at present.

According to this investigation (accepting the philosophy of Justinian and rejecting that of Aristotle), we must enlist not only our own staff in the formation of municipal policies; we must also recruit the citizens for whom those policies are formed – over and above the prior condition that the administration has already been elected by those very same citizens themselves. An important question thus arises, namely, as to how the three parties, elected council, paid employees and the general constituency of citizens, may effectively work together to get done what the Rand report specifically suggests, and that is implicit in Justinian's maxim: 'Matters concerning all should be agreed by all.' It is by no means a remote and theoretical proposition for scholars; New York City is fighting for its existence in a civil war aimed at destroying itself and, whichever side from this remote distance we choose to cheer, it is only to shout for our own downfall here in Britain. For if we look more closely home, at our own National Economic

Development Office, we are looking at the same need for tripartite co-operation: government, trade unions and the general constituency of employers. Our need in Britain is just as pressing as that in the City of New York: our example in antiquity is also Justinian and not Aristotle, and an inspection of the literature will reveal a confusion of thinking among us no less impressive than among the burgesses of Manhattan, since enemies on pence today must be allied on pounds tomorrow.

The demand that the formation of public policy in this country should also involve not merely the elected members of the council but also the mass of its paid servants has been already put forward by the Trades Union Congress. The fact that this august body has since changed its mind is of no importance, for a proposition that has been under discussion for over two thousand years is bound to have its random ups and downs:

> The TUC, which has already called for half the members of company boards to be elected by worker-representatives, is now moving to the position where it wants half the councillors on local authorities to be elected by workers employed by those authorities, through their trade unions. This radical step would mean that registered voters would elect only half the members of their local councils, and would affect the control of most councils. It has been agreed in principle by the TUC's local government committee which met this week. It is likely to cause even more passionate discussion than the TUC and Labour Party's proposal for supervisory boards to oversee company management, on which half the members should be workers' representatives elected through their trade unions. The argument for a similar fifty–fifty arrangement on councils apparently rests upon a simple principle: that what is demanded for the private sector is appropriate for the public sector – and not simply the nationalized industries. The TUC will almost certainly take a similar line over the new health authorities, seeking the same split between those employed in them at all levels, and outside representatives. (*Guardian*, 5 June 1974)

This is to stand the Book of Ecclesiasticus on its head all right. No longer are those who maintain the city by their trust in their hands nor by the work of their craft to be denied their

235

place in public counsel, their high seat in the congregation nor their understanding of the sentence of judgement. No longer shall the bureaucracy alone appear before princes and be occupied in prophecies. These suggestions of the Labour Party to remove from the bus driver, the gas-fitter and the road-sweeper those brands of inferiority laid upon them by countless generations of scribes (since they are but a special case of promoting worker-representatives to the coalitions of administrative power), seem also to turn the Instruction of Duauf inside out. However this may be, nobody seems yet to have suggested that the same programme of reform should be carried into Parliament itself. What about half the members alone being elected every five years by the historical constituencies and the other half being sent there in some way yet to be worked out by the paid servants of the total parliamentary system, itself still yet to be defined? I do not know the answer to this question, and I do not propose to seek it, for the simple reason that I do not feel the TUC's proposals do other than reinforce the Instruction of Duauf; nor do they help to remove the brands of inferiority from the council workers, after all. Everything that Duauf approves of to ensure that his little boy will watch the others do the hard work; everything Ecclesiasticus has to say about those whose flesh is wasted by the fire as distinct from those whose praise is declared by congregations; everything Aristotle tells us about men of honour engaging in public affairs needing to be distinguished clearly from mechanics and peddlers, those of wretched lives and virtueless businesses; all of this would go on as before, perhaps more pitilessly, if we do no wiser than reinforce the scribes and the directors with the more able and determined of the artisans and labourers.

We must seek the accommodation of scribe and artisan in a new manner if we are to do anything useful about the troubles of New York and of places nearer home. The traditional formula for finding peace when the civil war has actually broken out is by arbitration. The ambassadors of the conflicting parties, watched by those with marginal interests, meet at the negotiating table and engage in precisely those dialectical contests for which the education of the scribes has prepared the Pepis of this world from time immemorial. It was not until 1972 that the miners of Britain tried another tactic; having seen their own gladiators of reason dragged ignominiously around the arena in 1926, the grandchildren grew wise in their own generation and opted for stopping the movement of coke and of oxygen. The schoolteachers tried starving the little children and the lecturers demoralizing their degree candidates; each replied according to their power and to their opportunity. But to what is it, more precisely, that they so effectively reply? Is it the authority of the scribe? Or his self-interest? Or his obstinacy? What is the underlying *cause* of the civil war, as distinct from the manifold *occasions* of its outbreak? These are formidably difficult questions, and they admit of no final answers. Inevitably, they are confused by the ancient hatreds of authority; now that we know what Duauf had to say to Pepi so long ago, who would regard that as surprising? We agree they are confused by the self-interests of a lot of people, especially in a country which appears seriously to believe that the whole world owes it a living. And they must be confused by all who attack their opponents, on whatever grounds. The Earl of Birkenhead himself once remarked after a meeting with the miners' leaders: 'I should call them the stupidest men in England if I had not previously had to deal with the owners.'[12]

But there are other issues apart from those of economic interest and of distributive justice; some of them are set out in earlier chapters and touch upon communications at the point of work. Whether we consider hospitals (Chapter 3), the floor of the factory (Chapters 10 & 11), the foreman's cabin and the manager's office (Chapter 12) or the classrooms of the adolescent (Chapter 13), we find the same result: the most important single influence on relations at the point of work is the quality of open-mindedness. Whenever the persons involved in the collective task, whether studying the theorem of Pythagoras, operating a telephone exchange, healing the sick or protecting the handicapped, making furniture, generating electricity, mining coal, winding armatures or assembling gas-cookers, or whatever other efforts by which they help to create the wealth of the nation, feel free to seek from each other what they may need to know, then those persons seem to be less tormented and perplexed than others elsewhere who believe themselves not to have that freedom. Those who are able to learn by receiving replies to their own questions seem, at least for the moment, more satisfied with what they are doing than those who cannot. Participation is the child, not of power, but of communal need.

There may be more in this self-evident proposition than meets the eye. Learning is a complex social process; like quicksilver spilled on a polished table, it will run all over the shop. An action learning set formed to study five complex problems reveals at an embarrassing velocity the characters of its five constituents, not only to each other, but to their own selves. Those who seek to know their hidden environment through the guidance of their colleagues end by knowing better the darker recesses of their inmost beings. In the same fashion, those who come together on the opposite sides of a negotiating table to test at what point the others may yield and, to achieve this goal, will study every observable detail of their opponents' conduct – not only turning it to advantage during the negotiation in hand, but carefully indexing it for future reference – might also be persuaded to learn something of the externals of what has brought them together. There is more to conflict than conflict itself; causes are not the same as occasions, nor are outcomes less complex than origins. Human sickness, like human conflict, may bring pain and distress, but we must not forget that our expectation of life today is double what it was in the time of William the Conqueror because we have learned by studying the sick. Those who have watched over dying children know that time has no greater sorrow, but from our vigils we have learned to save much infant life. Beyond our dark emotions may glimmer a little light of reason, and humanity has overcome adversity by not being forgetful of it. It is this miraculous gift of learning from experience of which we have so desperate a need today; when the changes that beset us have no parallel in history we should greet our conflicts not merely as the habitual masochistic wallowings in which we are licensed to indulge, but also as opportunities, trivial enough, no doubt, to understand a little more about the world we inhabit. It is an advantage of action learning to offer us such opportunity.

We might take the recent action of the schoolteachers as a starting point from which to approach our inevitable conflicts in a new spirit, namely, as those eager to learn from what is happening to them. There is much about our education system that, after a life's experience of it, I have little difficulty in accepting, but I cannot believe there to be many teachers who feel that depriving children of their midday meals is going to solve many of the problems that afflict the service. Nor can there be many who believe that their display of industrial muscle has, in some way, put the Department of Education and Science in its place or taught its minister a personal lesson, so that now all manner of other questions will speedily be resolved. But all agreements, all negotiations, are between a number of different parties and are called for the resolution of divergent issues or for the accommodation of opposing interests. If the teachers press for more money, the authorities can bring up the need for a better service. I do not imply by this that the only way in which the idea of a better service can be raised with the profession is through the settlement of a dispute; nothing is further from my mind. But it is a fact that when personal interests become involved, the imagination is likely to quicken; issues that would be regarded as insignificant or unworthy (to some) and as overwhelming or unmanageable (to others) assume different and, perhaps, reasonable proportions when introduced at an appropriate hour. I see no reason why negotiations started by one party, the employees, in its own interests, more pay, should not be taken by the other party, the education authorities, to raise such issues as those implied in Fig. 9.

It might be said that such a suggestion is provocative in the extreme, deliberately calculated to inflame what is already a source of conflict. Are not feelings high enough already, forcing the teachers to withhold the service of the children's meals, without throwing into their faces the criticisms implied in that display of observational data? If we need to know why the estimate of teaching ability made by school-leavers of their staff seems to be so closely correlated with their personal liking for them, cannot we pursue the question by 'scientific research'? We can, of course; scientific research is a wonderful thing. But since it is the body of professional teachers who alone can apply the results of it there may be some virtue in getting that body involved as soon as possible. And their involvement (as the New York City findings also suggest) has more than one dimension: it must not only be an intellectualized detachment, but must also draw upon an emotional commitment, or a belief that only the teachers themselves can do the job as it should

239

be done, even although they may need help to do it, or even to start upon it. And, should such a commitment need to be roused within the hearts of these professionals, what better occasion for its arousal than when those same hearts are being searched by their owners? It is a virtue of action learning that, like truth itself, it is a seamless garment; with its help, all parties alike, scribe and artisan, manager and workman, should tackle their common foe, the external problem. Their own opinions of each other, personal and interested, stained by the antipathies of unforgettable tradition, teased and exacerbated by every civilizing process of the educational establishment, reinforced by every decision of our industrial tribunals, are, it may be, pretty intransigent; advance will not be easy.

We occupy a changing world. When Carlos II, king of Spain, died in 1700, a helpless imbecile, he bequeathed his vast empire to the grandson of the king of France, since it was regarded as a piece of personal property to be disposed of as the owner thought fit. It was as if the will of our present Queen now provided that Britain and its remaining possessions should, on her death, pass to a grandchild of Queen Juliana. It was not then at all bizarre in principle; it is our modern ideas about the rights of individuals that have changed so fundamentally. The first serious challenge to this convenient proposition came with the French Revolution; in 1793 the militant democracy of Paris (that might, only a century earlier, have had its ancestors given away to a foreign king by the testament of their own) aroused the governments of Europe by cutting the head off Louis XVI. The progress of popular government in Britain has, since that time, been marked by such legislation as:

(a) *Democratization of franchise*: starting with the Reform Acts of 1832 and 1867, most adults in Britain now have some say in how they are to be represented in the government. The rallying cries are various: Votes for Women; One Man, One Vote; Abolish the House of Lords; Write to Your MP about It; Will *You* allow the trade unions to run the country?; Devolution for the Scots!

(b) *Democratization of local government*: the Municipal Reform Act of 1835 saw the end of the close corporation, run by the 'shabby, mongrel aristocracy'[13] mal-

240

versating public funds for parliamentary electioneering, not seldom by simple bribery. It was followed by local reforms of many kinds, including the County Councils Act of 1888 and the abolition of property qualification for Justices of the Peace in 1907. The very latest move is the recent abolition of the office of alderman.

(c) *Democratization of contract*: the Trade Union Act of 1871 was the first major piece of legislation permitting workers to get together for collective bargaining, and was followed by the Trades Disputes Act of 1906 absolving the unions from having to meet any losses caused to employers by strikes. These moves led, if circuitously, to the Whitley Councils of 1917, in which representatives of the workers were given seats on the bodies that determined the wages of civil servants. Wages councils are now an essential feature of the economy.

(d) *Democratization of ownership*: although some services had long been provided by the government out of public funds, it was not until the nationalization of the mines in 1947 that much of our productive industry was publicly owned. Since then, the mixed economy has, at least in a legal sense, spread the idea of ownership to members of the public not, perhaps, keenly aware of their possessions. It would, nevertheless, have been revolutionary to suggest to the Duke of Marlborough that the suspected coal measures under his new palace at Blenheim were the property, not of his formidable Duchess, but of the people as a whole.

There are, no doubt, those who would see all of the changes implicit in these four streams of legislation as somewhat less than wishy-washy. Taken together, all the same, there is no mistaking a common historical and cultural trend. Universal suffrage, local control, statutory wage agreements and public ownership would have seemed just as outlandish to the Duke of Wellington as they would have done to Aristotle, but they are with us today and can only be particular illustrations of a secular decline in the ancient authoritarianism of emperors and kings, popes and archbishops, princes and aristocrats.

As I understand it, all the talk about industrial democracy, something so long anticipated, so deeply confused and so indefinitely postponed, is merely another stream of evidence. Democratization of the process at the place of work – as distinct from suffrage, control, arbitration and ownership – is being born from these established forms. Its emergence may be hesitating and unaccompanied by the excitements of, let us say, repealing the combination laws: the TUC may say one thing about industrial democracy today and something different tomorrow. But the idea has been carried down to the present just as, in their own time, were the measures set forth above, and precisely in what form, or at what time, it will be seen as having taken root in the economic and social plantations is a question for future historians. Our present need is to understand the trend, not to misinterpret and oppose the course of democratic nature. Only if we recognize from the outset how little we know about getting the scribes and the artisans together, not always to attack each other, but to tackle the substantive troubles of their common world, shall we get away from such troubles as those of New York City.

The four extracts at the head of Chapter 15 suggest that over the past 200 years the quality of life has deteriorated alike for managers and work-people. It seems to be agreed that the bulk of the damage was done in the first fifty years of the period and that there has been no significant success in retrieving the deplorable harm so recklessly contrived. It therefore calls for a saintly optimism to recruit courage enough even to recommend that a fresh trial should be given to such retrieval, and, were it not for a few objective observations that all may confirm, such optimism itself would be denied. These assets of hope are the thesis that, in groups small enough, people seem to spend much less time in conflict than similar people attempting similar tasks but in large groups; the relation between the readiness of men to work and of their managers to listen to them; and the law that supervisors pass on to their work-people the treatment they perceive themselves receiving at the hands of their own superiors.

With this precious arsenal of behavioural insights, the manager who sets out to improve relations in his own command must next identify the nature of the disease that he is to be brave enough to treat, and this, it is certain, cannot be diagnosed by reading the pages of a textbook. Of all approaches action learning is probably the most promising, since it is organic and will not shrink from seeking the part of the manager himself in the total syndrome. Nevertheless, behind all the local, specific and temporary manifestations of discord and inefficiency will loom the shadow of Culture M. To the extent that *The Wealth of Nations* was, as Burke suggested, the most important book ever written, so, to that extent, will the evil it identifies persist. This, we have noticed, is fourfold:

(a) the unimpeded exercise of individual liberty;
(b) the specialization of trades and professions;
(c) the limitless divisibility of working tasks; and
(d) the mechanical pacing of human work.

It is useful to sketch, very briefly, the inheritance of Culture M upon the factory floors of today. If, as I have suggested, our higher education system is not only pervaded by it, but is now the most characteristic expression of Culture M, it is quite unthinkable that the shop-floor should have escaped its influences. I deal with the four factors in the order set out.

What was seen by Adam Smith as the unimpeded exercise of individual liberty must be expressed by the trade unions as their belief in free collective bargaining: while this must necessarily be curtailed so long as the government adhere to any form of wage restraint – indeed, of any national wages policy – the cultural inheritance remains. Seven generations or more being subject to the exercise by others upon one of their own particular blends of individual liberty will not normally be without effect, and any action learning programme that assembled those on whose ancestors such liberty had been exercised would soon identify what useful steps, if any, could now be taken to minimize its less fortunate consequences. If British manufacturing industry is now having to pay the price for whatever past injustices, let us at least make an effort to understand what those shortcomings have been. It is of no use to declare that the past is over and best forgotten; we must be more constructive and trace the disabling consequences of history, and we must recommend courses of conduct or procedure that may help to overcome them. I believe that an invitation to all workers, anywhere in Britain, to contribute to a list of the individual freedoms they would like to exercise would produce some useful ideas. In Japan such contributions have ranged from variable hours of work, through the attachment to each small work group of a handicapped person to remind its members of their own better qualities, to the provision of life-sized and resilient images of the senior management of the enterprise, placed at convenient traffic junctions and well supplied with good quality canes that may, if desired, be taken home after being used to assault one – but, on any occasion, not more than one – of the images. Individual liberty is a manifold thing: the Prussians once held that a citizen possessed it when he was free either to observe or to break the law of the land.

The second element of Culture M is the intensive specialization of trades and professions, and this has really entered into the soul of trade unionism, appearing as the insuppressible sprite of job demarcation. It would be incorrect to attribute all the ills brought down upon the head of humanity by its capricious visitations to the industrial upheavals of the eighteenth century, since we read of men following their special trades in the Book of Genesis; we read of Tubal-cain, 'an instructor of every artificer in brass and iron'. The sagacious 'Let not the cobbler go beyond his last' can be traced back to Pliny the Elder, nineteen centuries ago. Nevertheless, these concentrations upon doing one particular kind of work were to maintain the standards of it rather than to exploit a commercial advantage over the client. The residues of such self-respect still appear pretty intractable, as when the work-study expert sets out to 'de-skill' the factory task, and we must recall that our first action learning programme in Belgium followed the discovery that the managers of Flanders would seek posts in other factories at a lower salary in order more effectively to use their professional qualifications.

The ancient tenacities do not, of course, explain all the intransigence aroused by much innovation: the organizations formed to defend their members against rampant exploitation are now closing ranks to defend themselves and the jobs of those who do the organizing. But if the restrictive influence of Culture M is to be overcome at all, it will be by such activities as action learning projects that form operational teams to study and to treat complex afflictions. We need not think here only in terms of such high-level exchanges as took the logistics analyst of the oil company to think about the long-term policies of the international bank. In the Hospitals Internal Communications Project (see Chapter 3), the porters and the washerwomen joined with the nurses and the doctors to work out how better to serve their patients. It is not, in my view, that the trade unionists will dig in their heels against co-operating with other kinds of workers; my fear is that the administrators in charge of the systems so desperate for better co-operation will ridicule the very idea that the shop floor has anything to contribute, and by their unfavourable reception of action learning drag up all the latent resistances of Culture M.

The third element of Culture M is the limitless division of the task, the 'break-down' of the work-study engineer. It is still in the pink of condition, and has been given a new lease of life by the rise of automation and the computer after two generations of nourishment drawn from the assembly line. There are, naturally enough, counter-movements, particularly in what is called 'Group Technology', evolved largely in Sweden in the last decade, although others (including IBM at their Endicott plant during the Second World War), have long been aware of the difficulty of controlling a flow of work from which all interest has been removed by the simple expedient of calling in the efficiency experts. It is quite unrealistic, however, to imagine that repetition can ever be removed from human work. All we can do is to find means of countering the depressing effects of it, as was attempted by the professor of economics who had to give the same lecture twice every day and who added interest to it in the evening presentation by taking out both sets of his false teeth. Since it is those, the trade unionists, required to do the monotonous tasks who are most likely to suffer the effects of them, it would appear that any action learning programme that, within the same working organism, brought together management, supervision and artificer to tackle some complex production sequence, would help all the parties concerned with it. A set of four or five such exercises conducted in close proximity but with different technologies or products might show us how to counter the more corroding effects of hyper-specialization; better still, whether efforts should be made to be shot of it altogether. It is because action learning is an educational contract between equals, rather than the imposition of expert dogma, that it promises so much to the shop floor. There must be plenty of manufacturing superintendents in British industry who would be glad to have their shop-stewards suggest to them how to eliminate some of their daily troubles with true hope of support from the floor.

The fourth element of Culture M is the machine pacing of human effort, to put up with which has now become one of the main objectives of our higher education system, with its insistent mortgage upon the future expressed as lecture lists, reading assignments, tutorials and examinations, and all set at a rate by authorities far removed from the students. It has become so difficult to vary the speed of this interlocking train of superimposition that the students have virtually given up attempting it, and are now attacking the total system at a more vulnerable point, by demanding that they are awarded a degree whether they clear the last hurdle or not. However this may be, the more apparent consequences of this element of Culture M on the factory floor can be cumulatively disastrous: the speeding up of a system to produce, or intending to produce, an increment of one per cent only may cause a stoppage that costs a week's total production.

There is also evidence that beyond certain critical rates the liability of spoiled work rises sharply. Nobody would suggest that the trade unionists are unable to defend themselves against the unhappier consequences of accelerated work rates. The majority are past-masters at it, drawing the incentive rewards without necessarily increasing the output to correspond with them, or using the new rates in one part of the plant to lever up those in another not immediately affected by the recent agreement. Indeed, an observer external to the scenes of British industry might well ask whether, whatever turmoil and excitement has been brought to the shop floor by the threat of speeding up the work process, there is reliable evidence from the productivity returns that output is rising in proportion; he might even produce returns to suggest that it was in fact steadily falling. It is precisely in such conditions that action learning, again, can prove its value; perhaps the suggestion made above (with reference to the third element of Culture M) – that several sets be established in the same neighbourhood to examine the assumptions of Culture M as they bear upon productivity in the contemporary world – could look at that culture in the round. Certainly the design of a satisfactory consortium would be straightforward enough, using several ranks of employee and several different settings. The trade unions have troubles enough with Culture M not to be indifferent to the suggestion that they could work, across employment grades, across unions and across factories, in a co-operative effort to find out something about those troubles and, perhaps, how to ameliorate them.

This chapter has so far treated of participation as action learning in several fashions that might be argued as 'rational-deductive'. I therefore suggest that an effort is made – initiated perhaps by the Action Learning Trust or by ACAS (Advisory Conciliation and Arbitration Service) – to activate some central register of sick institutions, forming a consortium for the study and treatment, by action learning approaches, of their troubles. Just as doctors do not cure sickness, but merely do what they can to stimulate the natural recuperative powers of the invalid, so experts cannot put sick institutions to rights. They can, of course, close them down, exactly as doctors can bury their patients. There was a time when they could suppress the signs of trouble by, for example, shooting the rioters. But that is no longer possible, since there are too many sick institutions; even those that appear to be free of conflict may live from one year's end to the next on the brink of it.

In the Hospitals Internal Communications Project, it was arranged that small teams, of doctor, nurse and administrator, from one hospital should visit the others in order to identify and suggest for treatment some of the problems of the others. No team claimed to be expert, and all hospitals admitted to internal problems that they would like better to understand. In the sick factories the choice of suitable visiting teams would in itself be an interesting exercise. My own suggestion is that it ought to contain representatives of management, supervision and of the shop floor, chosen, not so much to look into their own difficulties but into those of other factories in the consortium. It would be idle to pretend that such a consortium would be easy to launch. But I believe that, once it were launched, it would be easy to run; the teams from any one sick institution called upon to examine the troubles of another would not find their mission a waste of time. The consortium would need to be defended from the experts with ready-made solutions, all available before any trouble was even notified. It would also need to be encouraged to carry on with its mutual support and criticism long after the visible dispute or crisis had faded from public attention. Such an experiment will be started in some country or another before long, simply because there is no alternative road to understanding. We can close the factory down, we can invoke the law, we can sack the malcontents, just as our fathers and grandfathers have done before us. Action learning now offers us the chance to understand.

PART IV

The five chapters that make up the final part of this book concern themselves with the organization and logistics of action learning. They try to specify the characteristics of managers that are invoked in its programmes, the place in such programmes of the senior managements under whose aegis the action learning is encouraged, the kinds of staff work that are called for and the personal qualifications of the staff called upon to carry out that work. Since there does not yet exist a valid literature of action learning, much of what appears in this part of the book must be taken as no more than a marshalling yard from which to set out on a campaign of rigorously monitored explorations. We really know very little about the learning and development of experienced persons. The concerns of scholars have not been much with the utility of how they spend their own time and that of their charges, but only as to whether or not certain arbitrary propositions that are known to appear in approved books can be reproduced in a variety of dialectical disguises, or detected beneath a variety of verbal camouflage. The very presentation of this book itself as a string of argument and abstraction bears witness to the tenacity of the scholastic tradition, forcing its writer to adopt the very evasion of real time action with real persons engaged in the treatment of real problems that learning-by-doing so persistently denounces. Just as Agesilaus declined to listen to the man who could imitate the nightingale because he had heard the nightingale itself, so there would be few who, having themselves practised action learning, would hope to gain much from reading what is said here. For all that, we need to know what others are thinking and feeling and doing about action learning, and this part of the book may be taken as a pointer to the activities of one person. It should not be seen as more than an attempt to encourage the true pioneers of action learning to learn with and from each other. It cannot be the learning itself.

18.
Managers and how to help them

Am I my brother's keeper? (Gen. ch. 4, v. 9)

In many ways the saying, 'Know thyself' is not well said; it were more practical to say, 'Know other people'. (Menander, *Thrasyleon*, c. 300 BC)

Make it thy business to know thyself, which is the most difficult lesson in the world. (Cervantes, *Don Quixote*, Pt II, Bk IV, ch. 42)

I have never for one instant seen clearly within myself; how then would you have me judge the deeds of others? (Maeterlinck, *Pelleas and Melisande*, Act I, Sc. 3)

The approach of action learning to its mission of helping managers is so simple that it takes any run-of-the-mill professor of management about five years to misunderstand it enough to make conversation at an ordinary meeting of teachers; the big shots, with international reputations to defend, will probably take ten years to attain the orders of confusion expected of those who charge a thousand dollars for a one-day stand. All action learning claims is that, since managers are employed to run businesses, or sections of businesses, or to run non-business organizations, like hospitals or schools or government agencies, or parts of such non-business organizations, they will fulfil their contracts of employment more effectively only by asking how they fulfil them at any particular moment, and by making use of whatever those studies reveal to them. The primary and inescapable obligation of the manager is to run whatever it is he has been appointed to run. Action learning suggests that, since he has to do this in any case, he might just as well find out how he is doing it at the moment and, with what he discovers, try to do it a little better the next day, or next week, or even next year. By asking himself how well things went today, he ought, without great difficulty, to contrive that they go better tomorrow.

All that I believe I have added to this primary piece of simplicity, to turn action learning into the programmes of endeavour set forth in the opening chapters of this book, is what is needed to deal with the questions, 'How can the manager know how well he is doing today?' and 'How can he then contrive to improve upon it?' In each instance, I suggest that he gets the help and advice of a few other managers, all of whom are honestly bent upon the same purpose, namely, to run something better tomorrow by finding out how well or badly they are running it today.

Like all simple ideas, not only is it readily misunderstood by those who claim to be expert in something or other, but it raises controversy in the most unanticipated fields. If, for example, I suggest that learning is manifest by improved performance, then it follows that what has been learned is measured by that improvement. Knowledge that has been acquired is exhibited in what has been done with it; this is why it is called action learning, and why knowledge is the ability to do things and not merely to talk about them, nor even to write books about them.[14] Hence I find myself having to waste a lot of time arguing epistemology with people who do not speak German, for in this formidable language the words for 'to know' and for 'to be able to do' come from the same root: *kennen* and *können*. Hence, too, my central thesis: if I want to help a manager know something, that is, to do something better, I try to help him find out what he is doing now and get him to improve upon it.

Hence it also follows that managers (like everybody else) learn only if they see the purpose of doing so, namely, if they want to learn. We therefore ought to know what it is that stops managers from wanting to learn, and when we begin on this we run into difficulty enough. I had plenty of subjective impressions as to what might discourage managers from learning while I was still at the Coal Board, but it was not until I went to Belgium in 1965 that the opportunity came to start constructing a catalogue of managerial shortcomings. 'What were the peculiar blockages to managerial learning, or the professionally-inspired handicaps to continuous improvement?' It was my good fortune to fall in with a Belgian psychologist, Frederick Musschoot, with whom I worked on an early programme of research and who, some years after our collaboration had closely matured, became a professor of psychology at the University of Ghent. The classification of managerial blockages that follows, and its relevance to the design of action learning programmes, was arranged directly we began to work together and formed a theoretical starting point for all future developments.

The majority of managers, by the age of assuming major responsibility, have lost whatever theoretical interest they might ever have had – perhaps at the university, perhaps elsewhere – in such ideas as marginal costing, queueing theory, cognitive dissonance, linear programming and so forth. Before all else, they remember their outstanding successes and their unhappy failures, which they interpret in accordance with their own scheme of the natural order. No matter how the triumph or the misfortune actually came about, the manager will have his own explanation of it. So convincing is real experience itself – as Pavlov showed with his dogs in conditions far less disturbing than those faced every day by real managers – that, once a manager has worked out to his own satisfaction the causalities of good and evil, it is next to impossible for him to abandon what he thinks is good, even although it will not work again, or for him to give a fresh trial to what was bad in conditions now totally different.

We therefore accepted, as the first occupational weakness of managers that our programmes were to be designed to correct, the idolization of their own past successes, the condemnation of their own previous failures, and their conviction that they knew the final reasons for these particular events to have worked out as they had done. The trait may be identified as a fixation upon the significance, to them, of their more important past experiences.

The second emphatic characteristic of managers that came out of our early content analyses of their conferences and disagreements was the charismatic influence of those who were regarded as successful. The majority of busy managers do not ask that any proposition they are expected to take up can be logically or experimentally proved. They want merely to know whether it has been accepted and used by another manager for whom they have respect. Some researches (of which the results have never been published) conducted by my department at Manchester during the studies of Dr Hussein (see p. 129) had shown some years before that new ideas were taken up by Manchester companies, not on their technical and commercial merits (as these were estimated to be), nor because the money could be got to finance them, nor because the manufacturing capacity was available. These were all taken into account as might appear essential. But the key consideration was simple: 'Was there a senior member of the board of the company who believed in the idea so strongly that he could, by his personal example and his past record of backing successful innovations, convince the others to go for it?' If so, it was unnecessary to push the venture upon any other grounds. 'Does he genuinely believe in the idea?' and 'Do we believe in him?' is all the management science that the typical company board needs to get by with. It is this trait, the influence of charisma, that is exploited in the action learning set. As soon as the fellows have learned to rely upon each other they have learned to listen, and to accept serious criticism of their first trait, the idolization of past success and the condemnation of previous failure.

This second emphatic characteristic carries with it, however, a less amiable satellite. Managers who come strongly under the charismatic influence of their acknowledged idols may tend to despise those who do not appear to be very successful; since their own subordinates, by the very fact of their subordination, have not done as well as they might, their opinions are not accorded as much respect as they may deserve. An inability to listen to what their juniors have to say to them is therefore linked with the charismatic influences of success. The researches of Dr Hussein show how devastating the inability to listen may be, and it has been a central objective of the action learning set to get its members to use all the weapons at their disposal for improving their communications with subordinates at all levels. More than one ex-fellow, now chief executive of an enterprise

254

employing ten thousand workers or more, has testified that the programme made him pay attention to what the junior staffs on his project had to tell him. The mechanism is simplicity itself, for when a senior manager goes to work, as he would in Belgium, in an undertaking with whose business he is unfamiliar, and whose own senior management must confess to not understanding the trouble he is about to investigate, he is at once driven closer and closer to the place of work for his information. Without exception, the time he is obliged to spend satisfying himself that he has got the facts he needs, and that he can interpret them systematically, greatly enhances his respect for the lower orders of supervision. In the Nile Project (see p. 54) the chief engineer of Egypt's largest automobile company found himself, in a study of the vegetable oil industry, having to enquire into the hand-gathering of seeds from low-growing bushes. He discovered, to his astonishment, that an illiterate foreman, whose ideas on sorting the crop he (the engineer) had dismissed as nonsense so arrant as to call for him to spend a day under the blazing sun to disprove in the foreman's presence, was, on the contrary, quite right and was able to give the engineer some fresh thoughts about classifying his own work in progress.

The third disabling predisposition of managers is their impulse to spontaneous action in practically all conditions, and, particularly, when they have the uneasy feeling of being in the presence of something as minatory as it is ill-defined. The majority will gladly attend to the urgencies of the moment, however inconsequential, rather than clear the decks for a sustained attack upon some long-term and defiant trouble. This seems to be the equivalent of Gresham's Law: 'Short-term issues drive out the long.' Thus one encounters the top-level director cheerfully helping somebody two levels down with a job that has to be finished by next morning. I found, early in my days at the Coal Board, an impressive illustration of what can happen if the French chef, as it were, can be persuaded to stop washing the dishes and to sit and think about running the cuisine for the next six months or so. One colliery in a pretty homogeneous sample of seventeen from the same administrative area, whose weekly accident returns I was carefully following after the start of a safety campaign in which all were participating, suddenly took a remarkable turn for the better. Closer study showed that output had also begun to improve at about the same time; both records, of production and of safety, continued to show improvements and after several months readings enough were at hand to show the trend to be highly significant. Letters of enquiry sent from London received no reply. This did not surprise me, since most colliery managers had enough to do without having to reply to non-operational questions posed by bureaucrats two hundred miles away or more. Nevertheless, the figures were so significant that I decided to call at the colliery itself when next in the coal-field. When I did so, I found that the manager, in the very month before the returns had started to demonstrate their sustained and favourable turn, had been afflicted with a painful onslaught of arthritis and was virtually unable to go underground; the Coal Mines Act still required that he did so, but his visits were no longer what they once had been. He was now obliged to sit in his office and receive the reports of his under-officials, who now met as a team and, by their collective presence, made it impossible for him to give the first instruction to enter his head, but rather obliged him to reflect upon what he thought he was doing, and to consult a number of other persons in the act of getting it done. Probably for the first time in its eighty years of life, that pit was not being run on the immemorial principles of 'management by jerks'.

An action learning programme should thus be designed around these characteristics of the manager, negative although they may be. To those who then object that we are building on weakness rather than on strength we can only reply that this, too, is the settled policy of the medical profession – to treat the sick rather than the healthy. It is sometimes forgotten that science has its roots in the examination of things that go wrong. Thus, instead of paralysing the natural curiosity of our participants in the fetters of some high-flown syllabus, action learning obliges each to look critically at his own past experience, dragging it out for the inspection of his colleagues; whatever the project, his next moves, whether diagnostic, prescriptive or therapeutic, should be so debated with his fellows that his first perceptions of his own past are constantly and inexorably under review. Since the others may be anxious to exploit his own suggestions about what to do next, or his own explanations of what happened last, to advance their own projects, he will constantly be called upon to explain why he is following the course of action he has chosen. From time to time every participant will come to a halt; either he will run out of ideas or find himself obstructed within his receiving enterprise, and such checks will oblige him to listen with a new intensity to his colleagues. In such experiences he will become painfully aware of the magnitude of the task that he has undertaken, but will also see that the only persons who can help him are his colleagues, those comrades in adversity who also look to him for help; in consequence, all learn not only to listen, but to listen to criticism about themselves. When this reinforces the weekly reviews of what has actually happened on the job as compared with what was expected to happen two or three weeks back, or how present hope is translated into future outcome, the fellows may start to reflect in the long-term as well as to be carried away by the impulse of the moment. And, finally, the continuous cross-examination by the other fellows forces each of them to verify his facts and to justify his proposals; in both of these he is soon driven to admit his dependence upon his subordinates, particularly if he is working on a project in his own enterprise.

Thus the disabling characteristics of managers are made the social chemistry of the action learning set. It follows that any supporting studies to speed the interactions must then suggest themselves. The joint confrontations with reality on the job and with deeply-involved colleagues in the set offer scope for the psychology of perception and of personality structure, such as to explore attitudes to authority, senses of security and armouries of defence mechanisms. The movement away from charismatic adoration to self-dependence and the appreciation of subordinates enables the fellows to explore the psychology of interpersonal influence. The cooling zephyrs of reflectiveness, brought to still the fevered calls of 'Action now!', may be supplemented by some light reading in the theory of systems, so that, the occasion requiring it, the manager can begin to link in one conceptual scheme the operational observables that might previously have been seen as independent, or even arbitrary. Such intellectual back-up should be offered only when it is asked for, but if it is not asked for something is amiss with the set discussions, perhaps with the set adviser, if one is still employed after the fellows have learned for themselves the cleansing exercises of honest self-disclosure.

19.
Climates at the Summit

To resist him that is set in authority is evil. (The Instruction of Ptahhotep, *c.* 2675 BC)

Oft hath even a whole city reaped the evil fruit of a bad man. (Hesiod, *Work and Days, c.* 700 BC)

As the judge of the people is himself, so are his officers; and what manner of man the ruler of the city is, so are all they who inhabit therein. (Ecclesiasticus ch. 10, v. 2)

Where there is no vision the people perish. (Prov. ch. 29, v. 18)

How shall I be able to rule over others, that have not full power and command over myself? (Rabelais, *Works*, Bk I, ch. 52)

Life always gets harder towards the summit – the cold increases, responsibility increases. (Nietzsche, *The Anti-Christ*, Aphorism 57)

There is a tale about a man considering a challenge, whether he would be able to walk a hundred paces with his severed head carried under his arm. No conditions were specified as to which arm, nor would he have been disqualified had he shifted the load from one arm to the other, since heads are quite heavy things to carry a hundred yards or so. Having consulted the management scientists, he decided that, so long as he could take the first step without dropping his burden, he might win the bet. Those who think about getting an action learning programme under way arrive at the same conclusion; if only they can get started the programme will then run on its own. We notice, for example, that Roy Gilbert has this to say (see p. 88) about the Public Service Board's efforts in Australia. Further examination of the point reveals that, of all the influences determining whether or not any programme will ever start, the first is the belief of its organizer that action learning will work, but the second is the willingness of the top management to try it out. If we suppose that one or two brave souls who have already proved to themselves, like Roy Gilbert, that action learning does work are as a result willing to campaign in the cause of its diffusion, then the first step that will perplex them is the convincing of the power structures. It seems very heavy going to persuade the normal top management that its staff are capable of learning with and from each other when allowed a free hand to tackle what appear to be obstinate and, not seldom, insoluble problems. The tycoon, like the professor, does not often so respect the integrity of subordinates that he is willing to allow that they may succeed where their superiors have so far failed. The effect is, of course, one of the established truths of antiquity, that the organization takes upon itself the qualities of its leadership: adventurous bosses attract adventurous followers, and the pusillanimous leader magnifies timidity. Our reliable authority, the Book of Ecclesiasticus, offers fresh support: 'As the judge of the people is himself, so are his officers; and what manner of man the ruler of the city is, so are all they who inhabit therein' (Ecclesiasticus ch. 10, v. 2).

The present book, too, has its evidence to suggest that those in charge set an example to their employees. In recounting, for example, what went on in my time at the Coal Board, I draw attention to the astonishing influence of Sir Hubert Houldsworth, even if the final source of our astonishment is the neglect of his teachings by those who inherited his office (see p. 110); the work of Dr Hussein (see p. 137) and that of Dr Sikka (p. 154). These examples demonstrate how the morale of the supervisors and of the work-people is linked to the willingness, or even the ability, of their bosses to listen to what is being said to them. There is a vast and popular mythology about the charisma of leadership, with illustrations from the Book of Proverbs (ch. 29, v. 12 & v. 18):

If a ruler hearken to lies, all his servants are wicked.
Where there is no vision, the people perish.

to the songs of the Victorian music-hall:

When Father turns, we all turn . . .

and the popular sayings of today, such as that fish always goes rotten from the head, or that in cleaning a staircase one ought always to start sweeping at the top, or that the bottleneck is always at the top of the bottle, or that there are no bad soldiers but only bad officers. Given so enduring a myth – and it has come up during the development of action learning as the Principle of Insufficient Mandate (see p. 137) – it is natural that we should have tried to specify as closely as our pioneering gracelessness will permit just what may be the disabling effects of top management upon the success of action learning or even, perhaps, upon its survival. In what follows I draw upon the doctoral studies of Thomas Joh, a Korean at the University of Brussels who spent several years tracing the consequences of forty projects carried out between 1969 and 1975. Those interested in the methodology elaborated by Dr Joh are referred to his original thesis;[15] it is important to add that Dr Joh was in no way associated with the programme, and his doctoral supervisor was the professor in another school quite independent of the Fondation Industrie-Université by whom the programme was promoted in the first place.

All the enterprises studied by Dr Joh joined the Inter-University Programme of their own volition, offered a strategic problem for treatment by a fellow from another enterprise and offered their own fellow to work elsewhere in the consortium. One might therefore suggest that, at least immediately following the kick-off, all the top managements who had had to decide whether or not to participate were inspired by the same benevolent curiosity; the coalitions of power in charge of major firms do not offer their vitals for examination by apparent strangers as an amiable or careless flourish. Bravado, or even defiance, perhaps, but indifference, or even frivolity, certainly not: life at the summit is a serious, or even desperate, business, like the struggle of Prometheus to bring mankind, against every pain and adversity, the benefactions of art and technology. The research shows that, while so noble an image smiles upon the faces of some directorates, there are also those of whom one's first impression is different; Dr Joh presents a twelvefold classification of summit attitudes, and the objection that, to be able to identify so many shades of variety in so small a sample must throw doubt upon the discriminating criteria, may readily be met by collapsing some of the twelve into larger sub-groups that then face each other in sharpest contrast. The twelve set forth in the thesis are (in English translation):

(i) *Carte blanche confidence*
Top management, from the outset, manifest complete confidence in the programme and in the approach of their visiting fellow; they are personally and collectively anxious to work out their own roles in the preparation of the exercise, notably by reviewing several possible topics of investigation before nominating to the consortium as a whole the problem they have selected, and then by making known throughout their own enterprise their personal support for what is to be done, and their willingness to be engaged in its detailed progress. They are fully aware that their visiting fellow enters as a learner, not as an expert or technical adviser, and that his project, while manifestly a learning experience for him, is also one for his host enterprise, including its top management. They do not conceal from the fellow their belief that he is trying to do what may be a most difficult task, and will, from time to time, invite him to confidential discussions about how he sees the top managers themselves as an effective team.

(ii) *Active co-operation*
Top management are open and receptive, rather like those in (i) above, but do not see themselves as learners in the same spirit as their visiting fellow is a learner; they will go out of their way to ensure that the visitor is given all the support and encouragement that he needs to get on smoothly, including advice about securing the goodwill of their own colleagues and heads of departments.

(iii) *Encouraging attentiveness*
Top management are no longer actively forthcoming but will always do their best to meet requests from the visiting fellow for their support; they generally reveal that they understand how the visitor is getting on, but seem to suggest little to the fellow in their discussions with

him that he did not know before; they manifest a paternal detachment and seem concerned not to be perceived by their key subordinates as now trying to make the running in the project as a whole.

(iv) *Circumspect alliance*

While continuing to meet specified requests for help from their visiting fellow, top management give him the unmistakable impression that they are not, and will not necessarily be, committed to any particular line of action that may suggest itself as the investigation unfolds; they withhold illuminative comment and suggest no initiative even when, to the fellow, the iron has now become sufficiently hot for effective striking.

(v) *Non-hostile scepticism*

The attitude of the top management is now even less encouraging than in (iv) above; they demand that the suggestions of the visiting fellow should have the endorsement of the subordinate staff of the enterprise, backed by evidence that, were top management unlikely to withhold their consent to what is proposed, the changes would be sure to succeed; there is, in short, no evidence whatever that the top management are willing to take any risk, however small, nor that they have any ideas of their own they would like to try out.

(vi) *Lack of interest*

Top management give their visitor no attention and he may have difficulty even in making an appointment to introduce himself to his very client, so that he is led to ask himself from the first day why the enterprise has participated in the programme at all; this response of the power structure is of continuing interest to the other members of the set to which the fellow belongs, and enables him to persist in his apparently fruitless mission purely on account of its appeal to students of management ritual. There seems to be an atavistic reassurance that *merely to be in the programme* will drive off the embarrassment offered to the fellow for investigation; alternative manifestations of the same ritual protection are in paying consultants to write reports about the problem with no intent to act upon them, purchasing books about the subject that are both incomprehensible and never opened, and sending staff to management courses from which they return in frustrated bewilderment. Top managers have nevertheless done *something* in all such cases to assuage their troubled consciences, like sinners at the confessional or even like Mr Henry Ford leaving an ambiguously acquired fortune to advance the understanding of human happiness; what may therefore seem at first sight to be exactly what Dr Joh has called it – lack of interest – may be of greater potential interest to the student of anthropology than any of the five more positive categories that are set out above to precede it.

The six orders of top management responses identified by Dr Joh so far seem to follow a linear scale of descending manifest involvement, from extreme personal concern to total collective indifference. The remaining six orders are rather more miscellaneous, but seem to differ from the first six in the matter of *predisposition*: top managements have their own ideas before the fellow starts to make an independent assessment of what may be called for, and these predisposing ideas may lead to a manner of cold war between the fellow and his hosts. It would be totally unrealistic to imagine that real managers offering real problems to be examined in real time by real fellows would not introduce such predisposition, and I believe that, if there is ever to be a science or even an art of management, it will be delineated only by managers themselves taking on projects in the difficult climates identified first by Dr Joh's researches as the following six:

(vii) *Directive autocracy*
Top management unequivocally regard the fellow as an expert executive hired to them under a commercial agreement to put into effect their own unilateral decisions; they simply refuse to consider any fresh or contradictory evidence emerging from the enquiries made by their fellow, and may go so far as to require all communication with him to be conducted in writing.

(viii) *Diagnostic inflexibility*
While not, perhaps, regarding their fellow as a hired expert subject to their detailed instructions, top management nevertheless persist in refusing to consider that the original formulation of their problem might be misconceived, or that it is so much bound up with other afflictions of the enterprise that it cannot be investigated

on its own. While top management may not have made up their minds in advance as to the solution they want implemented, they are convinced as to the statement of the problem, and yet mistakenly so.

(ix) *Manipulative guidance*

Top management have their own preconceived solution to the problem (and it may be both effective and intelligent) and they seek to insinuate it into their enterprise so as to maintain the goodwill of their fellow; their concern is to maintain his co-operativeness while employing him as their instrument of innovation for changes that might have had a rough reception without his 'scientific' lubrication; while the fellow may be denied much practice in the skills of diagnosis he will receive much instruction in the guiles of micro-politics, so long as he does not encourage himself to believe – as his receiving top management will encourage him to do – that the success of the project is due entirely to his rapid grasp of what was wrong and what he ought to get done about it.

(x) *Tactical procrastination*

Top management give the impression of for ever wanting to gain time; they examine with elaborate argument and in labyrinthine detail each new turn of the project, motivated, apparently, by either or both of the following: the fear that any action that might be taken as a consequence of the project might irretrievably wreck some existing balance of power within the enterprise; or the hope that their visiting fellow, by continually being headed off such-and-such lines of enquiry, might one day, by the deliberate contrivance of a foreseen accident, hit upon the desired solution already agreed but not disclosed by top management within themselves. The lessons of micro-politics so instructive in (ix) immediately above are also to be learned from tactical procrastination.

(xi) *Evasion and vacillation*

While apparently not opposed to discussing superficial details and even ready to make minor amendments to current practices, top management systematically avoid any investigation of the deeper and more contentious problems of their enterprise; they are particularly unwilling to entertain any suggestion that the project itself is merely an expression of a need to review long-term

or strategic objectives. Such attitudes are often characteristic of regimes that are coming to an end and when,
for the sake of ordinary decency, the patient should be
allowed to pass peacefully away.

(xii) *Defensive rationalization*
This is the active form of (vi) above, *lack of interest*;
top management now seek to explain away, by whatsoever argument may occur to them – including any inconsistent among themselves – each element of any
diagnosis made by the fellow and each fact brought up
by him in support of that diagnosis, and every such
piece of special refutation may seem quite plausible
taken entirely alone; they will not, however, face the
responsibility of asking whether, taken as a whole and
despite the writing-off of details, the total evidence does
not suggest effects calling for attention. The inconsist-
ency of top-management responses is not only a further
lesson in micro-politics for the visiting fellow (and for
his set), but offers insights into top management defensiveness; a dawning admission that perhaps the problems lie within the coalition of power itself may first
manifest itself in such slippery efforts to explain the facts
other than as they may be.

It is not pretended that any of these responses of top managements to the unaccustomed probings of another manager
illustrate any propositions not already well understood in the
literature of psychology. The majority of persons do not find it
easy to accept bad news, such as that they are not doing what
it is their settled intention to do, nor even what they think they
are doing. Those occupying the two sides of some precarious
balance of power do not want it upset if they are told that there
may be more than one new rallying point from which to choose.
The sincere idolization of one's own past success and the haunt-
ing apprehension of one's own previous failure, whereby the
vision of today's truth is seen always through the mists of
yesterday's ghost, make learning and change alike equally improbable. The mounting challenge posed by the work of the
fellow is invigorating up to such-and-such a point, since it can
be met, but threatening thereafter, since it calls for new and
disturbing approaches. The project shows that, while there is
without doubt a serious problem at the heart of the enterprise,

it is by no means what it was imagined to be when the top management resolved to have it looked into, and those who imagined that the fault would be pinned on others now find themselves holding up the joker for everybody else to see. These truths so familiar to the student of human frailty are exemplified over and over again in the responses of top managers to the diagnosis of their torments; any one of them can checkmate the endeavours of the fellow to bring them sustenance.

As we begin, alike with the rough-and-ready wisdom of the sets and with the refined analysis of such as Dr Joh, to understand better the resistances and the necessities of those in power, perhaps we shall be able to diffuse more effectively the benefits of action learning among them. Perhaps the work of Alan Lawlor and the Institution of Works Managers, in which the managing directors and chief executives of the participating companies are also forming their regular sets, will help us to see a way forward (see p. 66).

20.
The Vocabulary of Managerial Confrontation

Knowledge is of two kinds. We know a subject ourselves, or we know where we can find information upon it. (Boswell's *Life of Johnson*, 18 April, 1775)

My enterprise takes only calculated risks; the manager sounds the fire alarm with one hand and posts the insurance money with the other. (Fellow in Belgian Inter-University Programme, 1967–8)

The Platonic idea of value was not only the most elusive in the whole programme; it was also, in the end, seen as the most important. Few were able to define what they believed in at the outset, and those who did all changed their minds before the end; some agreed they believed in something but were not sure what it was; others said they believed in whatever was useful at the time; the remainder found the concept of value as very confusing in itself. (Report on Belgian Inter-University Programme, 1967–8)

If I expect Y to happen after I have done X, but what actually happens is Z, then the difference between Y and Z is my ignorance of the system. (Translated from the French of Philippe Verset, Fellow in Belgian Inter-University Programme, 1967–8)

The only means of strengthening one's intellect is to make up one's mind about nothing – to let the mind be a thoroughfare for all thoughts. (Keats, letter to George and Georgiana Keats, 1819)

> *. . . but the full sum of me*
> *Is sum of nothing: which, to term in gross,*
> *Is an unlesson'd girl, unschool'd, unpractis'd;*

269

Happy in this, she is not yet so old
But she may learn; happier than this,
She is not bred so dull but she can learn;
Happiest of all is that her gentle spirit
Commits itself to yours to be directed . . .
(Shakespeare, *Merchant of Venice*, Act III, Sc. II)

In Chapter 11 I describe how Dr Hussein listened to several hundred shop-floor workers in and around Manchester tell him what they thought about life in their factories. When what they had to say was classified, Dr Hussein found that most of it could be sorted under thirty-four different (or apparently different) headings. These thirty-four classes can then be used for quite specific ends, such as to find out what are the things that managers in such factories ought to be doing to attract more favourable attitudes among their workers. The research method has been used in other contexts, and one of the more interesting is in classifying what the fellows have to say to each other in their sets. There are conditions in which these can be fully recorded and their contents sorted at leisure. It should be a principal objective of our research policies to discover how it is that senior managers learn with and from each other as they tackle obscure and difficult problems, but so far I have been so occupied in getting action learning programmes set up that I have not been able to give these questions the attention they deserve.

Since, however, the most important feature of action learning for me is that I should continue to learn how more effectively to encourage it, I must be able to introduce the ideas of action learning through channels of communication that are open to me. Most managers have already attended some kind of seminar, and demand of me from the first contact an exposition of my syllabus; professors, on the whole, go further by asking, not only for the syllabus, but for a sight of past examination papers. It is always hard to explain that I have neither. After an interlude of confusion (that can be most encouraging as it changes into ridicule and opposition), I usually find it constructive to talk about previous programmes, giving specific details about what the participants achieved in their projects. The discussion invariably turns to the achievements of the fellows in their sets: 'What do they say to each other? What concepts do they employ to exchange ideas and impressions, or to decide when it is time to dispute what somebody else is trying to say? If, as the programme pretends, the members of the set are to offer each other criticism, advice and support, in what terms is any of this communicated? And since, moreover, the set will be together week after week, by what criteria can they help each other to see if they are making progress towards some recognizable goal?'

The answers that I shall give to these questions have been found in much the same way as Dr Hussein first identified the thirty-four topics that he used later in a rigorous factor analysis of shop-floor attitudes, except that they remain largely the fruits of my own subjective judgement. I have listened to many hundreds of hours of set discussions, many of them over and over again as tape recordings, and I have followed the progress of several sets over the entire course of eight months during which they regularly came together. As a result of this, I have attempted to make a two-way analysis of the contents of the discussions within the sets and about the projects. The first dimension tries to identify the concepts that the fellows seem to use in communicating with each other, and the second tries to write some kind of sequence into their progress, as they move from initial bewilderment to final mastery. With the enforced modesty of a pioneer I have kept the categories in each dimension down to half-a-dozen, and shall cheerfully accept any future correction to my artless taxonomy that can be shown by empirical studies to be called for.

I start by listing my six concepts, which, in some form or another, I have recognized from the days of the Hospitals Internal Communications Project. They are

(i)   the nature of information;
(ii) the nature of risk;
(iii) the significance of values;
(iv) the qualities of a system;
(v)   the synthesis of a decision; and
(vi) the learning process.

In so far as I might need to defend the transactions within an action learning set as lending themselves to a classification useful to those trying to exploit those transactions on behalf of managers striving to help each other with their problems, I would suggest these six concepts as the first items in that classification. Each of them admits of the most elaborate intellectual treatment; all command an extensive literature, alike descriptive and theoretical, which I do not intend to quote from here. Indeed, I can think of few ways more likely to suppress the hesitating enthusiasm of the recently-enrolled fellow for the practical task that lies ahead of him than to threaten him with a course of lectures in each of the six concepts as the necessary preliminaries to embarking upon his action learning project. My intention here is briefly to illustrate how any set-discussion (whether consciously aware of it or not) must constantly evoke all of the six concepts.

The working material of managers is information, just as wood is the medium of the carpenter. The value of a message to a manager is the amount of information in it; if the message is of no value to him, it has no information for him, although it might be full of facts or data. Consider the message 'Today's Derby Winner, Brown Charlie'; if the race is to be run at 15.00 and the manager gets it at 12.00, it is of very great value to him and so is full of information. Exactly the same message at 18.00 is of no value at all, although the facts or data are the same. (We go into the question of the *reliability* of the message lower down, when discussing the nature of risk.) Thus, it is important that managers do not mistake data for information. They must be clear what they need the messages for, in the first place, because merely collecting facts or reading reports is often a waste of time. One virtue of an action learning set is its impartial mutual criticism. Fellows continually question the approaches of their colleagues, pressing each other to define what they are searching for and whether what they are collecting is really of value in identifying their problem or its treatment. In addition to discriminating between useful and useless messages, fellows also help each other to recognize reliable sources of information. In particular, they can be of great comfort to each other as they progressively discover that the senior managers with whom they work often know very little indeed about what really goes on in their commands. As time elapses, the fellows in the set learn to distinguish between many shades in the spectrum of epistemology: information, data, hearsay, rumour, mythology, personal opinion, hallucination, distortion, omission, calculated misrepresentation, public relations, advertising copy, official statistics and so forth. An action learning project, suggesting broad goals for achievement, carried forward on periodic set-discussions, is an admirable instrument for helping the fellow to separate the useful message from the useless; as with the other five concepts, the set should be encouraged from time to time to dwell upon particularly illuminating instances, that arise at first hand, of speciously attractive messages that turn out misleadingly false and of dismally unexciting circulars that are later revealed to contain the clue to some spectacular breakthrough. No discussion on the utility of the messages to be picked up in one's work environment can ever be wasted time, particularly among an action learning set trying to understand its working material.

This brief discussion of information as the value of the message at once enables us to identify the nature of risk. Fellows are constantly trying to define what they are trying to do, what is now stopping them from doing it, and what they are able to do about it. For all three of these they need information, which they secure through the messages they generate or intercept. But quite often they see that the information they can actually get is less than what they need; they do not always see that the difference between these two measures has to be filled in by guesswork, or by taking a risk. The difference between what one knows about something and what one ought to know in order to take useful action about it is a measure of the risk that one accepts – or needs to accept. Our message 'Today's Derby Winner, Brown Charlie' might *if true* and to hand three hours before the race be all one needs to solve one's problem of making something for nothing. But if the truth-content is dubious (because it comes from a source that is right in its forecasts only five times out of ten) then one must take a risk if one chooses to base one's decision on it. The recognition of this immediately leads from the value of messages (information) to the value of information: 'What is it worth to take the trouble of finding a little more information, if that cuts down the risk because it brings what is known closer to what ought to be known?' But getting more information may not only cost money; it also consumes time, and there is a deadline after which the bookmaker will not take the bet. Risk is a most fertile topic for discussion in any action learning set; it not only lends colour to the arguments about the nature of information, but can lead into clarifying revelations on what the different fellows find surprising. Whenever, in his periodical accounts of how his project is going, a participant discloses to the set that something has occurred to surprise him, he should be pressed to explain what it was, and why it was found so different from what he had expected. Surprise, or the difference between what was anticipated and what took place, is always an indicator of concealed risk; fellows should always let the rest of the set share all the surprises that turn up.

It was agreed, at the end of the first Inter-University Programme in Belgium, that the single concept that had seemed to the fellows of the greatest importance was that of value, in the sense of those personal preferences that determine, or tend to determine, human behaviour irrespective of the accidents of the environment, or of the period. There is in all persons a set of predilections, called here a value system, that seems to endure from one task to another, even although it has been conditioned by previous experience to have become what it now appears to be. Action learning sets need make little effort to generate abrasiveness; fellows will disagree with each other over all manner of everyday work, but, as the facts are better understood or more accurately featured in the discussion, such discord will recede. But when, without being aware of it, different fellows, whether by inheritance, upbringing, education and experience manifest different codes of choice or of conduct when all appear to be in the same circumstances, they may spend long in manoeuvring round each other in what appears to them all a singularly fruitless and exasperating fashion. When these residual differences can be traced to different personal value systems, the set may be on the verge of a great enlightenment. There is little doubt that the complex 'atmosphere' of the typical board-room in which the Belgian fellows spent so much of their time is determined by the value systems of its directors, and to grasp the micro-politics of the board-room one must first grasp its value systems. While it might be rash for any fellow to try debating with those in his field project the significance of their value systems to the fortunes of their enterprise, all the participants in the same set should try frequently to help each other examine their own. It is an unhappy truth that one sees in complex and threatening conditions – such as being a fellow in an action learning programme – only what one wants to see. What one wants to see, moreover, is strongly determined by one's value system, and it is no bad thing to enlist the help of dependent mates sometimes to put one right upon what that system might be. It may be worth recalling here that the single question voted by the fellows of the first Belgian programme to have given them most to reflect upon was: 'What is an honest man, and what need I do to become one?' This has quite a lot to do with the significance of value systems.

It may appear at first a little supererogatory to dwell in any preparation for action learning upon the qualities of systems, since the one characteristic that most distinguishes practice from theory, action from talk about action, achievement from intention, is the multi-dimensional nature of getting things done against the essentially simple specification of what those things are to be. Since *doing* necessarily follows *intending* it is in the future, and none can tell what the future will bring forth; reality, moreover, has a nasty knack of not fully making itself known to those who would change it. Hence, the wise man, trying to match the outcome of his actions as closely as possible to his desire for them, shows no less interest in what he *cannot* see under his nose than in what he can; he therefore asks of what wider system the visible aspects of his field of adventure form part. Behind all that is observable and that so excites the clever man already familiar with it lie countless recondite causalities. The theorist may hope to ignore them, to ensure the fuller and more elegant elaboration of his model, but they are still there when the man of practice tries to change the totality in real space and real time. It is an advantage of action learning that, not only has the fellow to put up with the contemptuous indifference of Nature herself to his incomplete preparations for changing her, but also that the others in his set want to dwell upon those shortcomings in order to understand better their own.

The reports, criticisms, encouragements and general cross-fire of an action learning set, with its transitory alliances and oppositions, are always the preliminaries to some member or another marshalling his resources to get something done: it is time for a decision – in action learning it is *always* time for a decision, for all discussion about what one is in the set for brings its increment to resolution. The first idea that the participants come across is that so common in the petroleum industry: upstream and downstream, acquisition and disposal, production and marketing, which, in action learning, become seeing it and doing it. A decision has to be *designed* and then *negotiated*; the problem or the opportunity has first to be *diagnosed* and then *treated*, with an ephemeral *prescription* in between. All our work suggests that the guile of realistic diagnosis – 'What are we after? What stops us? What can we do?' – demands just less than 50 per cent of our total effort, and the artfulness of effective negotiation – 'Who knows? Who cares? Who can?' – most of the remainder. Hitting upon the right prescription once the job has been properly sized up and the micro-political resources of the chessboard judiciously recruited is a piece of cake; it not only suggests itself, but will be offered to the fellow by the management of the enterprise in which he pursues his project.

The frustrations and the joys of the participants at their set meetings will be in direct proportion to the progress they are making in the real world with whatever messages they are getting in response to the six questions of design and negotiation: 'What are we after?' asks the fellow of his client and of his receiving management, and if he questions ten of them he will get ten different answers the first time, with another ten altogether the next. His melancholy and wandering account of this interrogatory hotch-potch will be received by his fellows with transports of ecstasy, for they have been baptized in even worse confusions, and, at this point, all are ready to seek from the others the moral support and the intellectual guidance needed to weather the crisis. To be able to confess, to others in the same predicament, that one had never before clearly thought through the central obligation of one's professional task – 'How do I set about knowing what we ought to be doing?' – will cleanse the ego of so much guilt and self-deception that Satan himself might well shed tears over what is left behind when the set breaks up. Nor is this all. An action learning project, with its relentless demands, week in, week out, for the fellows not only to work on their decision scaffolds at the job but to come together and examine the solidity of each others' progress, strips away the shoddy disguise of make-believe.

I do not say that action learning will contribute much to the literature of mathematical decision theory; I do not believe that it needs to. But I am quite clear that, in bringing home to managers their central responsibility of organizing the improved use of the resources at their disposal, there is nothing to approach an action learning set assembled round the treatment of real problems by real persons in real time. No wonder that one of the fellows in the first Belgian programme observed: 'At last I understand why Henry Moore makes his people have holes through them. I feel just like that when the set forces me to tell them about my decisions.'

Finally, the concept of learning: that one cannot change the system of which one is in command (at least in any new sense) unless one is oneself also changed in the process, since the logical structure of both changes are in correspondence. The change in the system we call action; that in the self we call learning, so that learning to act effectively is also learning how to learn effectively. The project experiences and the set interactions provide encouragement enough for both; this should lead the participants to study the elementary literature of learning, from which they should soon get confirmation of what may already be dawning upon them: that learning consists much more in the reorganization of what was already familiar (even if not thoroughly understood in the sense of being operationally applicable) than it consists in acquiring fresh knowledge altogether.

When one member of an action learning set begins to reveal to the others that he persists with some wrong-headed interpretation of his lack of progress, they may become very impatient with him (for the good and simple reason that he may also be impeding their own advance) and a spontaneous discussion of his perversities may break out. All manner of darknesses may then become suffused. It is not that the culprit is lacking the *nous* to put the questions nor to understand the answers; he simply does not want to believe what is so self-evident even although, as much as anybody else in the set, he can identify the truth that it proclaims. Action learning sets do not pretend to offer psychotherapy as such, but when, by their routine monitoring of progress, some members begin to suspect that among them there is one who persists in the same misinterpretation of his own evidences, what may then be set in train can often be described as good quality home-spun psychiatry, the first moves in setting up a cottage industry for straightening out amateur psychopaths. Its great value is the utterly altruistic nature of the concern that the fellows have for each others' blockages of this kind; the very term, 'bloquage', although admittedly not very good French, became one of the in-words of the first Belgian programme, and the fellows still enquire of each other, in a most civil fashion, as to any embarrassment theirs may be causing, just as the upper classes would discuss their servants or a bench of aldermen their piles, in the days gone by.

These, then, are the six concepts that form so much of the supporting framework of set discussion; they become to the participants so vivid, so distinct in the endless to-and-fro of debate that the fellows may safely be encouraged to enrich their direct experience of them by collateral reading, or even, when they have the time, to attend formal lectures about them. What the action learning programme does is to establish the relevance of these disingenuously appealing ideas, at one moment appearing so simple and at the next so hopelessly complex. Perhaps in time we shall discover that there are still better points of argumentational reference, so demonstrating the learning processes going on within action learning itself.

The second dimension of our vocabulary of managerial confrontation suggests the time sequence that any successful project might follow, as the set moves down its individual tracks from opening in confusion to winding up in confidence. Again, I cannot claim to have made the factor analysis of the observable behaviour of the sets which might enable me to assert with confidence that the phases suggested in the timetable bear sufficient correspondence with reality for an emphasis upon them to be useful to prospective fellows. They may, indeed, be artefacts of the design of programme that was first adopted in Belgium, and, since that design was chiefly settled upon in order to persuade the businessmen to come into it, my taxonomy of progress may be worse than specious; until, however, it had been replaced by another based upon some form of sequential analysis, I shall continue to use it as a guide to suggest the critical stages through which the projects must all develop, or, in the French term, 'unroll'.

I again identify six successive periods. To what extent they overlap (or, in the manner of a fishing rod, fit into each other) seems to me impossible to determine. All I can be sure of is that they are a useful guide to the fellows as they desperately struggle to conserve the time that yet remains to them, so that, if their correspondence with the field operations is slight, their effect on spurring the set to achievement can be demonic. Particularly in exchange programmes, when the fellows may feel the necessity of rising to a challenge as interesting as it is formidable, they recognize that their time is the most precious asset, calling for a budget to account for every hour. However this may be, they still find useful the early structure that I subjectively observed in the Belgian programme, a diagnostic phase of three months, followed by a therapeutic of the same length, preceded as a total exercise by an induction phase and interrupted halfway through by a visit overseas (for no purpose other than to discuss with interested strangers the contents of their diagnoses).

The original phases of diagnosis and therapy have been elaborated, each into three, and the six are now identified:

(a) analysis, to choose the main questions needing exploration;
(b) development, to find some paper answers to these questions;
(c) procurement, to get the means of filling these answers;
(d) assembly, to marshal these means into an organic whole;
(e) application, to bring this organism to life; and
(f) review, to check its achievements against the main questions.

The usefulness of any of the activities prosecuted in any of these stages can be determined only by what turns up in the next stage. If the questions posed at the outset cannot even be found paper answers it would seem that the questions are not very useful, and thus a fresh start will have to be made. At any stage in the six, the enquiry may be driven back to any other, even to the beginning; this does not, of course, mean that the work so far done is all wasted. Unlike the Pentecostal Procession of Echternach, which passes along the streets of that ancient town by three steps forward and two steps back, thus covering *exactly the same spot* five times (either to or fro), whatever it may be that the fellows are doing as they move up and down, it is far from covering exactly the same spot. 'What if . . . ?' may always *seem* to be the same question; every experience of trying to answer it shows how much it is changed by that experience.

The analysis stage must be entered by a narrow gate, generally the specification of the supposed problem by the management that has so far failed to resolve it. It is surprising how many people are ready to admit that they cannot find the answer to such-and-such a question; there are fewer who ask themselves, or anybody else, whether they are asking the right, or even a useful, question. When the fellow begins on a project misled by a tightly-specified but wrongly-conceived task, he is in for a rough time, particularly when the main embarrassment to his hosts has little to do with their activities, but lies within themselves and within the mythology of their enterprises. It is hard to point out to any directorate that it is addressing itself to a useless enquiry, and virtually impossible to follow this up by adding that the fault is with the directorate itself. But if the fellow begins to suspect that the proper questions have not been built into the task he must elaborate for himself, the set will help him. In practice, he will be led back to the central (and mis-stated) question through one subsidiary to it on which he does not differ from his hosts; we find that, in casting around for useful starting questions, it is well to lay in an arsenal: centrally characteristic, or those that make the project what it is thought to be; locally specific, or proper to that project in that particular enterprise; and beneficially interesting, or, while not all that vital to the project itself, probably worth working on for other reasons. These three categories form an order of priority and, if the fellow finds that those in the first have been wrongly chosen or specified, he must concentrate on one of a lower order for a start. The set will help him catch up after his enforced late start.

Once each fellow has started to list the key questions, he will find an abundance of paper answers flowing in to him; some he will have thought of, but many will be offered by his hosts.

These paper answers mark the development stage; many of them will suggest reframing the key questions, or altering their order of priority. His friends in the same set will want to offer him all manner of interesting answers as well, most of which they are trying to derive from their own key questions. It is at this stage, should it not have arisen before, that the fellows will begin to see the immense differences between the backgrounds against which the four or five of them are working, in contrast to the similarity of the micro-political issues that are emerging in each of the different participating enterprises themselves. They will also be getting their first lessons in operational utility, looking at the paper answers to ask not, 'Is this likely to be the right approach to the question?' but rather, 'Will I get backing for this so that I can now enter the next – or procurement – stage?' For of one thing each fellow can be sure, and at all times: No receiving enterprise will start to put real resources at his disposal unless it believes there is virtue in what he is proposing. No project yet was ever a high-velocity fiasco. Indeed, if any fellow should report to his set that things are suddenly forging ahead and his clients are taking his ideas up with enthusiasm, he will be met with so chilling an avalanche of disbelief that he will return to look more critically at his records of both the stages of analysis and of development.

The entry into the procurement stage finds the project at its most testing time. Even if nobody has been deceived by the choice of key questions and even if everybody has been helpful in the search for the paper answers, it is their willingness to contribute to the sinews of achievement that really counts. The world is not short of people ready to talk, especially to talk about the embarrassments of their superiors; and it is most emphatically not short of people ready to press advice down on others about their troubles.

The procurement stage is radically different from the first two; they call only for intelligence or even perhaps only for cunning, whereas getting hold of the resources calls for commitment, which has little to do with cunning but a lot to do with values and sincerity. 'Never embrace an uncertain cause' was the advice I was given by an acquaintance at Cambridge who was later to enter the House of Lords (it was not Lord Bowden), and there are those fellows in action learning programmes who, as they flounder in their procurement stages, will hear it re-echoed. But, as always, the comradeship of the set will help each of its members in trouble to outwit the wolves in sheep's clothing among whom he has fallen, for each will read the disappointments of his friends like an open book.

At the end of the procurement stage of one particular fellow, another may still be trying to sort out his key questions and a second busy chasing the paper answers that will reveal his need to return once more to the very start. But in the set discussions it is imperative that there is some marching in step; all must, in some sense, be shoulder to shoulder with the fastest man. At the end of the procurement stage, therefore, it has been our custom to assemble the fellows before an entirely unknown collection of colleagues, preferably the fellows from another set in another programme, so that all may make a comprehensive review of where they are and of what they need to do to catch up. They may agree to cut down the number of questions they are trying to pursue in their projects, leaving it to a working party, set up within their receiving enterprise, to deal with others. This may turn out to be a move of great value, since it may engender a vigorous thinking process in the receiving enterprise that diffuses action learning along unexpected lines. As a rough-and-ready rule, it might be said that, since there are six stages identified from past projects and since most programmes last of the order of six months, then the procurement stage should be well under way within the third month, so that the laggards may well expect to face some awkward choices. In the Belgian programme, which was quite artificial judged by the high-level support that it was given, an attempt was made to complete a reasonable procurement inventory by the end of three months' full-time work, through the prospect of an American visit on which each fellow would have the chance to present his diagnostic report (questions, answers and resources promised) to an informed, professional audience of businessmen and academics alike.

After diagnosis, therapy; after design, negotiation; after talk, action. The dichotomy is false: therapy has started with the first questionings; diagnosis continues until the end of the treatment; design may anticipate negotiation, but negotiation will modify design; talk may prepare for action, but those who act learn to talk in a different tone for the future. But the dichotomy is also true: diagnosis, design and talk call only for intelligence, perhaps only for mere cleverness, or not seldom for cunning alone; therapy, negotiation and to act call, additionally, for courage, for belief and for commitment. Practice may prove one's diagnosis to be wrong, even ignorantly wrong, and there are many to shrink from being proved other than wholly right on every single pronouncement they are ultimately forced to make. It does not do any professor much good to be shown ignorantly wrong, particularly in front of other professors with whom he battles for a share of a fixed total budget. Academics therefore are inclined to stick to the diagnostic preliminaries, so that, in our three later stages, we have little in the way of theory to guide our footsteps. Nevertheless, our observations of the Belgian programmes, with their high-level participants wrestling with strategic difficulties of the first magnitude, suggests that we should treat the therapeutic stage of our achievements in three conceptually distinct parts.

We leave the third stage of diagnosis, procurement, with three sets of resources: the plan, composed of the (suitably modifiable by further experience key questions and the paper answers to them; the resources of which we have the promises exacted by the procurement stage itself; and a vague sense of expectation throughout those likely to be involved in the therapy. The first task of the fellow is to weld these three assorted assets into a working organism or, at least, to emphasize the construction from them of such an organism, since, during the procurement stage, he will have been obliged to say what he intends to do with the resources he is looking for. Again, what would seem an impossible task if thrown at an isolated individual becomes an interesting challenge when the fellow has the support of others in his set all after doing the same thing. At this stage, when the fellows can rely within their receiving enterprises upon a small camarilla of conspirators, they may be able to speed the construction or assembly stage by clandestine meetings of supporters from different firms, also ready to learn with and from each other. During the therapeutic or negotiation phase of any programme, the clients can also learn with and from each other, since they will carry more responsibility for the project once their fellow starts to implement his plans than they will while he is still formulating them. It is now that the fellow will begin to reap the reward for having nursed well his client from the start, and kept him well informed of his plans and difficulties as the diagnosis has advanced. It is now that the shrewd fellow begins to unload as much as he can upon the client and the rest of his hosts, playing the micro-political game for which the diagnostic phase was his apprenticeship. And yet, although every hour that passes makes the next still more important, with the end of the project looming up before him and all the critical steps yet to be taken, he will not try too assiduously to structure what needs to be done.

It is a policy of opportunity that he must follow, with fresh questions in the following order: 'Have I got my resources into the shape that I want? Do the people working with the client and myself really grasp the plan? Before I actually get them to try the changes that I am so sure are the right things to do, can I be satisfied that they are the burgeoning team I want them to be? How far am I forcing my ideas on to them? How far am I reflecting what they genuinely believe and want to get done, whether or not I had ever been here to help them?' All these mark the construction stage. He must then ask 'Now I am pretty sure that they are together and anxious to make a start, how do we get started? Who settles the deadline? Who cuts the tape or presses the switch or lights the touch paper?' These are the criteria of the application stage, and such questions should not be pursued until the fellow is reasonably sure that there exists a firm assembly to make the new system survive its own birth pangs. And finally the review stage: 'What has it all meant? What have we done – if anything? Does it bear any relation to what we set out to do in defining and answering those first questions? If not, where did things start to go wrong? Or have we been overtaken by events, so that, fast as we were changing the enterprise by our deliberate efforts, it was changing even faster on its own?' It would be useful, even if the helter-skelter of the second phase – of negotiation as opposed to design, of therapy as distinct from diagnosis – made it all but impossible, for the fellows within any particular set to emphasize month by month these three aspects of implementation: assembly, or building something out of the resources; application, or getting that something to work; review, or comparing what it is doing with the expectations of the project. In any case, even if these suggestions seem hopelessly theoretical, the fellows themselves will impose some kind of timetable upon the progress they will anticipate all ought to achieve; each will trim his endeavours in his own way to the bed of Procrustes that marks the duration of the programme.

21.
Projects, Fellows, Clients and Options

Some therefore cried one thing, and some another: for the assembly was confused; and the more part knew not wherefore they were come together. (Acts ch. 19, v. 32)

Mystery, Babylon the Great, the mother of harlots and abominations of the earth. (Rev. ch. 17, v. 5)

Others apart sat on a hill retir'd
In thoughts more elevate, and reasoned high
Of providence, foreknowledge, will, and fate,
Fix'd fate, free will, foreknowledge absolute;
And found no end, in wandering mazes lost.
(Paradise Lost, Bk II, line 557)

The essence of action learning is to extract from the *new* task itself a sustainable desire to know what one is trying to do, what is stopping one from doing it, and what resources can be found to get it done by surmounting what seems to stand in the way. I say here a 'new' task, despite my opinion that, as time goes on, action learning will increasingly be practised within the Own Job options first clearly identified in the GEC programmes (see p. 65).

The element of newness in continuing to do the job that one was doing before coming into the action learning programme will, of course, be membership of the set, for whatever option is followed the fellow must, in the sense in which I define action learning, extract the sustainable desire from the new task with the help of a small number of others seeking the same essence.

'Learning-by-doing' is an insufficient description of what I have been on about these last twenty-five years; it is rather 'Learning to learn-by-doing with and from others who are also learning to learn-by-doing'. The distinction is far from trivial. Among other awkward questions it asks, in a painful and ungentlemanly fashion, precisely what is the role of the professional teacher in action learning. This is a highly controversial business, particularly at a time when the industrial and commercial world seems to be turning from traditional management development towards the practices of learning within the enterprise and on the job itself. It is not only that this departure may appear to threaten the prospects of the traditional teacher to make a living. The embarrassment lies elsewhere. Those who have been professional teachers of management, spot-lighted on the rostrum in the Winter Gardens, fitting together the elaborate details of the syllabus, stamping with the hand of yesterday the examination scripts of their apprentices, impressing the contents of their own memories upon the committee set up to get things changed, scattering like sheep the case-discussants by letting off the well-used and trusty muskets of the ambush, have much to readjust. Action learning has no place for such Napoleons; its working material is not the knowledge of the teacher but the experiences and the needs of the learners, and we must not underrate the differences between them. Nor must we be satisfied with the verbal explanation of the professional instructor of those eager for his help – that he will now run things differently, no longer putting across what he had planned to do in accordance with the syllabus, but instead trimming every word to the needs of those who come to him with their project hang-ups. This may be his true intention, honestly professed and illuminated by example of his reformed approaches. We must nonetheless be on our guard; authoritarianism is a personality trait and does not easily submit to defeat by conscious argument, and in action learning I am seeing it revive itself in subtle but destructive disguise. The professional may no longer be telling his audience what they ought to know about variance analysis, inflation accounting, industrial psychology, company law and so forth, simply because he no longer has any audience to tell it to; even if he manages to get an action learning programme off the ground those who join it may not want to know any of these things, and they may soon tell him so if otherwise he cannot master his desire to sound off about them. The inveterate hankering of the teacher to be the centre of attraction will come out in other forms; if he is no longer custodian of the working *material*, doling out the data, the principles and the methods, he will strive to regulate the social *process* by which the fellows help each other to learn with and from themselves as a set. My fear is that, in the very moment when the industrial world has become sufficiently mature to see that it has its freedom to develop with the help of its own resources, we are all to be impaired by the interested intervention of professional process-mongers.

My concern is not diminished by what I have learned of the recent history of the psychological and psychiatric professions and their practice. It may well be that action learning is not consciously intended for the treatment of mental illness (however that may be defined) and that the managers who join our action learning sets are normal, indeed, rugged, individuals, not readily vulnerable to the insinuations of others. But my primary thesis – that true learning consists mainly in the reorganization, or reinterpretation, of what is already known – does call for the learners to understand what may be preventing them from using more fruitfully that to which they already might have access, if only they knew also how to secure that access. Such a postulate might rightly be claimed as the original discovery of innumerable psychiatrists; it is merely a matter of choosing the appropriate phrases in which to dress it before laying it at a whole Harley Street of brass-plated consulting rooms. But what kind of a jungle is this Harley Street? Not one, let it be clear, in which a physicist-turned-coalminer feels much at home; it is a jungle lacking proof either by experiment or by outcome. Nobody outside the mind-shrinking game can possibly read its history since Freud and still believe that it is obedient to rules other than those invented by its manifold players for their own transitory prestige.

I am anxious to make my own position clear on this delicate point of professional dogma; when ordinary men, like hardworking managers, are confused and uneasy, but nevertheless obliged by circumstances to get something done, it is not some intellectual explanation of their emergency that they seek, followed by a logical plan of action that will get them off the hook; one cannot build intellectual edifices upon the foundation of disorder. At such times, borne down by responsibility, fear, confusion and helplessness, it is not argument one needs but support, not analysis but example, not lucidity but warmth; if argument is good, let it come *after* support, just as analysis may follow example and lucidity come after warmth. Once the simple human aid has been given and confidence starts creeping back, then may be the time to deploy the weapons of sophistication and dialectic; then may the professorial moonshine blaze forth in all its glory. But in the real world, riddled with anxiety and obligation, managers face few tasks that can be discharged solely in terms of argument, analysis and lucidity. Nor is it that support, example and warmth are lacking; there are funds of those precious qualities at hand and, often enough, with plenty to spare. What is lacking is a widespread *ability to use* them. We live in a callous world, tormented by the need to appear successful, to be able to stand on our own feet, and we seem to want to owe it to ourselves not to ask for help.

In a culture of book-learning we all know how to write each other memoranda; in the truly with-it culture of the business schools we are finding out how to communicate through the digital computer; only in the dangers of the mine, simply because we are all there in it together, do we understand that it is not by ratiocination that we help each other make better use of our potential talents. I do not believe that the hospital ward has quite the same ennobling spirit, for there are too many to impose their will upon others and suppress thereby the reciprocal help that lies at the very heart of action learning. As I see it, some process-analysts have much the same effect. By their displays of mastery they discourage the hesitating fellow from blurting out precisely what he needs to disclose in order that he may now understand how to give, and, more important, how to receive the support and friendship that alone can help him how to learn. The difficult lesson for the teacher to grasp is this: that intellectual weapons are all very well for brandishing at the pageant, especially if one is on the bandwagon or out rattling the collecting box; they should, however, be slung aside as soon as the hand-to-hand stuff starts. And then, if he is to join in at all, it is on the same terms as the others, the humble instrument of Almighty God with as many fears, confusions, responsibilities and shortcomings as the rest. In this conclusion, I seem to be supported by such slender researches as the psychiatrists can muster; where the clients are encouraged to get on with their tasks rather than to discuss their behaviour the treatment is significantly more effective. This is why I have long put the accent upon tackling the problems offered rather than upon deliberately stressing the interactions of the sets. Although a man may need to know that he does not listen to what others are trying to say to him, he needs to know it not *per se*, but to be a better manager by solving the troubles in which he is up to his neck. The help he needs he will best get from those whose first need is also to solve problems, not to discuss social relations. Action learning has a duty to British management to see that the energy released in its attacks upon real time problems by real people is not siphoned off into the drains of academic and professional consultancy.

The assignment of a task that, as work on it advances, becomes more and more closely specified as to purpose, setting and resources is essential to action learning, at least in its opening stages. As learning to learn-by-doing becomes more closely assimilated to the daily endeavours of management practice, so that it is as much a habit as addressing one's colleagues in whatever may be the local language, there is less and less need to chalk the tasks that loom ahead with the same boundaries and the same arrows as are helpful for mapping the first exercises.

Unless the efforts of the fellows are firmly anchored to some objectively observable programme of achievement, they may well drift off into some academic Valhalla; the constant tap on the shoulder which the fellow will be given by his colleagues in the set will serve to keep his attention from becoming mere introspection *as such*; as each fellow questions the other about his progress and his blockages, so he continuously points out to him what he has *done* and what next he needs *to do*. I do not mean that these increments of the past and for the future are explicitly specified: not at all. But the other fellows, themselves having plenty of ground to get covered, must, by the very nature of their coming together, be more interested in his progress than in his sentiments. They may, it is true, from time to time, console him with their admissions that they, too, have felt as he does, but this is a wishy-washy encouragement compared with helping him along the recordable stages of his project. Nor does this encouragement necessarily come to him from the other fellows; he, in helping them, may see more clearly how to help himself, or, in seeing them surmount the difficulties that arise under their own feet, attack more cheerfully those that confront himself.

The conundrum that provides the task of every fellow, whether he is working at some aspect of his own job, on a similar job elsewhere, on a different job in his own enterprise, or, as in the Belgian programme, on a different job altogether in a different organization altogether, must be a problem and not a puzzle. Puzzles are the quarry of the respective experts, and all experts in the field of the same puzzle should come to approximately the same conclusion, since the solution of the puzzle may be said to exist before anybody starts to work on it. Given the same books to examine, five different expert accountants should come to much the same conclusion about how much profit (or loss) such and such a company might have made in such and such an accounting period. But if, unfortunately, it is a serious loss, five different expert consultants might give very different sets of advice to the directors, even although all of them are honest, reasonable and experienced in company doctoring. If the five accountants seriously diverge all one needs to do is to inspire each to check the others' arithmetic and find the errors of calculation – or even of copying; the five consultants may disagree because each is drawing upon different values and different interpretations of similar past experiences. The accountants are merely sorting out a puzzle; the consultants are advising upon a problem. Puzzles are the working material of experts, and problems are the concern of leaders; action learning is not for experts, who thrive on programmed instruction.

Thus, the conundrums of action learning are to be problems, to excite the interest of the participants in what they cannot see rather than enhance their skill in elaborating what they can see already. The project task must therefore be open-ended (admitting of a range of alternatives, each leading to still others), inter-departmental and of serious concern to those who offer it. Unless those who are beset with the problem offered in any action learning programme are genuinely concerned to get something done about it, the fellow who has the misfortune to draw it will, despite learning much, suffer endless frustration. Indeed, it is an essential part of the programme proper that those offering the project should see themselves as learners from their participation just as clearly as will the fellow who is to tackle it. It should be clear before the enterprise joins the programme that the project it intends to offer, too, will open up learning opportunities for those within the enterprise as much as for any from outside. My own belief is that if, within the set, the emphasis is put upon the progress of the fellow rather than upon his personal shortcomings or upon the processes of the dialectic in which he becomes caught up, the receiving enterprise will, in consequence, reach a better understanding of its own internal dynamics and resistances, its collective enthusiasms and inertias, even if this means that the fellow will need to attack the formidable array of discouragements that may manoeuvre themselves across his path. With the levers of his set and the fulcrum of his client he will surprise himself at what he is able to move.

The choice of client goes with that of the project. However loosely the project may first be stated it must have an 'owner' of some kind. He need not be the most senior member of the organization with a concern for the problem, for, in many problems posed for action learning consortia, that distinction would lie with the chief executive. All the same, the client should be a member of, or on close terms with, the coalition of effective power that may be said to run the firm offering the problem to be studied. There are three possible, if alternative, qualifications for a client: that he is well informed as to why the problem *is* a thorn in the flesh of the power structure, that he should be well known across the enterprise for his readiness to see that something is done about the trouble, or that, once the trouble has been defined and resources got together for attacking it, he has the power to put behind the shoulders of those ready to make the first shove. Understanding, eagerness and force are all called for to do anything at all about a problem, even if it is to seize an opportunity that promises; the client should preferably command all three, but it is essential that he commands the second. Provided that he is genuinely motivated to act, the fellow will supply the information and between them they will enlist the power. There is no such thing as an unmotivated client, except no client at all. There is often the *wrong* client, when the problem has been wrongly specified or wrongly attributed; the fellow may then have the task of persuading the coalition of power to change the client. In Belgium, as some of the projects developed and much detailed data had to be collected or discussed, encroaching unreasonably upon the time of the client – for there is always a paradox in the bigger the client the less time he has for the fellow – we fell into appointing assistant clients, called *responsables* or *coordinateurs*; they were generally invaluable to the fellows and some enterprises came to look upon the offices as preparations for the holders to become their fellows in the next programme. As his project develops, the fellow must regularly show his client the progress he is making with the diagnosis, and discuss with him the possible choice of *client-group* (known in Belgium as the 'structure d'acceuil') in anticipation of the therapeutic or implementation stages of their collective task: all is to be expressed by the *client-group* – the evolution of the strategy, the identification of those who know, those who care and those who can, acting under the patronage of the client, upon the advice of the fellow, all held together by the political cunning of the co-ordinator, if one such has been appointed. The key to it all is the confidence the fellow has in his client and the trust the client reposes in the fellow, and of the memorable analects of the Inter-University Programme it is the remarks made by fellows about their clients that stand first:

Nurse your client and hasten slowly; lasting change takes longer than you think.
Never moralize about your client's problems; help him to solve them.
My client has enough embarrassments already; he has no time for all these details of technique.
Start by selling yourself to your client – all but your soul.
You must never lose the confidence of your client; it is your only strength.

When a number of separate enterprises, as in Belgium, or a number of units within the same company, as in GEC, have tried action learning in successive years, they will start to see the virtues of bringing occasionally together the clients from different projects. The period of cultural preparation, as we may call it, necessary for the diffusion throughout top management of the notion of the enterprise as a learning system stimulated by an organized assault upon some current affliction, may well be ten years, even in these times of precipitate change. For those who, like myself, are still trying to find out how better to use the vast stores of experience locked away in the managerial store, a gathering of hard-bitten clients and their fellows has plenty to offer; their willingness to come together may be taken as the most discriminating criterion of the success of the whole programme.

The choice of participants, or fellows, is evidently the central responsibility of those who would wish to try action learning within their enterprise or public service; it is like casting the Prince of Denmark for a performance of *Hamlet*, however important may be the choice of Ophelia and Polonius. Nevertheless, I believe that action learning is not understood by those who see the development of the fellows as its sole objective. Such concentration upon certain favoured individuals I believe to be a hang-over from the bad old days.

It is our quest for diversity that calls for the selection of the right fellow. While he must accumulate to himself in the action learning programme all the virtues that he can, he is also to inoculate all with whom he comes into contact with the simple notion that it is by reflecting upon what one is doing that one sees how to do it better. This he will do as a matter of course while working on the project assigned to him in the programme proper. It is more difficult to do in the normal course of his work, such as after returning from a sophisticated programme or during the progress of an Own Job exercise should he be, for example, joined in a Management Action Group organized by the Institution of Works Managers. Thus, if the full potential of action learning is to be realized, the selection of the fellow must notice not only his ability to improve himself but also to develop others. This may seem a strange demand to impose upon an educational system that has emerged from simple competitiveness, but is easily explicable when seen against the suggestion that the first quality of any leader is to ensure that his team learns the lessons of their own experience. The chief executive may well have to anticipate tomorrow more accurately than others, but here he can take advice. It is only after making the guess that the trouble starts, namely, of getting everybody (including himself) to see that tomorrow is not yesterday. This process of collective learning is his first and constant pre-occupation, and it is the main strength of an action learning programme that its participants secure new insights about the enterprise as an autonomous learning system.

It therefore follows that in any major action learning programme the choice of fellows must be a stage in their career development, as well as a resolution by each participating organization to do something about at least one of its major troubles. It may by now be clear that the attack upon the selected affliction has two purposes: to do something about it *per se* and to exploit it as the opportunity to engender within the enterprise a process of collective learning. These are the pay-offs that will accrue to the firm. But what is meant by the career development of the fellow? What are to be the pay-offs that accrue personally to him? His first qualification for joining any action learning exercise is that he wants to join it, not because he is being sent, in recognition of his services to the firm or because his name has come up in accordance with its training policies or routines. And he must want what the programme has to offer, namely, to understand better how the constant troubles that beset him (and the organization) can be seen as the developmental opportunities for all to seize, and, in particular, to exploit as an aid to mastering conditions of ignorance, risk and confusion. The ideal fellow must be seen, and must see himself, not as a more polished expert, but as a future leader. Those who would like to join the action learning programme as fellows because they wish to know more about techniques, cash flow, computer programming, 'industrial relations', VAT and so forth, should be encouraged to look elsewhere: action learning is not for teaching the solution of technical puzzles; that is the job of the management schools.

Since we are trying to describe the part played in an action learning programme by its key participants, it may help to clarify the functions of the sets to which they belong by reporting some of the subjective impressions that the fellows have exchanged with each other at the end of several Belgian consortia. (At the end of the very first programme, in 1968, the remark of the year was voted as that heading the list.)

What is an honest man, and what need I do to become one?

Whatever help I had from others – and it was plenty – I am still on my own and always shall be; only I can decide how to live my life.

It is no longer disturbing for me to accept support from a colleague without having to promise help in return.

There is something to be said for the suggestion that managers should try to understand themselves as well as other people.

After three months with the other fellows I recognized that they could read my thoughts more easily than I could read them myself.

It is quite reassuring to discover that for years I have only been deceiving myself, never anybody else.

I was convinced at the start that the changes were impossible; now, by the use of my own patience and the backing of my set, we have made them all inevitable.

Beware of making premature alliances: first find who knows his job.

Remember with respect your first impressions; you may change them but they were the true voice of all your past experience.

It is agreeable to be bothered by troubles now; I get so much out of my set forcing me to deal with them.

At first I felt uneasy about my freedom to tell the truth.

Why should anybody in a firm like mine want to tell the truth? Now I see no harm in it. Indeed, sometimes we find it quite helpful.

It is a pleasure for somebody now to be rude to me; it always puts my project in a new light.

Our managers are not untruthful by nature; they simply must pretend to know even if they have no idea at all.

It may be necessary for morale not to worry too much about the future, but we still ought to do something about it.

Experts are there to answer questions, or to pass them to other experts. But managers must decide what questions to get answered.

There is a difference between believing in nobody, on the one hand, and not knowing whom to believe in, on the other.

It is always the boss who decides whether the staff behave well or not.

The boss who encourages you to do everything intends you do nothing.

I see now that not only have I been doing the wrong things for years; our salary system was designed to make me concentrate on my doing them.

Not everybody switches off now whenever I start talking to them.

The choice of these epigrams for illustrating all the fellows had to say to each other as a result of their action learning investments may seem proof that I wish to stress the psychotherapeutic nature of the set experience, thereby contradicting the emphasis with which I try to open this chapter, namely, that the set is more concerned to help the fellows with their projects than to examine their behavioural blockages and to free their fettered powers of communication. This is not my purpose. The Belgian programmes were composed largely of senior engineers and lawyers who were strongly motivated to get something done about the projects they were assigned to. Their primary objective was action, since they were drawn from a closely-knit industrial and commercial culture in which all their bosses (company presidents) knew each other and met frequently. So insistent were those who had paid for the programme that it produced tangible results among the troubles presented for treatment, that all the fellows were taken, in the middle of the programme, to America, where they spent three weeks in presenting their draft findings to a range of businessmen and academics, all with a view to improving their proposals for concrete action upon their return to Belgium. Their main desire was to meet the business analysts, the consultants and operations research men who were employed by the major American corporations to advise upon comparable difficulties; at the majority of these presentations, about fifty in all, the accent was unmistakably upon the project and what to do about it, and any references to the obliquity of perception or infelicity of expression of the fellow himself were little more than the normal banter of any team of intimate colleagues. My argument is difficult to make, and I could not support it by producing a weight of documentary evidence about project design and implementation, for the very simple reason that we found, quite early on, the preparation of elaborate reports to be an obstruction to future progress; the fellows were encouraged to keep brief notes in their diaries and to discuss their import frequently with their clients. But they all discovered that, once committed to the duplicator, their suggestions about what to do next had become embarrassingly out-of-date by the time they had been studied and approved. It was this inevitable delay, coupled with the comparatively brief life of the programme (nine months), that opened the search for serial structure referred to in the previous chapter (see p. 279).

Action learning must experiment with many project options, not only because only by trial and error are we likely to find out much that is useful to our understanding of how experienced persons are likely to learn, but also because such exchanges as were possible in Belgium are not likely soon to be replicated in Britain. Learning to learn-by-doing must be an austere business if it is going much to help the vast number of middle managers in the medium and small firms upon which the economy depends; whereas there are still plenty of troubles to be accepted as the most effective media for development, it is unrealistic to imagine that there will be much opportunity to exploit their solutions by full-time exchanges. Thus it is that all manner of ways have been devised, stumbled upon, ordained and even experimented with for confronting experienced and overworked managers with interesting and profitable ways of rethinking their professional missions, or arousing and sustaining a desire to know what one is trying to do, *and* what is stopping one from doing it, *and* what one might be able to do about it. The programme that, while preserving at its heart the practice of regularly assembling the participants in sets, has also encouraged the greatest variety of options among its projects, has been that of the General Electric Company. In this, mixed in the same sets, have been full-time outsiders working on the problems offered by a company within GEC; an Indian manager released from his Calcutta office of the main company; managers from the Midlands studying the afflictions of their own units and sometimes of their own jobs – and hence necessarily working part-time in the programme, although perhaps time-and-a-half overall; managers transferred from one GEC company to another; managers moved outside of GEC altogether to work upon a difficulty common to that other organization, a consumer or customer, and GEC itself, the supplier or manufacturer. In the first programmes these mongrel sets used to come together regularly at the GEC College of Management, where they had been assembled for an induction programme, to carry them quietly through the disorienting barrier dividing the impetuous confusion of the employing unit out of which each had come from the organized incomprehensibility of the receiving unit into which each had been sent. Experience was to show that, in complete contrast to the Belgian programme, and to the Indian that started about the same time as GEC, these British managers did not regard the later gatherings of their four sets as particularly useful. It would be heart-warming to learn that this was due to the iron solidarity of the four sets within themselves; despite their mongrel character (or perhaps on account of it) out of 704 possible attendances, from two sets each of five fellows and one set of six meeting on thirty-four different days and one set of five meeting on thirty-two, the total recorded was 700. Nor is that all the evidence of internal cohesion; at the end of the third national programme, the GEC experiment has split up into eight local programmes, each encouraging a still greater variety of project options.

In the consortium of London hospitals the field activities were based, not upon individual fellows and individual clients, but upon two teams of three from each hospital, doctor, nurse and administrator comprising each; the senior remained always in the home hospital, the junior visited other hospitals from time to time. A Norwegian programme run from the Administrative Research Institute of the Commercial High School in Bergen used the same idea among small firms; this option has the additional benefit of appearing to build team-work among the visitors as well as to encourage some institutional learning among those whose problem they take as their project. In a recent coalmining programme a set of adjacent collieries had, like their British counterparts twenty-five years before, lent each other various officials to examine problems unfamiliar to them in their own mines. These options were hardly team exchanges in the sense of the London hospitals' programme, since each visiting official of the three was marking some specific weakness of functioning not seen to be closely bound up with the interests of his two companion visitors. Just as there were three visitors, so also were there three pit clients all reporting to the manager. From time to time, various samples, drawn from different pits, met under the managing director at the coalfield headquarters. Such a design might well form the starting point for action learning within any very large enterprises, with the colliery managers replaced by departmental heads and the visitors drawn from the ranks of the supervisors; such a set of options was, in fact, evolved during the follow-up of one of the first Belgian exercises, and had been reported as *Project Management Efficiency*.[16]

In the small and medium-sized firms, action learning may spread and proliferate in fertile anarchy, offering the experimental scope that has been denied the educational world since its first polarization by the Instruction of Duauf. In the bigger concerns, however, things may go differently and action learning may become orderly and respectable, run by a priestcraft from lavishly equipped temples on the banks of slow-moving rivers; from such pinnacles of the established hierarchies will be issued the policies for all to pursue, and I forecast the following orders of precedence becoming accommodated by the four main options traced above. We summarize them briefly.

(a) a familiar problem studied in a familiar setting: a fellow examines some aspect of his own job;

(b) a familiar problem is tackled in an unfamiliar setting: the colliery manager swaps his underground transport official to work with a few other such officials on the transport problems of a set of collieries;

(c) an unfamiliar problem is put up for solution in a familiar setting: a production engineer agrees to work with the personnel department as client to simplify the wage structure of their company; and

(d) an unfamiliar problem studied in an unfamiliar setting:
the commercial director of an agricultural bank helps
those on the spot to understand and treat the technical
obstructions to innovation in a shipyard.

These four options may readily be matched against the four ranks
of managers normally employed in large undertakings. Option
(a) is suitable for plant, unit or section managers, those who
form the backbone of the concern but have little prospect of
promotion; sets composed of such men make up most of the
Management Action Groups of the Institution of Works
Managers, although some members of these are directors in their
own right. Other sets of options (a) are drawn from within the
same enterprise. It will then be necessary, to ensure that action
learning does not degenerate into authoritarian project work, and
that from time to time the sets meet similar sets from quite
different enterprises and, preferably, from quite different industries. I hope that the Institution will show the way in such
inter-industry own-job action learning by admitting the farmers
to their Management Action Groups. The take-over of land by
the financial institutions is bound to raise all manner of farm
management problems, and I see nothing but good emerging
from those who run our farms and our factories supporting each
other with professional advice and criticism. They can still meet
while doing their own jobs.

Option (b) will widen the horizons of the functional experts
in their particular specialisms. Technical change will always
provide an internal spur to fresh thinking, but it is not unknown
for some skins to be so thick that the spur is not felt until it
has brought about a fatal poisoning of the blood. There are
pay-offs for both sides when the man in charge of producing
diesel engines for heavy trucks spends time helping his fellow
engineers organize their production for fishing smacks or for
railway locomotives. There are thousands of experts who have
no wish to enter what is called general management, and option
(b) offers them development from within their chosen trade; the
pairings of the Nile Project suggest that two such specialists
could be client to their own problem and fellow to that of another factory. It would be interesting to experiment with sets
of two or three such bartered couples; they might breathe new

vigour into some of the moribund professional institutions, extending the lofty debates of the presidential durbars into a hundred set meetings at West Hartlepool and the like.

Option (c) is suitable for senior departmental managers due to join the policy-making board of an organization, or the committee of departmental chiefs advising that board. Their demonstration of the abilities to run their functional department effectively proves only that they understand how to answer the questions that have been posed by the policy makers of the enterprise. It is no proof that they have grasped the complexities of deciding suitable policies to be implemented, nor that they see those policies, even after they have been decided, from an angle wider than that of their own departmental doorway. The illustrations given in the public services of Australia show how wide might be the application of this particular option in the cells of central and local government.

Option (d), foundation of the pioneering Inter-University Programme of Belgium, has already been extensively described. It is entirely suitable for the high-quality manager likely to become the chief executive, called upon to display the wisdom of summitry, to be more interested in what is invisible than in what all the others around him see so clearly that they can think of nothing else. Option (d) may be for the few alone, but it is the laboratory in which we dissect the question-posing mind.

22.
What Action Learning is Not

Agesilaus, being invited once to hear a man who admirably could imitate the nightingale, declined, saying that he had heard the nightingale itself. (Plutarch, *Lives*, c. AD 100)

But there were false prophets among the people, as there will be false teachers among you, who will secretly put forward wrong teachings for your destruction ... And a great number will go with them in their evil ways, through whom the true way will have a bad name. And in their desire for profit they will come to you with words of deceit, like traders doing business in souls: whose punishment has been ready for a long time and their destruction is watching for them ... these men, like beasts without reason, whose natural use is to be taken and put to death, crying out against things of which they have no knowledge, will undergo that same destruction which they are designing for others; turning out of the true way, they have gone wandering in error, after the way of Balaam, who was pleased to take payment for wrongdoing. But his wrongdoing was pointed out to him: an ass, talking with a man's voice, put a stop to the error of the prophet. These are the fountains without water, and mists before a driving storm; for whom the eternal night is kept in store. For with high-sounding false words, making use of the unclean desires of the flesh, they get into their power those newly made free from those living in error ... (2 Peter ch. 2)

... there were very few names of any real distinction on the management education front ... the two giants were probably Revans and Rice because, for all the theoretical talk, they were operationalising completely new designs which respected the integrity and the mental constructs of the managers themselves. ... The clarity and simplicity of (Revans') insight were in-

tolerable. What he said, for all its directness, was truly incomprehensible to those who had elevated the process of running things to an academic study. (Alistair Mant, *The Rise and Fall of the British Manager*, 1977)

I have tried to list in this book what I believe to be a coherent set of ideas, supported by some accounts of the translation of those ideas into managerial action, that are sufficiently distinct from many other ideas to deserve identification under the general title of *action learning*. At no time have I claimed that any single one of these ideas was original to me and I do not wish to make this claim now that I have survived long enough to see them being applied all over the world. But to fortify those who might themselves wish to try action learning against the buffoonery of financially interested professors of business management I believe it is essential to state quite specifically in what way action learning differs from other approaches to management development (or to the wider understanding of our social and economic problems) with which the business world has been made familiar.

In *job rotation* the learning vehicle is a series of differing functional tasks carried out under the tutelage of some local expert, whether manager, specialist or head of particular branch, and rich in the mysteries traditional to those experts. One sits next to Nelly. But while sitting next to Nelly may give one the most vivid impressions of both what Nelly is doing and of what Nelly believes herself to be doing, it does not tell the learner whether what Nelly is actually up to is either sound practice or profitable investment. Good managers will pause from time to time to assess whether what Nelly is doing is of much use or not, and whether it might be done in some other way if it is of use, or how to stop it should it be a waste of effort. The purpose of action learning is not to multiply avuncular instruction by the acknowledged experts in the current mythology; it is concerned to evaluate what is going on by bringing to bear a fresh criticism. Since so much in management development is now based on job rotation, those who are trying to introduce action learning face a formidable task; what is totally new is taken as the immemorial old simply because it demands moving from one setting to another, at least in those forms of action learning involving exchanges between work-places. In condemning it as an inferior form of job rotation because it does not call for the embalming solicitude of the canonical crackerjack, the establishment's dismissive contempt is voiced: 'So *that's* what action learning is! A new name for *job rotation*! Well, we've been doing job rotation for donkey's years, and there's nothing for us to find out. Anyhow, we know our own business better than you do.'

In *project work* the top management usually sets up a working party, composed of persons from within the firm itself – and so well supplied with those who have probably created the very problem they are now newly assembled to solve. The composition of the team, that is usually the outcome of some internal political negotiation and not the disinterested selection of an external fellow involved with many similar fellows on totally different problems, necessarily forbids detachment. Its terms of reference, too, are generally confined to making recommendations for some higher body to implement, in whole or in part as may be felt expedient. Its progress is almost certain to be monitored by some expert or another, caught up in the power games ceaselessly played within the firm but, unlike a visiting fellow in the same conditions, necessarily committed to some faction with a stake in the issue under dispute. It is usual for the individual members of the project team to attend as emissaries of their particular departments and to speak to an approved brief. In organizations that have been carefully designed to observe the highest principles of the management sciences, there will be invisible checks upon the loyalty of these departmental representatives to their own chiefs; this will ensure that, so far from the project team striving to identify what the trouble is about, it will seek the most agreeable compromise between all that the various factions are willing to accept. While it is likely that such project work may be a useful apprenticeship to the skills of micro-politics, it cannot have the objectivity essential to the inter-enterprise set, let alone the detachment of the exchange between enterprises. When, in addition, the project team is seconded by some academic expert from a local business school or college management department, helping them to design a 'scientific' plan of operation, we may rest assured that the entire exercise will have firmly built into it all those experiences of the expert that he wishes to remember and none of those he wishes to forget.

To cut a long story short, we must, in designing projects of the traditional kind, assure ourselves that we are doing something apart from exchanging one set of misconceptions for another, even although it is being done under the expert direction of scientific authority. I believe that, as research grants become less readily available to the universities (whether from the established research councils or from private firms interested in their own specific troubles), there will be a move away from the canonical research project in its dual role of industrial therapy *and* postgraduate thesis towards the more mobile approach of action learning. Instead of tightly-designed and authoritarian *pièces de théâtre* staged by one enterprise alone and supervised by one expert alone, we shall see organizations working together in small action learning consortia. It may well be that some of the managers nominated as fellows will be registered for further degrees, and that their work in the action learning programme will form the theme for their postgraduate dissertations. My forecast will be that the quality of the work done in the action learning consortia compared with that of the traditional academic projects will be so much higher that the thesis examiners will draw attention to it in their annual reports upon the condition of the system for awarding postgraduate degrees.

There are all forms of *simulation* at present being employed in management development. They include case studies, business games in which computers assess (or claim to assess in accordance with such-and-such rules) the consequences of decisions taken by the participants, group or team exercises in competitive achievement such as to assemble some prescribed model from a fund of distributed elements, and much ingenuity has gone into constructing them. Like the more popular television team games they undoubtedly appeal to the instincts of rivalry and exhibitionism, so that it is not flattering to be told that action learning is merely what could be done with less effort and more security in 'a good case study run by a professor thoroughly familiar with it'. Cases and their quantitative counterparts are edited descriptions by unknown authors of inaccessible conditions for which the participants cannot possibly be responsible and upon which they cannot deploy their most effective managerial talent, namely, their power of observation. But if they cannot enrich their diagnosis of what the problem might be by independent observation of its setting, much less can they test the validity of their treatment by taking any real-time action to apply it. There is a danger that participants may come to believe that they would in practice follow the courses of therapy they so vigorously advance, whereas, with their own personal interests truly at risk in the real world, what they might do would bear little relation to what they assert in the classroom about some never-never land. If not provided against, moreover, simulation may have a retrograde effect upon the subject's grasp of his own learning process. Those experiences that lead to behavioural change as well as to the expression of different opinions require that the learner shall see the practical outcome of his own actions or decisions, and in the simulation, including the case study, this is impossible.

Since an essential process in any action learning programme is the set discussion, itself inextricably associated with the projects deep in managerial reality, it is not seldom asserted that *group dynamics* and its many derivatives have long supplied us with all that action learning may have to offer. Because the set helps its manager-participants to correct their obliquities of vision and to master their infirmities of resolve, and employs for these useful purposes the managers themselves, would not the set be greatly helped if the participants openly and courageously embraced all that the behavioural sciences have to offer? I cannot dispute this claim, as I do not know what all the contending schools of inter-personal psychology are on about. I can only stress that action learning is about real people tackling real problems in real time, observing the impartial discipline of the business setting, and looking after a lot of people without much interest in group psychotherapy of any kind. Such exercises as sensitivity training, transactional analysis and so forth are not, it seems, *by their very nature*, riveted firmly to the here-and-now demands of industrial or commercial achievement. My criterion is simple: 'Does the programme require that, after the therapeutic episode, the subject tries himself out afresh in the real world and produces the evidence of improvement that will convince *external and disinterested observers*?'

For all I know, there may be many novel approaches to social exaltation and to the advance of individual ability now going the rounds of the psychology schools, and it would be foolish of me to claim that action learning has advantages over them all. I merely wish to emphasize my incompetence to judge of these recondite affairs by listing the names of a few of the latest psychotherapies that have caught my brash attention:

actualism, analytical tracking, bio-energetics, crotch-eyeballing, encounter groups, *est*, Feldenkrais, functional integration, Fischer–Hoffman process, gestalt therapy, Gurdjieff, human life-styling, integral massage, neo-Reichian bodywork, organizational role analysis, polarity balancing, postural integration, primal therapy and screaming, psychodrama, scientology, Silva mind-control, Synanon, T-groups, Tau Chi Theta, transcendental meditation, wife-swapping, Yoga (hatha and raja) and Zen.

There is now some evidence that *business consultancy* will be increasingly presented to stress those aspects of the historic profession that are not unlike action learning. In listing what I feel to be the contrasts between them, however, I do so, not to claim any superiority for what I have so long been advocating, namely, my belief that managers learn more effectively with and from each other than from third parties such as professors or consultants, but because I believe that it will be through the more progressive consultants that the theory and practice of action learning will most rapidly and securely advance. First, the business consultant, like the medical adviser, normally seeks a long-term attachment to his client; action learning is a one-shot effort, hoping to engender long-term organizational learning. Second, the consultants are specialists of repute in what are seen to be the particular troubles of particular firms. Action learning offers new experience to substantive managers temporarily formed into a team and tackling unfamiliar troubles in the hope of understanding better their own. Third, the expert consultant is primarily there to clear up the troubles; in action learning the fellow encourages the client to work out with him his own solution. Fourth, the expert is always on the look-out for those same short cuts that he spotted on the previous assignment; the action learning fellow strives to expand the horizon of his client in similarly striving to expand his own. Fifth, the consultant must always be constrained by his contract with the top in his confidences with the middle and junior managers; in action learning the lack of any such contract may lead to the fellow becoming 'the walking conscience of the receiving enterprise'. Sixth, the expert consultant who temporarily runs into trouble (or out of ideas) will turn to other professional specialists; in action learning the fellow has the whole consortium at his disposal. Seventh, the managers of the enterprise calling in the consultants may resent the imputation that they do not know their business, and an armed truce may best describe their relations with the visiting expert; in action learning it is known that the fellow is himself a manager out to learn, so that he is not resented. Eighth, the consultant, even although he may know in his own heart that all the material in his report and recommendations with claims to merit has been contributed by his clients themselves, must offer the outcome of the work as his own; in action learning the consortium is designed on the fundamental assumption that all are to learn with and from each other.

Nor is *simple common sense* quite all there is to action learning, even although it is the comparison that I find most flattering. For what some people call common sense is merely the ineptness of their competitors, while common sense to others is in fact their exceptional professional mastery of some important resource or technique. True common sense, or wisdom, as I prefer to call it, is certainly what action learning sets out to cultivate, and only a stupid person would underrate the difficulty of cultivating it. By wisdom I mean the deliberate effort to explore what cannot be seen in the problem; this differs fundamentally from cleverness, which enlarges upon what is already known to be there. Wisdom is interested in posing fertile questions, cleverness in elaborating brilliant answers. And what some may call common sense is the wrongheaded application of the answers that were brilliant yesterday; it is a primary goal of action learning to qualify the idolization of the past.

Action learning has much in common with *operational research*, industrial engineering and work study, save that its main source of ideas of all kinds (both in identifying critical questions and in supplying to them the appropriate replies) are the managers and fellows in the total learning community; this tends to make an action learning consortium more fluid than a project in operational research, and to bring into the discussions of what might be going on a range, not only of opinion but of executive power, that might strike the professional OR-man as totally irresponsible. 'How can such unqualified people possibly know what this is all about? What understanding of science do they bring to the argument?' The answer to such questions, which are commonly posed by experts, is that it is for the experts themselves to find the answers: the apparently unqualified are part of the total system and it may well be their very ignorance or bewilderment that has led to the OR-man becoming involved in the first place. The most vital factor in the solution offered by the expert is its acceptability, and the expert cannot use his own failure to understand this to insist still more upon the need for scientific purity. The importance of putting one's ideas and suggestions to continuous test, that is the essence of every action learning programme, shows that *utility* rather than *elegance* is what managers seek. There is a sense in which the difference between these two qualities, between what is good enough to be getting on with and what is true enough to convince the philosopher (but that might be too true to be any good) is, on the one hand, the psychology of management and, on the other, the difference between action learning and operational research. The action learning fellow will argue: 'So-and-so has convinced me; I will follow his example.' The operational research professional will argue: 'So-and-so has proved it; I now understand how to do it.'

We may conclude that action learning is less structured and more empirical than most of these other approaches. It certainly imports less from outside the direct experience of the managers themselves, and it claims no syllabus as its own. It leaves those who need to do the managerial task to work it out among themselves, appealing to each other about what they are up to, what is in their way and what they can find to do. Whereas we may liken the traditional management schools and their manifold approaches (including all of those set out above) to an assortment of prestigious clubs, we cannot claim action learning as much more than the managers clustered around the factory tap, drinking each others' health in cold water.

Epilogue

To describe a living subject is like painting the Forth Bridge: no sooner is the first description finished than it must be amended. So it is with this book; the chapters drafted two years ago must be brought up to date. But since the first need of any book is to get itself published, I shall add to one chapter alone, as it were; this epilogue tells briefly of what is developing in Belgium.

The publications of the Bureau of Labor Statistics of the US Department of Labor, universally regarded as the most authoritative source of economic information in existence, tell that, since the late 1960s, the Belgian manufacturing economy has shown the steadiest improvement among the 11 countries whose performances are monitored. Averaged over the 11 years, 1968 to 1978 inclusive, the average annual growth rates of these countries in manufacturing productivity (percentage growth of output over input) were: Belgium 8.0; Japan 7.4; Netherlands 7.4; Denmark 6.6; France 5.5; Germany 5.2; Italy 5.2; Sweden 4.4; Canada 3.8; UK 2.4 and US 2.4. The result is statistically significant, and is reflected in other measures, such as maintenance of exports, high real wages, modest increases in labour costs, shorter working week and milder inflation. These Belgian results have been achieved despite the lowest capital investment among the 11 countries, an absence of natural resources (since Belgium has now closed its last colliery and has no internal sources of energy) and no labour to take from the farms into its factories. The Fondation Industrie-Université, which promoted the senior action learning programmes of Belgium, in which it is now estimated that well over a thousand top managers have been involved, is now staging within Belgium a study by its managers, on action learning lines, to trace the origins of their country's manufacturing success in terms of managerial activity. If land, labour and capital, between them, cannot explain Belgium's climb to the summit, the reasons for it must be found in the lead offered by the managers themselves, and the search has now begun. Since improved productivity may be one of the keys to a fuller order book and more work tomorrow, what the Belgian managers are now looking at ought to be of concern to

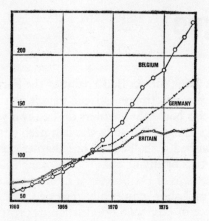

Source: US Dept of Labor; Bureau of Labor Statistics, Office of Productivity & Technology.

Figure 11. Showing, for Belgium, Germany and Britain, trends in manufacturing productivity between 1960 and 1978.

managers throughout all manufacturing countries; discussions are now taking place with those elsewhere, and it is hoped that a few British firms may be persuaded to join with their foreign counterparts in an action learning approach, to evaluate the assumptions that now underlie the creation of wealth in a manufacturing economy. Even though the present performance of Belgium seems to contradict the principles of Adam Smith, Alfred Marshall and John Maynard Keynes, the figures of gross domestic product per person employed ought to hold our attention for a moment. According to the Bureau of Labor Statistics they were, for 1978 (in US dollars): Belgium 25,376; Germany 25,527; Japan 18,023; UK 12,492 and US 21,836. These may not be specifically for manufacturing, but they show Belgium's figure to be ahead of America's, more than double that of Britain and only marginally short of Germany's.

The reason for the Belgians (and, perhaps, the Germans also) wishing to trace the effect of managerial activity upon manufacturing performance is suggested in Figure 11, showing, with 1967 as the base of 100 for all three countries, the productivity trends since 1960 in three not dissimilar economies. What, we may well ask, happened to British management at the very time the major business schools stepped forward as its saviours?

314

REFERENCES

1. INNOVATION AT THE COAL BOARD

1. Other senior members of the administration betrayed their deeper attitudes to education by misreading the official 'Notes for Speakers' offered for their support on public occasions: 'this unique millstone on the road of progress' . . . 'yet another far-sighted measure for us to work out of as soon as possible' . . . at press conferences announcing new scholarship and training plans in 1948.

3. THE HOSPITAL AS A LEARNING SYSTEM

2. *Hospitals: Communications, Choice and Change* ed. R. W. Revans, Tavistock Publications, London, 1971.

4. BELGIUM BREAKS THROUGH

3. Such comment as that by W. G. McClelland 'Sales per person and size of organisation', *Journal of Industrial Economics*, Oct. 1957, p. 221, shows that the general thesis (about the disabling effects of size) was not understood, even if the specific objections to it that could be raised in particular industries were elegantly presented. My early papers on size-effects made no impact and not until E. F. Schumacher (formerly a colleague at the Coal Board) came forward in 1973 with *Small is Beautiful* has the size-effect attracted the attention it seems to deserve. Recently, however, Professor S. J. Prais, in 'The Strike-proneness of Large Plants in Britain', *Journal of Royal Statistical Society*, Vol. 141, Pt 3, 1978, has most generously acknowledged (p. 382) my thesis, advanced 20 years ago as 'an exceptionally lucid discussion of these matters'.

5. THE NILE PROJECT

4. *The Nile Project*, Saad Ashmawy and Professor R. W. Revans, OECD Development Centre, Paris, 1971.

7. INDIA SEEKS FOR EDUCATIONAL INDEPENDENCE

5. *Manpower Journal*, Institute of Applied Manpower Research, New Delhi, June 1978: R. N. Mishra, *Action Learning*, Lok

Udyog (Monthly Journal of the Bureau of Public Enterprises) Sept. 1976, New Delhi.

9. PROSPECTS AND POSSIBILITIES

6. S. E. Morison and H. S. Commager, *The Growth of the American Republic*, OUP, 1950, Vol. II, p. 144.
7. Department of Health and Social Security: *Management Arrangements for the Reorganized Health Service*, HMSO, 1972.

12. THE MORALE OF SUPERVISORS AND MANAGERS

8. R. W. Revans, *Studies in Institutional Learning*, Brussels, Feb. 1969. Unpublished report of the European Association of Management Training Centres, now available from the author.
9. *ibid.*

17. WORKER PARTICIPATION AS ACTION LEARNING

10. M. I. Rostovtzev, *Social and Economic History of Rome*, OUP, 1926, p. 169; M. I. Rostovtzev, *Social and Economic History of the Hellenistic World*, OUP, 1941, Vol. I, p. 413; Vol. II, p. 898; Vol. III, p. 1549.
11. Drake, Keaney and Morse: *The Analysis of Public Systems*, MIT Press, Cambridge, Mass., 1972.
12. A. J. P. Taylor, *English History 1914–1945*, OUP, 1965, pp. 141–2.
13. E. L. Woodward, *The Age of Reform*, OUP, 1938, p. 441.

18. MANAGERS AND HOW TO HELP THEM

14. R. W. Revans, *Action Learning and the Nature of Knowledge*, Education and Training, London, Nov./Dec., 1977.

19. CLIMATES AT THE SUMMIT

15. *L'entreprise face au changement et a l'innovation.* Doctoral thesis of Thomas Joh, Faculty of Social, Political and Economic Sciences, University of Brussels, 1977.

21. PROJECTS, FELLOWS, CLIENTS AND OPTIONS

16. *Project Management Efficiency*; unpublished report of project in Inter-University Programme of Belgium, 1969. Copy available from the author.

Bibliography

Ashmawy, S. & Revans, R. W., *The Nile Project*: an experiment in educational autotherapy, ALP International, Nov. 1971.

Baquer, A. & Revans, R. W., *I Thought They Were Supposed to be doing That*, a comparative study of co-operation of services for the Mentally Handicapped in seven Local Authorities (June 1968 to Sept. 1972), King's Fund Report, 1972.

Baquer, A. & Craig, J. B., 'Action Learning: Staff Training based on evaluation of the services by the providers', *Journal of European Training*, Vol. 2, no. 1, 1973.

Bates, E. M., *Measuring Stress Levels in Health Organizations*: a study funded by Hospitals and Health Services Commission, University of New South Wales, Sept. 1976.

Boorer, D., *A Question of Attitudes*, King's Fund Centre, Nov. 1970.

Boorer, D., Craig, J. B. & Kirkpatrick, W., *Nurses' Attitudes to their Patients*, King's Fund Centre, July 1971.

Burgoyne, J., Boydell, T. & Pedler, M., *Management Self Development*, ATM occasional paper, Feb. 1978.

Casey, D., 'The Emerging Role of Set Adviser in Action Learning Programmes', *Journal of European Training*, Vol. 5, no. 3, 1976.

—, 'Individual Growth in Company Context', *Personnel Management*, Oct. 1978.

Casey, D. & Pearce, D. (eds), *More Than Management Development*, Action Learning at GEC, Gower Press, 1977.

Clutterbuck, D., 'Whatever Happened to Action Learning?' *International Management*, Nov. 1976.

Coghill, N. F. *et al*, *Worker Participation and Control in Hospitals*, a paper presented at 2nd International Conference on Participation, Workers' Control and Self-Management, Paris, Sept. 1977.

Cortazzi, D., *Illuminative Incident Analysis*: a technique for team-building, ALP International, June 1973.

Foy, N. 'Action Learning Comes to Industry', *Harvard Business Review*, Sept./Oct. 1977.

—, 'The Union Man Learns Action', *Management Today*, Oct. 1977.

Garratt, R., *The Developing Use of Action Learning in Urban and Rural Development*, ALP International, 1976.

Lawlor, A., *Improving Productivity in Retailing*, Redditch College, August 1975.

317

—, *Management in Action Programme – A Practical Scheme of Development for Managers and their Companies*, Redditch College, Nov. 1976.

—, *Managerial/Supervisory through Learning by Doing*, Redditch College, Oct. 1974.

—, *Organizational Development through Autonomous Learning*, Redditch College, June 1974.

—, 'Management Clinics', *Journal of Industrial and Commercial Training*, 1975.

MacLoughlin, A. H. & Johnston, R., 'An Evaluation' (Re Northern Ireland Training Council Bursary Scheme for specialist managers), *Industrial Relations Journal*, Spring 1976.

Mansell, C., 'How GEC learns action', *Management Today*, May 1975.

Mant, A., *The Rise and Fall of the British Manager*, Macmillan 1977.

Marsh, J., 'A new work dynamic is emerging', *Hydrocarbon Processing*, 1977.

Mishra, R. N., 'Action Learning', in Lok Udyog, *Monthly Journal of the Bureau of Public Enterprises and the Public Sector* (India), Sept. 1976.

Musschoot, F., *Action Learning in Small Enterprises*, ALP International, 1973.

—, *Attitudes of Senior Public Servants towards Change, Role and Tasks of their Local Administrations*, Institute Administration-Université (Brussels), undated.

Paine, L., *Coordination of the Services for the Mentally Handicapped*, King Edward's Hospital Fund For London, 1974.

Pedler, M., Lawlor, A. *et al, Report of the Sheffield Action Learning Clinic*, Yorkshire and Humberside Regional Management Centre, in association with the Institution of Works Managers, 1977.

Rapier, E., *Action Learning in Sweden*: an attempt at an evaluation, EFI Working Paper no. 6073, Aug. 1976.

Revans, R. W., *The ABC of Action Learning*: A Review of 25 Years of Experience. Published by R. W. Revans, Manchester 1978.

—, 'Action Learning and the Nature of Knowledge', *Education and Training*, Nov./Dec. 1977 and Jan. 1978.

—, *Action Learning: Its Silver Jubilee 1952–77*, Yorkshire and Humberside Regional Management Centre, Inaugural Lecture, Oct. 1977.

—, *Action Learning Trust*: a note on the need for *Encouraging the Development of Entrepreneurs* as well as the skills of the Managers, Oct. 1977.

318

—, *Hospital Performance and Length of Patient Stay*. Action Learning Trust, 1977.

—, *Action Learning in Hospitals*: Diagnosis and Therapy, McGraw-Hill (UK), 1976.

—, *General Principles of Action Learning*, ALP International, 1975.

—, *Participation in What?* ALP International, 1974.

—, *Studies in Factory Communications*, ALP International, Aug. 1973.

—, *The Emerging Attitudes and Motivations of Workers*, OECD Manpower and Social Affairs Directorate, Paris, 1972.

—, *Hospitals: Communication, Choice and Change*, Tavistock, 1972.

—, 'Action Learning – A Management Development Programme', *Personnel Review*, Vol. 1, no. 4, Autumn 1972.

—, *Developing Effective Managers*: A new approach to business education, Praeger Publishers, 1971.

—, *The Choice of Action Learning Projects, Clients and Fellows*, Fondation Industrie-Université, Feb. 1970.

—, 'Management in an Automated Industry', *Journal of Dyers and Colourists*, Vol. 84, Feb. 1968.

—, *Studies in Institutional Learning*, European Association of Management Training Centres, April 1967.

—, 'Management Education: Time for a Re-think', *Personnel Management*, July 1976.

—, 'Helping Each Other to help the Helpless: an essay in self-organization', *Kybernetes*, 1975.

—, 'Human Relations Management and Size', in *Studies in Industrial, Economics, Human Relations and Modern Management* (ed. E. M. Hugh-Jones), North Holland Publishing Co., 1958.

Revans, R. W. and Cortazzi, D., 'Psychological Factors in Hospitals and Nurse Staffing', *International Journal of Nursing Studies*, Vol. 10.

Revans, R. W. and Coghill, N. F., *A Study of Para-Clinical Attitudes among Consultants*. Addendum to the report of the West Middlesex Hospital upon the Hospital Internal Communications Project, 1969.

Skeet, M. and Crout, E., *Health Needs Help*: results of a study into the role and preparation of volunteers working within the re-organized National Health Service, Blackwell Scientific Publications 1977.

Sutton, D., 'Teaching and Learning in Management', *Management Education and Development*, Vol. 7, pt 1, April 1976.

Wieland, G. F., 'Manager-Directed Surveys for Organizational Improvement', *Journal of Nursing Administration*, Nov./Dec. 1972.